Children's Literature

Children's Literature

New Approaches

Edited by

Karín Lesnik-Oberstein

palgrave
macmillan

First published 2004 by
PALGRAVE MACMILLAN
Houndmills, Basingstoke, Hampshire RG21 6XS and
175 Fifth Avenue, New York, N.Y. 10010
Companies and representatives throughout the world

PALGRAVE MACMILLAN is the global academic imprint of the Palgrave
Macmillan division of St. Martin's Press, LLC and of Palgrave Macmillan Ltd.
Macmillan® is a registered trademark in the United States, United Kingdom
and other countries. Palgrave is a registered trademark in the European
Union and other countries.

ISBN 1–4039–1737–X hardback
ISBN 1–4039–1738–8 paperback

This book is printed on paper suitable for recycling and made from fully
managed and sustained forest sources.

A catalogue record for this book is available from the British Library.

Library of Congress Cataloging-in-Publication Data
Children's literature : new approaches / edited by Karín Lesnik-Oberstein.
    p. cm.
    Includes bibliographical references and index.
    ISBN 1–4039–1737–X (cloth) – ISBN 1–4039–1738–8 (paper)
        1. Children's literature, English – History and criticism. 2. Children – Books
and reading – English-speaking countries. I. Lesnik-Obserstein, Karín.

PR990.C496 2004
820.9'9282—dc22   2004045802

10   9   8   7   6   5   4   3   2   1
13 12 11 10 09 08 07 06 05 04

Printed and bound in Great Britain by
Antony Rowe Ltd, Chippenham and Eastbourne

To the memory of my father Max Lesnik Oberstein

Contents

List of Illustrations

Acknowledgements

I would first like to thank all the contributors to this volume: their enthusiasm, dedication, and generosity made it a great pleasure to work with them. Many thanks also to our commissioning editors at Palgrave Macmillan: Eleanor Birne first conceived of this volume and was tolerant of my repeated insistence that it should be truly 'new'; Emily Rosser then supported the project to completion. Becky Mashayekh also at Palgrave Macmillan was kind to me during a difficult time for me personally, and Paula Kennedy responded patiently to my queries.

Thanks to Professor Peter Brooks for encouragement in the early stages, and for generously suggesting further contributors, including Professor Miller. I am grateful to Routledge for giving permission for Professor Miller to reuse material published previously by them. Thanks to Dani Caselli and Hilary Fraser for help on specific editorial issues, and to Neil Cocks for suggesting the structure of this volume. All at Reading's 'Centre for International Research in Childhood: Literature, Culture, Media' (CIRCL) are central to what this book is about: our past and present MA and Ph.D. students and the teaching staff, especially Tony Watkins, Stephen Thomson, Josie Dolan, Neil Cocks, Sue Walsh, and Sarah Spooner. I have learned, and continue to learn, so much from them. The Reading Theory Discussion Group continues to offer an arena of genuine intellectual excitement and debate: my thanks go to all its members.

My dear friends gave me unstinting support during the time I worked on this project, as at all times: I cannot thank them enough. Finally, my beloved family are always there for me whatever I do: all my love to Bobe, Sarit, Saskia, Martijn, Zev, Ayal, and Hoyte. This book is dedicated with love to the memory of my father: the integrity, deep engagement, and rigor of his scholarship are an abiding inspiration.

Notes on Contributors

Daniela Caselli is a lecturer in English Literature at the University of Salford. She has published widely on the work of Samuel Beckett and inter-textuality in the *Journal of Beckett Studies* and *Samuel Beckett Today/ Aujourd'hui*, and has co-edited a volume of the *Journal of Beckett Studies* with Professor Steven Connor and Dr Laura Salisbury. Her work on childhood includes articles on the work of Djuna Barnes and ideas of simplicity (in *Critical Survey*) and the child in Barnes's criticism and fiction (*The Yearbook of English Studies*). Dr Caselli is working on books on Beckett, Dante and theories of intertextuality, and on Djuna Barnes and concepts of modernism and gender.

Neil Cocks is at present Head of English at Southeast Essex College in Southend-on-Sea. He completed his Ph.D. on the history of the Nineteenth Century Boy's School Story at the University of Reading in 2000. Publications include articles on Kipling's '*Stalky and Co.*: Hunting the Animal Boy', in: Karín Lesnik-Oberstein (ed.), *The Yearbook of English Studies* on 'Children in Literature', vol. 32 (Maney Publishing for MHRA, 2002); forthcoming: 'Death and Absence in *Tim* by H.O. Sturgis' in *Nineteenth Century Contexts*, and forthcoming work on childhood and archaeology, and on the painter Frida Kahlo and gender.

Lila Marz Harper gained her Ph.D. from the University of Oregon, and she is now an instructor at Central Washington University, USA. Her book, *Solitary Travelers: Nineteenth-Century Women's Travel Narratives and the Scientific Vocation*, was published (June 2001) by Fairleigh Dickinson University Press/Associated University Presses, and was included on Choice's Outstanding Academic Books of 2001 list. She is currently working on a critical edition of Edwin Abbott's *Flatland*. Other publications have been in the areas of Victorian literature, women's biography, natural history/science and travel writing.

Jacqueline Lazú is currently an assistant professor of Modern Languages and Latin American and Latino Studies at DePaul University where she specializes in Latino, Caribbean and Diaspora literatures. Some of her courses include: Latino/a Literature, Caribbean Literary and Cultural Perspectives, Latina Motherhood, Latino/a Theatre. Originally from Hartford, Connecticut, she recently completed her doctoral studies at Stanford University where she wrote a dissertation entitled 'Nuyorican Theatre: Prophecies and Monstrosities'. The work explores articulations of national identity in the theatre of Puerto Rican writers in the USA. Most recently, Dr Lazú submitted a piece to the upcoming Oxford University Press *Encyclopedia of Latino Literature* on 'Nuyorican Poetry and Theatre'. She has recently started work on her first book, a highly anticipated first history of Puerto Rican theater in the United States.

Karín Lesnik-Oberstein is a senior lecturer in English, American, and Children's Literature at the University of Reading. She is also Director of the University's 'Centre for International Research in Childhood: Literature, Culture, Media' (CIRCL), and of the MA in Children's Literature. She researches in the areas of childhood and children's literature, literary and critical theory, gender studies, and philosophy, from inter- and multi-disciplinary perspectives. Her books include: *Children's Literature: Criticism and the Fictional Child* (Clarendon Press, 1994, repr. 2000); (as editor and contributor) *Children in Culture: Approaches to Childhood* (Macmillan/St Martin's Press – now Palgrave Macmillan, 1998); (as editor and contributor) *The Yearbook of English Studies* Special Section on 'Children in Literature', vol. 32 (Maney Publishing for MHRA, 2002); and articles and chapters on a wide range of issues around childhood and children's literature.

J. Hillis Miller is currently UCI Distinguished Research Professor of English and Comparative Literature at the University of California at Irvine. He joined the Irvine faculty in 1986 after having taught for 14 years at Yale, and before that for 19 years at Johns Hopkins. Professor Miller has written many books and articles on nineteenth- and twentieth-century English, American, and Continental literature, and on literary theory. His most recent books are *Others* (Princeton University Press, 2001); *Speech Acts in Literature* (Stanford University Press, 2001), and *On Literature* (Routledge, 2002). He is currently at work on a book on speech acts in the work of Henry James.

Sarah Spooner has almost completed her Ph.D. in Children's Literature on the work of Arthur Ransome and ideas of Landscape, Heritage, and Nostalgia, at the University of Reading. There, she also teaches undergraduate courses and the MA in Children's Literature.

Christine Sutphin is Professor of English at Central Washington University, USA. Her major field of study is Victorian literature. Her most recent publications include 'The Representation of Women's Heterosexual Desire in Augusta Webster's "Circe" and "Medea in Athens"', *Women's Writing*, 5(3) (1998): 373–92; *Portraits and Other Poems, an Annotated Edition of Selected Poems by Augusta Webster* (Broadview Press, 2000); and 'Human Tigresses, Fractious Angels, and Nursery Saints: Augusta Webster's "A Castaway" and Victorian Discourses on Prostitution and Women's Sexuality', *Victorian Poetry*, 38 (Winter 2000): 511–31.

Stephen Thomson is a lecturer in English, American, and Children's Literature at the University of Reading, and teaches undergraduate courses and the MA in Children's Literature. He writes on literary theory, literary history, philosophy and social science, but his publications on children's literature specifically include: 'Substitute Communities, Authentic Voices: The Organic Writing of the Child' in Karín Lesnik-Oberstein (ed.), *Children in Culture: Approaches to Childhood* (Macmillan – now Palgrave Macmillan, 1998); 'The Real Adolescent: Performance and Negativity in Melvin Burgess's *Junk*' in *The Lion and the Unicorn* on 'Contemporary British Children's Literature', 23(1), January 1999; 'The Adjective "My Daughter" in T.S. Eliot's "Marina"' in: Karín Lesnik-Oberstein (ed.), *The Yearbook of English Studies* on 'Children in Literature', vol. 32 (Maney Publishing for MHRA, 2002). He has a book forthcoming on children's literature and critical theory.

Sue Walsh is a lecturer in English, American, and Children's Literature at the University of Reading, where she teaches undergraduate courses and the MA in Children's Literature. Her publications in the field include 'Animal/ Child: It's the "Real" Thing' in: Karín Lesnik-Oberstein (ed.), *The Yearbook of English Studies* on 'Children in Literature', vol. 32 (Maney Publishing for MHRA, 2002); ' "Irony? – But Children don't get it do they?" The Idea of Appropriate Language for the Child in Narratives for Children', in *Children's Literature Association Quarterly*, for the special issue on 'Narrative Theories and Practices in Children's and Young Adult Literature', 28(1), 2003, 26–36; forthcoming: 'Belonging to the Tribe, or Not: Moderns and Primitives in the "Taffy" stories' in Judith Plotz (ed.), *Kipling Centennial Studies: 'Just So Stories' and the Puck Books at One Hundred* (Children's Literature Association Quarterly Centennial Studies Series, 2004/2005).

Chronology

A chronology of significant publications for Children's Literature Criticism and Theory (since 1900):

Sigmund Freud, *Three Essays on the Theory of Sexuality* (1905).

F.J. Harvey Darton, *Children's Books in England: Five Centuries of Social Life* (1932).

Philippe Ariès, *Centuries of Childhood: A Social History of Family Life* (1959).

Sheila Egoff, Gordon T. Stubbs, Ralph Ashley (eds), *Only Connect: Readings on Children's Literature* (1969).

John Rowe Townsend, *Sense of Story: Essays on Contemporary Writers for Children* (1971).

Ariel Dorfman and Armand Mattelart, *How to Read Donald Duck: Imperialist Ideology in the Disney Comic* (1971).

Bruno Bettelheim, *The Uses of Enchantment: The Meaning and Importance of Fairy Tales* (1975).

Margaret Meek, Griselda Barton, and Aidan Warlow (eds), *The Cool Web: the Pattern of Children's Reading* (1977).

Fred Inglis, *The Promise of Happiness: Value and Meaning in Children's Fiction* (1981).

Chris Jenks, *The Sociology of Childhood: Essential Readings* (1982).

Jacqueline Rose, *The Case of Peter Pan or the Impossibility of Children's Fiction* (1984).

Martin Barker, *Comics: Ideology, Power, and the Critics* (1989).

Valerie Walkerdine, *Schoolgirl Fictions* (1990).

Allison James and Alan Prout (eds), *Constructing and Reconstructing Childhood: Contemporary Issues in the Sociological Study of Childhood* (1990).

Peter Hunt, *Criticism, Theory, and Children's Literature* (1991).

James Kincaid, *Child-Loving: The Erotic Child & Victorian Culture* (1992).

Karín Lesnik-Oberstein, *Children's Literature: Criticism and the Fictional Child* (1994).

Carolyn Steedman, *Strange Dislocations. Childhood and the Idea of Human Interiority, 1780–1930* (1995).

Chris Jenks, Allison James, and Alan Prout, *Theorizing Childhood* (1998).

Peter Stoneley, *Consumerism and American Girls' Literature 1860–1940* (2003).

1
Introduction. Children's Literature: New Approaches

Karín Lesnik-Oberstein

How and why does this book claim that its approaches to children's literature are 'new'? In order to explain this, I examine in this chapter what children's literature critics already claim they do, and then contrast this with the approaches in the chapters in this volume, to demonstrate how and why these differ from what has come before in most previous criticism.

The academic study of children's books, and the academic criticism of children's literature have been seen to be part of the post-Second World War burgeoning of the study of popular culture in universities across the world. Whether it be media studies, or the study of, let's say, sports, tourism, or popular music, areas which previously were seen to be the appropriate province solely of either amateur interest and participation, or professional training (in teaching or librarianship, for instance, or television, film, and radio production), have gained a substantial foothold in academia in terms of having their own undergraduate and postgraduate degree courses, textbooks, conferences, and academic teaching and research posts. Yet the academic status and position of some of these fields, and certainly of children's literature, remains somewhat uncertain in several respects, as many children's literature critics have commented.[1] First, the idea that it is somehow suspect to study children's literature in an academic context persists widely, both in the general media, in wider academia, and in some children's literature criticism itself. It is seen as claiming a complexity or difficulty for something that is regarded, by definition, as simple, obvious and transparent, and, moreover, as valuable precisely for being so. Secondly, even though academic courses and publications in the field now have a considerable volume and history, it is also still unclear even within the field itself, and despite extensive debates on the issue, what exactly constitutes an 'academic' study of children's literature and its criticism as opposed to, say, educational or librarianship courses and publications on children's fiction. In fact, it is disputed whether such a separation is either possible or desirable. Roger Sell, for instance, has recently (2002) argued in an introduction to a book he edited that 'especially as commentators on *children's* literature, the authors of the chapters which follow do not allow themselves to be wrong-footed by purely academic developments', which he sees as potentially 'driv[ing] a wedge between children's literature and the human world within which it occurs'.[2]

So, do other children's literature critics agree with Roger Sell? What does the criticism see itself as being for and about, and how does it see itself as setting out to complete those aims? Now almost exactly 20 years ago, Jacqueline Rose wrote that there seemed to her to be a 'project ... of a number of children's book writers and children's book critics, to establish the literary "value" and credentials of children's writers and children's book criticism ... [T]he ultimate fantasy, perhaps, of children's book criticism [being] that it should come of age and do what the adults (that is adult critics) have been doing all along ...'.[3] Certainly many eminent children's literature critics claim that developments of the kind Rose indicates have taken place, or are taking place, in the field, and that they see these developments as being fundamental. Peter Hunt, for instance, introduces his well-known book *Criticism, Theory, and Children's Literature* by arguing that '[c]ritical theory may not seem to have much to do with children and books; but ... [g]ood work with children's literature depends, ultimately, on coherent and thoughtful criticism, and good criticism depends on coherent and thoughtful theory'.[4] He goes on to quote Anita Moss's suggestion that 'if we believe ... that children's literature occupies a place in the tradition of all literature, we owe it to ourselves to explore what is going on in the field of literary criticism, even if we decide to reject it', only to insist further that '[w]e cannot "decide to reject it", because new theories in time change our habits of thought, and become the norm'.[5]

Peter Hunt here implicitly shares with Anita Moss the aim of the first part of Jacqueline Rose's description of the 'project', namely the wish 'to establish the literary "value" and credentials of children's writers and children's book criticism', but disagrees with Moss in terms of the idea of what 'literary criticism' is, and what it can, or cannot, be said to do. To Moss, literary criticism is worth investigating as part of the effort to have children's literature taken more seriously, but it also remains a separate field, an 'add on' which could be left to one side. To Hunt, on the other hand, it is something which is intrinsic to 'habits of thought', and although he feels that '[t]heory is an uncomfortable and uncomforting thing', he argues it seeks 'to explain what we might otherwise have thought was obvious[;] it draws attention to hidden problems'.[6]

What Hunt's and Moss's views do also share further here, however, is the idea that the relationship between children's literature criticism and (adult) literary criticism or theory is relatively recent or even entirely new. For Moss, whose article was published in 1981, it is apparently something worth investigating, but this has not yet happened: its use or possible rejection are something yet to be explored. For Hunt, in his 1991 book, the linking between children's literature criticism and its adult counterparts (both literary criticism and theory) also still has to take place, for he writes that

> [b]oth the children who read the books and most of the adults who deal with them either know nothing of decontextualized reading or literary value systems and cannot understand the point of them, seeing them as illogical and threatening. *But criticism is changing.* It has many valuable elements which can help us to understand how we understand; help us to work with texts and with people. ... The first chapter of this book examines the relationship between criticism, *as it is becoming*, and children's literature.[7]

This claim in both Moss and Hunt that the encounter between discussions about children's fiction and (adult) literary criticism and theory is new, or only just starting out, may, curiously, be seen to recur as a theme, as Rose also suggests in her comment about the 'project' of children's literature criticism. Children's literature critics in various ways claim repeatedly that this meeting of children's literature, literary criticism, and theory (however they define them), is yet to begin, or has only recently started. In 1985, Aidan Chambers, as still quoted, significantly, again in 1991 by Peter Hunt, wonders 'why those of us who attend to children's literature are, or have been, so slow in drawing the two [literary theory and children's literature criticism] together ourselves';[8] Roderick McGillis, in 1998, writes that '[a]ll these theoretical approaches may be, and have been, used by critics of children's literature. *Recent* criticism has forthrightly applied the work of structuralists, deconstruction, feminism, Marxism, Freud, Jung, and so on to children's books';[9] Fran Claggett, in her foreword to Lissa Paul's 1998 *Reading Otherways*, writes that Paul 'carefully elucidates the impact that recent and current critical thinking is having on the way we read a text';[10] John Stephens, in 1999, offers a summary of this thematic when he writes that

> [i]n the course of the nineteen-nineties, there has been a steady trickle of notable books which attempt to place children's literature within the context of those modern literary and cultural theories which post-date the various reader response criticisms, or within a particular facet of that newer body of theory ... we might also think of such books as reflecting a more general interest in newer theoretical ideas as well as having a leading or introductory function. In other words, can we look more widely at the framing of text by theory within contemporary critical practice, and discern some answers to the question, What [*sic*] are we interested in now?[11]

But David Rudd, in 2000, is still claiming that

> My methodological approach to this work has developed out of a more general concern with the way children's literature has been treated in the past. Many traditional approaches seem to me to be seriously inadequate, and for a number of reasons. ... many simply lack any methodological grounding, being prone to both whimsy and subjective judgement ... even where more systematic investigations are undertaken, they are frequently too narrow ...[12]

While Roger Sell, finally, concludes in 2002 that 'in 1968, John Rowe Townsend said there were two distinct categories of people who write about children's literature: "book people" and "child people" ... *Nowadays* there is also a third category "theory people" ...'.[13]

Several critics can here, then, be seen to repeat a discomfort or dissatisfaction with previous forms of children's literature criticism, as they see them, and to repeat too a claim to reform or renew children's literature criticism in ways that will address prior problems. 'New' or 'recent' literary criticisms, theory, approaches, or methodologies, as they are variously called, are seen as being ways to bring to children's literature criticism much-needed clarifications, corrections, or resolutions. It is here too then that we find formulated most clearly what the aims of these 'new' children's literature criticisms are seen to be, how these aims are judged not to have been achieved, or not to have been achievable, in prior criticism, and how the new developments are taken to address the problems in better ways. In other words, what is seen to be at stake in children's literature criticism; what it is *for*.

Peter Hunt, for instance, defines the aim of children's literature criticism as 'a way of approaching children's literature which helps us to make informed choices from first principles, as it were'.[14] In other words, for Hunt, children's literature criticism is about how to choose books for children. And this is, of course, the classical definition of the field, and what it is seen to be about, so unsurprising as such: from Plato on, in Western culture, this has been the point of the discussion of how and why to select books for children to read. In the first century A.D. the Roman educator Quintilian, for instance, recommended certain readings for children, in this case Livy, as 'clearest in style and most intelligible', while he finds Cicero 'agreeable even to beginners, and sufficiently intelligible'.[15]

In fact, I now go on to argue, this aim or goal – the choosing of good books for children – does not change from critic to critic, no matter how much they claim that they will be doing things differently, or applying new approaches or methodologies. The problem, I suggest, that they see in prior or other criticism is that, somehow, the wrong books are being selected for children, in the wrong way, or for the wrong reasons, and the role of the new or recent theory, as they will define and use it, is to show how and why to make the right choices instead. In other words, the new theory is permitted to question or change everything about the criticism, at least apparently, but the final goal of children's literature criticism itself – knowing how to choose the right book for the child – remains constant and unaffected. In this respect then I indeed argue that other children's literature critics continue to agree with Roger Sell's view, as quoted above, that children's literature criticism is there, ultimately, for the benefit of the child; it being able to confer that benefit, moreover, and crucially, through its knowledge of both the child and the book.[16] If I can demonstrate this to be the case, then three questions arise: first, what does it mean for critics to introduce a new theory without affecting the fundamental aim of the field? Or, secondly, to reverse the first question: what kind of theory permits its application without affecting the basic goal of children's literature criticism? In other words, what can and does the theory affect, if not that? And thirdly, and perhaps most importantly, does that fundamental goal of the criticism need to be changed at all? Ought it to be changed? Isn't the ability to know how to select the right books for the child exactly what children's literature criticism wants to achieve, and should therefore continue pursuing?

In order to begin to suggest some answers to these three questions, let us return then to the work of some of the critics I quoted above as examples of advocates of a reform through new approaches or theory. I consider in detail how they see the problems of previous, or other, children's literature criticism, and how they formulate their new theory, which is going to resolve those problems according to them, yet without, I suggest, impairing or changing their common final goal. Although referring to a range of critics, I look primarily at the arguments of two writers referred to by other children's literature critics as important theorists in the field, Roderick McGillis and David Rudd.[17] Of course, any selection of critical works to analyse will be arbitrary to some extent, no matter how much I try to rely on recommendations and citations from other critics in their writings as an indication of the perceived influence or relevance of their ideas to the field overall.[18] On a pragmatic level, I do not address extensively here the work of some writers frequently mentioned in the context of theoretical innovation, such as Aidan Chambers, Peter Hollindale, Peter Hunt, Maria Nikolajeva, Perry Nodelman or John Stephens, either because other contributors to this volume look at their ideas extensively in their chapters in this volume, or have already done so elsewhere in similar ways to my analysis here. Neil Cocks, for instance, in looking in his chapter specifically at ideas of the 'implied reader' in children's literature, considers Aidan Chambers's views at greater length; Sue Walsh examines closely the ideas of U.C. Knoepflmacher in her chapter on children's literature criticism and authorship, while she has analysed Perry Nodelman and Peter Hollindale's work in several articles elsewhere;[19] Daniela Caselli includes analyses of several recent writings on theoretical issues in relation specifically to J.K. Rowling's 'Harry Potter' books in her discussion of intertextuality, and Sarah Spooner, in her chapter, looks further at Peter Hunt's ideas on genre. Nevertheless, whatever the merits or demerits of my own particular selection, I continue to argue, and try to demonstrate, that in fact any texts of children's literature criticism, defining themselves as such, remain united in terms of an unwavering commitment to the fundamental aim of trying to find the best way to choose the right, or good, book for the child.

I return first, then, to Roderick McGillis's *The Nimble Reader*. McGillis defines the goal of his critical and theoretical effort as follows: 'the important thing is that we, as practising critics and teachers, raise to consciousness our own pre-suppositions when we interpret literature'.[20] In this way he seems to agree with Peter Hunt's view, as cited above, that there are processes in reading which are somehow unavailable to the reader, but something of which the reader can be made aware, and that this is what theory does. For, McGillis goes on to ask,

> [w]hat is our theoretical position? Why do we read texts the way we do? At the very least, we should be aware of the possibilities for reading texts and the implications of choosing a particular methodology.[21]

The reason we should be aware of these possibilities, moreover, according to McGillis, is that

> [t]o read with understanding we must have some means of entering the system of discourse that we confront, and to read with some chance of situating ourselves outside dominant beliefs we must have several means (strategies of reading) at our disposal ... if we read with the confidence of knowing why we read and how we interpret, then we have some chance of passing on such knowledge to our children, thereby encouraging them to become active readers too. Making children active, self-aware readers ... offers them the opportunity of understanding the codes and conventions they meet at every turn in their daily lives from their television viewing to their experience of urban sprawl.[22]

In this way, then, McGillis discerns two types of readers: 'innocent readers' who are 'imposed upon by what we read, ... powerless to escape the enforced quiescence reading can put upon us',[23] and readers who have been taught theory as a way to 'end their innocence',[24] which allows them to

> act ... my hope is that we all rouse our children's capacities to act. Reading is, after all, an activity. And to act is to affirm life.[25]

The idea here is that readers can be either 'passive', which seems to mean that they simply accept any text as it stands; they have no way of questioning it, or their reading of it. Or they can be helped, or taught, to become 'active' readers, which are readers who can become more aware of their own ways of reading, as well as of the 'codes and conventions' of the texts, so that they are no longer defenseless in the face of 'dominant beliefs': 'they have the opportunity of standing aside from the whirligig of the market system to understand how it impinges upon them.'[26] (See Stephen Thomson's chapter in this volume for an extensive analysis of ideas of 'ideology' in children's literature criticism.)

McGillis seems clear, then, on how people – both adults and children, 'innocent' and 'theorized' – read: how reading 'works', and that these are two fundamentally, and importantly, different kinds of reading. This sits uneasily, however, with his diagnosis somewhat earlier on, of the 'weakness' of children's fiction and its criticism, for here McGillis argues that he agrees with what he describes to be Jacqueline Rose's argument that

> both child and father are unknowable in any absolute sense. What we know is what we create, and we create both fathers and children through language: we create an identity in language. As Rose argues, creating an identity in language is not the same as reflecting an identity. Language does not simply state truths; it creates them. We forget this when we blithely assume that we know what is best for our children, that we know what literature they should and should not read.[27]

If McGillis's statements about how reading works, and that the child (and adult, but child by definition initially) is an innocent reader unless and until taught to read otherwise, are read as a statement of knowledge about the child, then his previous argument about its 'unknowability' is contradicted, for he cannot claim both to be unable to know the child, and yet know how it reads (before and after it is taught otherwise). But a subsequent statement suggests that McGillis understands the 'unknowability' of the father and child not in relation to a knowledge of how children read as such, but in relation to *what* they should read. After his assessment that 'blithely assum[ing] we know what is best for our children' is a problem, he continues directly by writing:

> [y]et much criticism of children's books insists on an evaluative stance … Evaluation implies moral worth, and just as children's books themselves have traditionally had a strong didactic element, so has the criticism of children's books. Good books make us better people than we would have been had we not read these good books. … Evaluation suggests a standard of value that transcends historical fashion.[28]

It is 'evaluation', then, which is a problem in this argument in terms of claiming to know what is 'good' for the child; a knowledge, according to McGillis, that Rose's argument, as he reads it, precludes. In other words, the 'unknowability' of the child would seem to him to have to do only with the *content* of children's fiction, and with not being able to determine which specific book is good for which child. Furthermore, McGillis also disagrees more generally with 'evaluative' criticism, which he sees as problematically resting 'on the belief in the "concrete universal", which the "objective critic" can explain to the uninitiated reader ... assum[ing] objectivity is unproblematic; it implies ... that a work of literature has a unified and single meaning; and it is confident that standards of value, which all readers can and should accept, exist'.[29]

This, however, can be read as raising several problems for McGillis's own overall arguments: first, in his discussion of 'innocent' and non-innocent readers, there would seem to be the clear implication that an innocent reader can only accept, passively, what the text has to give. For instance, McGillis writes in a later discussion of E.B. White's *Charlotte's Web* that, in this novel, 'form and content fit snugly together. ... [it] offers little in the way of an impediment ... [t]he reader may remain passive, in the clutches of a strong story told in a linear fashion',[30] and that it

> [l]ike nearly all children's books, contains comfort for the reader. Even in the presence of change and death, comfort is possible. This is one of the lessons of the book. ... [It] is an excellent book for young readers because it introduces them in a careful way to the interdependence of style and theme. The prose acts as a teaching device.[31]

This 'strong story' that overwhelms the reader into passivity and offers them comfort, however, looks very much like the assumption that the novel has the 'unified and single meaning' that McGillis was precisely criticizing earlier as an untenable claim on the part of the 'New Criticism'. He even knows what the novel will teach the child and, despite his repudiation of 'evaluation', that it will do so in an 'excellent' and 'careful way', even if he may be disagreeing with the importance or desirability of what he thinks it teaches.

Likewise, McGillis's ostensible disagreement with an 'evaluative criticism' and its assumptions both about what is 'good' for the reader and the 'universal' nature of its values, can be read as in contradiction with his entire critical aim: making readers – whether adult or child – 'active', no longer passively, helplessly, innocent. McGillis states, in a discussion of Terry Eagleton's *Literary Theory: An Introduction*, that

> I do not include the rest of [Eagleton's] sentence, which speaks of method and theory contributing to 'the production of "better people" through the socialist transformation of society.' 'Human transformation,' it seems to me, does not necessarily produce 'better people,' if 'better' means morally superior to others. What Eagleton must refer to is people better than those who subscribe to a capitalist system. I have no design to offer

a series of methodologies that we can use to 'better' our child readers in this way. It seems to me naïve to assume that either literature or theory can make people 'better,' either morally or politically.[32]

To make sense of McGillis's overall argument, I must now assume that he does not therefore see his aim of making readers 'active' as making them 'better', at least in the senses he specifies here, namely 'morally' and 'polit-ically'. But this must then also mean that, to him, his previous desire to teach readers 'to read with some chance of situating ourselves outside dom-inant beliefs' is neither politically nor morally better, nor is providing them with 'the opportunity of standing aside from the whirligig of the market system to understand how it impinges upon them'. It seems, then, that to McGillis, although he wishes to deploy theory to make readers 'informed and independent citizens',[33] and to 'introduce even the very young to the political implications of the books they read',[34] this does not make them 'better than those who subscribe to a capitalist system'. Readers who subscribe to the market system and those who 'stand aside' from it are here morally and politically equal.

I could, on the one hand, read this argument as McGillis's scrupulous attempt to deny possible accusations that he is encouraging the idea that some readers could claim some sort of inherent superiority of status and value over others. Perhaps he is anxious to insist that being a better *reader* does not make someone necessarily a better *person*. This would correspond with an argument that people are equal in worth in principle, no matter what their skills, attitudes, or achievements. On the other hand, this then does, I would argue, somewhat raise the question of the point of McGillis's whole enterprise. If his non-innocent readers are not, according to him, morally or politically better, then in what sense *are* they better than his innocent readers? In other words: if his theory helps readers to be better readers, but not better people, then how and where are we to understand this 'reader' as separate from the 'person'?

Crucially, therefore, McGillis seems to see his 'active' reader as neither polit-ically and morally improved compared with their prior state, or that of oth-ers, nor as based on the adherence to 'a standard of value that transcends historical fashion' which he disagrees with. This must then mean that, to him, his ringing statement in the final lines of his first chapter, that 'to act is to affirm life', is also not based on a transcendent standard of value, or on the equally criticized 'confiden[ce] that standards of value, which all readers can and should accept, exist'. In this case, I can either read an argument as per-mission to assume the critical endeavour of this volume to be qualified in its own terms as strictly personal, contingent and temporary, or I have to read the logic here as resting on the idea that the statements 'to act is to affirm life', and '[r]eading is, after all, an activity' are not 'standards of value' but simply some sort of truth. If I follow my prior reading, then most of what his volume states subsequently must be formulated in terms of this claim as personal, contingent, and temporary; if I follow my second reading, I must conclude that the logic here is self-contradictory and self-undermining for it would then rest on both a declared rejection and a simultaneous re-instatement of transcendent and universal 'standards of value'. In either case, though, I take the claim to be about how to teach children (and adults) to be better readers, and I also take the claim to include, as we saw above in the comments about *Charlotte's Web*, the assumption that better reading can be assisted or hindered by the texts themselves, as well as the ways they are read. In these terms, no matter how different it may look at first sight, McGillis too is relying on wanting to choose the good book for the child, and on knowing both what the book does, and what the child is, to do so: whatever else he is wanting to use theory to raise the consciousness of his readers about, it is not this.

Although McGillis, then, discusses a wide range of issues and approaches in *The Nimble Reader*, his value statements, as well as the claims to knowledge about the child and its reading, recur throughout, even when he continues to criticize precisely this in other critics' writings. With reference to parody, for instance, he first notes that '[y]oung children, so the argument might go, cannot appreciate parody and satire because their experience is too limited'.[35] He continues, however, by arguing that 'the point is that writers and illustrators show a respect for the young reader ... for the intelligence of children'.[36] Now such a statement might be read as a simple tribute to those authors and illustrators, and their opinion of children, whether correct or not, were it not that McGillis subsequently asserts that

> [t]he reader of parody cannot be drawn into the text in the sense of being carried away or rendered passive. The reader of parody must be active. The active reader is the reader on the alert for designs, both designs in a purely literary sense and designs on the reader herself. Reading parody, children receive one of their first lessons in criticism and critical detachment.[37]

Similarly, with regard to fairy tales, McGillis concludes that

> I suggest that the tales may liberate the reader from existing social structures by transforming those social structures into metaphor. The fairy-tale world is a metaphor of a possible reality, not an imitation of reality or a blueprint for reality. I think of Dickens's ironic depiction of the factories of Coketown as fairy palaces; the point is that the human imagination can transform these ugly factories if only it has the will to do so. Like all metaphor, fairy tales direct our attention to the play of language and convention.[38]

It may well be this pervasive and underpinning presence of the assumptions about active and passive readers, and readings, which prompted John

Stephens to suggest that '[i]t will remain to be seen whether the embedded examples of reader response criticism in ... McGillis ... designate a similar swan song for reader response in children's literature criticism'.[39] In any case, it is that 'embedded reader response', which keeps intact throughout *The Nimble Reader* a commitment to, and faith in, finding the good book for the child, or, as McGillis puts it himself in a well-known final conclusion,

> Do we really encounter prose before we encounter the old woman who lives in a shoe? Do children not babble and coo before they speak in sentences? Do children not chant and sing in the schoolyard and on the street at least as early as their first encounters with prose? Too soon they give up their singing. Too soon they accommodate a prosaic world. So what good is literary theory? Will it keep our children singing? Well, perhaps not. But understanding something of literary theory will give us some understanding of how the literature we give to our children works. ... And as long as we keep singing, we have a chance of passing along our singing spirit to those we teach.[40]

If, in my reading, McGillis's kind of theory does not, after all, succeed in its own aspiration to offer a different account from children's literature criticism's enduring common aim of knowing what the good book is for the child, I will turn now to David Rudd's *Enid Blyton and the Mystery of Children's Literature*. As we saw earlier, Rudd, more overtly than Roderick McGillis, expresses dissatisfaction with prior children's literature criticism and its approaches. One of his primary concerns is to do with 'one of the main weaknesses of cultural/media studies: that it rests on too narrow an empirical base ... It is particularly the case with critics of Blyton, many of whom make their pronouncements with no thought of consulting the primary readership, something that is perfectly captured in Brian Alderson's ... more general comment on "the irrelevance of children to the children's book reviewer." '[41] And he sees as a result of this that 'real children are often excluded from discussions that are of central concern to them, especially where discussion is seen to involve issues that blur the child/adult divide ...'.[42]

In this way it would seem that Rudd, from the start, much more straightforwardly than McGillis, and for all his critique of aspects of prior children's literature criticism, does not want to depart anyway from trying to find the good book for the child, and trying to find it through knowing about both the book and the child. But, surprisingly perhaps, Rudd does after all make a similar move to McGillis, in arguing at the same time that '[c]hildren, of course, are also constructed in a certain way, usually as helpless, innocent beings – girls particularly so'.[43] This construction, furthermore, is to be

49

understood in terms of

> [a] key term that enables us to speak of this force-field, comprising text, context, and readership... 'discourse'. This allows us to recognize the textual dimension of everything, not just the literary text *per se*... It is [Michel] Foucault's usage to which I am chiefly indebted... [in which] discourses are concerned with the authority with which people speak, what they speak about, and in what manner. In conveying knowledge, discourses simultaneously embody power and, thereby, a set of social relations. So certain ways of talking about a subject, deriving from particular institutional sites, actually form that subject...[44]

To Rudd, discourse (or a variation of the term he prefers to use: 'discursive threads') is important for several reasons, including that 'it recognizes that meaning and truth do not originate in the writer, the book, or the reader... [which] gets us round thorny issues like the "intentional fallacy" by refusing to read a cause–effect relationship from signifiers to underlying referents',[45] as well as 'suggesting a process rather than a thing... [t]o give an apposite illustration, if an adult tells off a child, the adult is not simply using these words to reprimand the child, but is also defining the child in the process; or, more exactly, is re-enacting and re-invoking the relations of adult to child, where the latter is the powerless, the dependant'.[46] Rudd therefore concludes that '[c]hildren, of course, are subject to just this discursive process, internalizing what it is to be a child who will later become an adult; and literature, especially literature for children, is ineluctably complicit with this'.[47] And he suggests, finally, that

> [t]his has serious implications, not only for looking at how children read but also at how we discuss their reading. We realize that there can never be an innocent interview in which truth is transparently revealed by the words spoken. Interviews are shaped by larger discursive elements... [T]hus there are differential power relations involved from the start...[48]

In short, to Rudd, it would seem here, children are produced by internalizing what adults say they are, and in this way his formulation may be read as very similar to those of Perry Nodelman, for instance, when he argues that children's books 'teach children how to be child-like', and that picture books 'are enmeshed in the ideology of the culture that produced them, and the childlikeness they teach is merely what our culture views as natural in children'.[49] Rudd and Nodelman, furthermore, also use similar terms when Rudd argues that 'this construction [of children] means that they can, thereby, be easily belittled and marginalized';[50] or, as Nodelman would have it,

> there surely never was a childhood, in the sense of something surer and safer and happier than the world we perceive as adults. In privileging childhood as this sort of 'other,' we misrepresent and belittle what we are;

most significantly, we belittle childhood and allow ourselves to ignore our actual knowledge of real children.[51]

Nodelman's formulations here deploy simultaneously two ideas about child-hood as identity, as Rudd's also do: on the one hand there are their overt arguments about the child as a construction, but on the other hand they also refer to a 'real child', as in the quotes above.

I must read both Nodelman and Rudd, therefore, as arguing that there are two kinds of children, constructed ones and real ones, and the question therefore arises of what Rudd means precisely by his constructed child and his real child.[52] This is a crucial question, it seems to me, if we are to under-stand how Rudd's central claim to having a new approach works. For I read him as claiming first that his approach is significantly different and better because he, unlike many previous critics, includes an 'empirical basis' – that is, he has interviewed children concerning their views on reading Enid Blyton – and, secondly, but even more importantly, because he rests his approach on his use of an idea of 'discourse' which also applies, according to him, to the child and to the empirical work that he has carried out. In other words, Rudd seems to me to be arguing that it is not the inclusion of empirical work itself which constitutes his 'new approach' to children's literature criticism in general (because children have been interviewed and consulted about their reading before, albeit, according to Rudd, not yet adequately in the case of Blyton), but the *way* that he has garnered and used this empirical basis in terms of his understanding of discursive threads. It is his view of the child as constructed, then, which he sees as reforming the empiricism that, he must be implying, he sees most other children's litera-ture critics having accepted as the child telling the truth about its reading. Instead, Rudd claims repeatedly that he does not see the interviews with children as '[t]he source of "the truth" about Blyton'.[53] If this is the case, however, then the question must arise of why these interviews are *with chil-dren*? For if children are constructed by adults, as Rudd asserts, I would sug-gest he surely would see the interviews as merely reflecting back to him what adults, including himself, have made the child to be. That is, how is Rudd to claim that he can see or hear in the interviews anything else than what he as an adult takes to be the child saying something about Blyton anyway? Or does the answer already lie implicit in the subsequent bracketed state-ment that '(they simply provide an alternative reading)'? For does the idea of 'an alternative reading' not already include a view of the child as 'other' ('alternative')? How is that idea itself to be excluded from being a construc-tion? In short, in interviewing people selected fundamentally[54] on the basis of an identity already assigned to them ('children'), they have already been defined as such: constructed as a 'group'.

The question for me then is how Rudd's constructed child is to be com-bined with the empirical base that he finds so important. I also still need to account for the status and definition of the real child that he also refers to, as I noted above. Perhaps this will be clarified for me in Rudd's further explanations about 'the involvement of children'

> [w]ho should be seen neither... as simply mouthing 'adult' discourses. For a start, each person is obviously a different weave of constituent discursive threads... Also, the child's very positioning means that it will use these discourses differently, producing hybrid forms, often mimicking and changing adult inflections. Lastly, these threads will themselves be intermixed with a more resilient child culture.[55]

But here, only further complications seem to arise for the conceptualization of the child in terms of 'threads of discursivity', in the sense that the definitions and uses of both these terms shift about constantly in this passage (as elsewhere in the book). For instance, in writing that children should not be seen 'as simply mouthing "adult" discourses', Rudd must be assuming that they also somehow articulate other-than-adult, or child, discourses. Moreover, 'mouthing' seems to imply, if not assert overtly, that children only imitate or 'pass on' adult discourses about them, rather than this being an 'own', innate or spontaneous discursivity.

But, if such other-than-adult discourses exist, then how does this work? For in Rudd's earlier explanation of discursivity, 'certain ways of talking about a subject... actually form that subject... certain ways of speaking become naturalized and literally "in-form" our thoughts, our way of addressing issues'.[56] If the child is produced ('actually formed') as subject by 'certain ways of speaking', then what and where are the 'other' ways for the child to speak? Are they produced by the mixing of the 'different weave of constituent discursive threads'? But how would this mixing evade their being 'adult' in origin, in terms of the way that Rudd postulated the power-relationships between adult and child? Equally, how would the child 'us[ing] these discourses differently, producing hybrid forms, often mimicking and changing adult inflections' stop the discourses being 'adult'? This would require Rudd, logically speaking, to postulate that 'hybrid forms', 'mimicking' and 'changing' are somehow either prior to, or wholly independent of, that on which they depend (the adult discourse which is to be somehow changed), both options being, effectively, a contradiction in terms.

It is perhaps in the final statement of the passage that it becomes most clear from whence these shifts and contradictions, as I have analysed them, stem: for, in the end, there is 'a more resilient child culture' mixed in with it all. This explains for me too how the constructed child lives, in Rudd's arguments, comfortably alongside a real child. 'Construction' here must mean something like a child-of-discourse, while a real child is a child-outside-of-discourse, in fact, after all; very nearly overwhelmed by the discourses of power, but residually resilient. So 'discourse' is not 'everything', as Rudd seemed to be stating earlier (when he insisted on the 'textual dimension of everything, not just the literary text *per se*'), because there is a reality 'underneath it all', however beleaguered, which Rudd can discern. I see this understanding of Rudd's ideas about the constructed and the real child confirmed in the subsequent arguments in the book, which refer repeatedly to a child who is real – which is defined as not produced by discourse, and not subject to Rudd's interpretation (his discourses of childhood), but simply *there*, known and identified in the text, for instance as follows: 'children do *not* write as Blyton did, although, once attuned to it, they can perform some creditable pastiches ...';[57] 'the problem is that this [Blyton's portrayal of children of the middle-classes] is certainly not a child's perceptions of its heroes; nor do I think it Blyton's';[58] 'although it might be argued that children won't discern these themes, they will certainly pick up on their emotional resonance: the insecurity of existence, knowing where one fits into the scheme of things, being accused of misbehaving, and so on';[59] or, as Rudd concludes,

> [t]o sum up ... I have made the move from adult discursive threads about nationhood and class to the way that most children seem to read the texts. For them it is the empowerment of children against adults that appeals, and, in this, 'St George' is the children's champion. ... In this way we can begin to explain George's overall appeal across the sexes, while also recognizing her extra appeal for girls in standing up against patriarchy. ... Whereas adults might find some of the above discourses ... suitably serious, the young reader would probably code them as 'boring'. Children enjoy the companionship ... I shall also suggest that for many readers the pleasure of the text is not merely a mental enjoyment, but a sensual one.[60]

Rudd consolidates this 'move from adult discursive threads ... to the way that most children seem to read the text' with quotes from his interviews, which must, then, in these formulations, also be read as being accepted as that very 'truth' (outside of discourse) that Rudd was earlier denying as possible. The question for me remains (besides the problem, discussed earlier, of the interviewing of children as such anyway), how Rudd's empirical base is doing anything new or different compared with interviews deployed in children's literature criticism previously. As Nicholas Tucker writes in his classic *The Child and the Book*, published almost 20 years before *Enid Blyton and the Mystery of Children's Literature*:

> [t]rying to discover some of the nature and effects of the interaction between children and their favourite books is by no means easy, though. One simple-minded approach to the problems has always been to ask children themselves through various questionnaires and surveys, what exactly their books mean to them. Turning a powerful searchlight of this

sort onto complex, sometimes diffuse patterns of reaction is a clumsy way of going about things, however, and children can be particularly elusive when interrogated like this, with laconic comments like 'Not bad' or 'The story's good' adding little to any researcher's understanding.[61]

I could speculate that Rudd's ultimate defense of his interviews against such critique – having disrupted his initial claim to their difference as lying in a status as discourse rather than truth – might be that they are at least 'better' interviews, not the 'powerful searchlights' Tucker rejects. But this would not affect the reasons and way they are used in that the interviews are still seen as a source of children's views about their reading, as Tucker notes. Seeing them as able to access those views better than other interviews does not constitute a claim to a difference of approach or theory, but only a claim to the superior application of the same approach.

Finally, Rudd offers two chapters ('The Mystery Explained (1): Writer of (and on) the Oral Stage' and 'The Mystery Explained (2): Writer of Passages') clearly signalled as providing a hitherto unavailable answer to, or explanation of, the popularity of the children's fiction of Enid Blyton; explanations, moreover, which form, it is suggested, part of a much more widely applicable 'new approach':

> [w]e, as adults, might only see bare words, outmoded and problematic discourse, but that is exactly our position as arch-Other. If, however, we do not try to understand her appeal, we are engaging in just the sort of arrogant colonialist discourse of which Blyton stands accused: of being dismissive, of disparaging what might seem to us quaint superstitions. And, in the very act of doing this we are solidifying the discourse that re-makes children's literature in our own image: one that celebrates the adult as the site of wholeness … At the other end of this binary see-saw sits the child: and, not surprisingly, the scales are heavily weighted against it … In Foucauldian terms, I have sought to unmask this power–knowledge coupling by teasing out its constituent threads.[62]

This passage, as well as the two chapters, do not to my reading, however, depart from the problems and contradictions developed in Rudd's prior arguments; for Rudd's reasoning here must rely on the claim that he is an adult who is also a child because he can see the 'adult' from the child's perspective ('our position as arch-Other'), which must also assume a real child who has a view of that adult as 'arch-Other' in and of itself (that is, not derived from adult discourse). There is no explanation here of how this occupation of the child's perspective by Rudd is somehow neither the 'adult-centredness' nor the 'arrogant colonialist discourse' which he precisely condemns.[63]

In fact, by introducing certain definitions and uses of 'orality' and 'psychoanalysis' as the two approaches that account for Blyton's popularity, in the two chapters on 'The Mystery Explained' Rudd comes to rely ever more heavily simply on assertions and statements about his real child and its reading, as well as the real adult and its reading. So the 'oral' turns out to be here both Blyton-as-storyteller (despite Rudd's previously noted rejection of the 'intentionalist fallacy' as part of 'recogniz[ing] that meaning and truth do not originate in the writer, the book, or the reader') 'captured' on the page,[64] with oral language consisting simply of a self-evident 'style' and features that are, however, mysteriously preserved in written text. Even more bizarre, furthermore, coming from a self-professed theorist of 'discursive threads', is the section where Rudd introduces a theory of brain-hemisphere functioning to confirm the 'oral' as the source of both Blyton and Homer's composition and 'appeal' (at one and the same time): 'What they [poets from Homer's time] were really "hearing", argues Jaynes, was their own right hemispheres, which literally took them over, delivering powerful images and sounds. This certainly seems so with Blyton ...'.[65] I find it hard to know how I am to read this as 'simply point[ing] to homologies amongst textual elements, be they "biographical" or "fictional" ',[66] as Rudd would have it.

Psychoanalysis, in the second chapter, has the same function as the 'oral'. It offers, in Rudd's argument, another access to the real child and its reading:[67]

> I have suggested that Blyton is essentially involved in creating fantasies that protect and strengthen young egos, though this is seen to be on behalf of children as a group. This not only helps the process of consolidating the Ideal-I, but also the complementary process of warding off the not-I: the threatening, unbound energies that Freud spoke of. Blyton's work is about staging fantasies of mastery ... Much children's reading, therefore, falls outside the way that many adults conceive it: neither slavish identification, passive consumption, nor ideological servitude. Basically, children are out to maximize their pleasure, by personalizing it, revisiting favourite moments.[68]

And Rudd concludes, finally, therefore, that

> [a]dult protests, then, add to the child's pleasure. ... The more that adults seek to control and define what children should be doing, the more that groups such as the Five will appeal. From the other side, Blyton's books are frequently disliked by adults because adults feel shut out of them. ... The adult reader ... cannot see that world beyond the seemingly threadbare words. ... This recognition, that there are some texts that might be good only for children, has been slow in coming. ... Blyton, of course, provides just such a point of retrenchment, of consolidation and emotional satisfaction. The sorts of play that children spontaneously engage in ... Blyton makes into stories. ... provid[ing] a landscape in which [children] could roam so freely, indulging themselves, celebrating their own world, while simultaneously turning the tables on the adults.[69]

Rudd here continues to be the adult who claims he *does* see beyond the 'seemingly threadbare words', and that he has found the knowledge of the real child that allows him to match these books, correctly this time, to that child. He writes of advocating the 'celebrat[ion of] a child-centred culture, where wholeness is expressly conceived at the level of the child working against the fractured world of adults',[70] which must again include the idea that he, Rudd, inhabits and knows both that 'fractured world' of adults and the wholeness of the child. There is no explanation of how this celebration could avoid being based on the very positions he so emphatically repudiated previously: on an adult definition of the child as 'other' to itself, and on an appropriation of that child for the sake not of the child, but of the adult who needs to see the child in that way.

As little as McGillis with his 'singing child', can Rudd, then, explain how his new theory has avoided making ultimately exactly the same moves as all the children's literature criticism they wish to reform: the finding of the good book for the child, through knowing both the child and the book. In this sense they have not disrupted the diagnosis that Jacqueline Rose made in *The Case of Peter Pan*:

> Children's fiction rests on the idea that there is a child who is simply there to be addressed and that speaking to it might be simple … [;] that it represents the child, speaks to and for children, addresses them as a group which is knowable and exists for the group, much as the book (so the claim runs) exists for them. … There is no child behind the category 'children's fiction', other than the one which the category itself sets in place, the one which it needs to believe is there for its own purposes.[71]

Despite the overt rejection, I am sure, critics such as McGillis and Rudd would make of any suggestion that they think that it is 'simple' to speak to the child, the underpinning of their arguments by the real child nevertheless constitutes that very idea of transparency – or simplicity – which Rose refers to again when she argues that '[c]hildren's fiction has never completely severed its links with a philosophy which sets up the child as a pure point of origin in relation to language, sexuality and the state'.[72] For this describes exactly the outer limits of the new-ness of the theories of McGillis and Rudd, and, in fact, I have suggested, of other children's literature criticism: the maintenance of the real child is part of a maintenance of a real world, which can be sensed and known. However aware many of these critics are of the problems of children's literature criticism – the conflicting and contradictory claims about what is good for children to read, and why; the inability of critics to find any 'evidence' or 'proof' for their claims, as opposed to those of any other critic; the necessity for critics to set themselves as having a superior memory or knowledge of childhood compared to other adults (except those critics with whom they happen to agree) – their attempts to develop a 'new' approach by appropriating or adapting a theory from 'adult' literary criticism is hampered fundamentally, I have attempted to demonstrate, by their commitment, finally, to finding the right book for their child.

But this leaves unanswered, after all, the third and final question with which I began this discussion. If I have now argued first that (and why) critics cannot, in fact, introduce a new theory – defined according to their own aims – without affecting the fundamental aim of the field; and, secondly, what kind of theory they turn out to have developed, which permits its application without affecting the basic goal of children's literature criticism; then I must also address, thirdly, and perhaps most importantly: does that fundamental goal of the criticism need to be changed at all? Ought it to be changed? Isn't the ability to know how to select the right books for the child exactly what children's literature criticism wants to achieve, and should therefore continue pursuing? My answer may already be clear from what I have analysed above, and, in fact, it is in a sense diagnosed by the children's literature critics themselves in their ongoing search for the new approach: also within the field of children's literature criticism itself, a pervading and continuing uneasiness with what it perceives to be its own problems and contradictions recurs. There is, after all, of course, no conclusive evidence of which critic predicts better than which other critic which children will like which book and why; or a critical method that addresses once and for all the demands made by children's literature criticism of itself to find the way to improved literacy, education, morality and emotional well-being through the reading of suitable children's books. Indeed, how could there be? What kind of account could any child – any reader at all – possibly provide that would, first of all, account for the taste, emotional response and memory of any other reader according to any given similarity attributed to them (gender, age, ethnic group, etc.)? And, secondly, how could any such account, even given that it existed, be seen in exactly the same way by that reader (is there only one, consistent, eternal account of a reader and a reading?), every critic and every other reader? My reply, therefore, must be that children's literature criticism as it stands, and as it defines itself, cannot succeed in achieving its own aim: finding the good book for the child, through knowing the child and the book. I suggest, the pursuit of that knowledge as the pot of gold at the end of the rainbow can only replicate the problems I have analysed above.

What then, finally, this volume wishes to offer as its 'new approaches', is a writing and thinking about children's literature that does not rest on – or re-introduce at some point, overtly or indirectly – the real child, and a wider real of which it is a part. In each chapter, aspects of critical interest are focused on – such as authors and authorship (Sue Walsh), ideas of 'history' (Christine Sutphin and Lila Harper), reading (J. Hillis Miller and Neil Cocks), the child, the family, and 'ideology' (Stephen Thomson), and national identity (Jacqui Lazú and Sarah Spooner) – in order either to analyse with respect specifically to those areas problems such as I have described above as occurring in children's literature criticism, or (also) to provide examples of how a criticism that does not rely on the real child might be formulated.

Is this an abandonment of the child? Leaving it to its own devices while some abstract philosophy is pursued, which would, as Roger Sell suggests, 'drive a wedge between children's literature and the human world within which it occurs'? This is only the case if that 'human world' is presumed to be, necessarily, in existence and knowable and reachable; that 'real world' that Jacqueline Rose referred to as part of a philosophy or 'a pure point of origin'. It is this real world – with its real child – which is set up by those whose faith lies in that philosophy to contrast with an 'ivory tower' of irrelevant abstraction, a heartless solipsism. It is that claim to their own moral selflessness, generosity and care that is defended here. As Peter Hunt once wrote, 'I *would* do good for others, but I can never be sure *what* is good for the others.'[73] Rather, then, than each critic endlessly re-finding finally, through whatever route, a child who can be known, and to whom their good can then be done, this volume will be proposing that an analysis of narratives – critical or otherwise – and how these can be understood to mean, in and of itself can contribute better to thinking through one's own actions and meanings. That actions and meanings will still take place is not in question, and neither that any analysis of them will by definition be partial, temporary and contingent. But the continued effort not to stabilize, to end, meaning is precisely the drive of the criticism in this volume, rather than precisely to end meaning by finally finding and fixing the child, which is what children's literature criticism has always wished for. Or, to put it in other words, as psychoanalyst Patrick Casement writes in relation to parallel issues in psychoanalysis,[74] this analysis does not see 'not knowing' as a nihilistic expression of despair about therapy ever getting anywhere, nor as an admittance that nothing can ever be known anyway, by definition, and that therefore therapy is some form of gratuitous or superficial storytelling. This would only be the case if 'knowing', finding the truth, remains seen as the ideal, the solution to everything, the thing that can be reached if only one tries hard enough, and, finally, the thing the therapist will find for the patient. Instead, 'not knowing' is seen as an essential element of a making sense which therapy *is*, a toleration which is essential to a recognition that meaning – both of the patient and the therapist – is not stable, consistent and there-to-be-found, but that it is continually being created. In being created it is nevertheless fundamental. It is this paradox that this volume too is attempting to sustain.

Recommended further reading

Ariès, Philippe, *Centuries of Childhood: A Social History of Family Life* (Harmondsworth: Penguin, 1973, orig. publ. 1959). The history that first formulated childhood as a historically and culturally variable concept.

Butler, Judith, *Gender Trouble: Feminism and the Subversion of Identity* (London: Routledge, 1990). Discusses gender as constructed in similar ways to Jacqueline Rose's discussion of the child as constructed in *The Case of Peter Pan*.

Derrida, Jacques, *Of Grammatology*, trans. Gayatri Chakravorty Spivak (Baltimore: Johns Hopkins University Press, 1998, orig. pub. 1967). Analyses philosophical ideas about writing, education and knowledge, particularly in relation to Jean-Jacques Rousseau's *Émile* (1762).

Freud, Sigmund, 'Three Essays on the Theory of Sexuality' in *On Sexuality*, trans. James Strachey, comp. and ed. Angela Richards, The Penguin Freud Library, vol. 7 (Harmondsworth: Penguin, 1991, orig. pub. 1905). Introduces psychoanalytic ideas about memory and identity which disrupt assumptions about a coherent, knowable, consciousness.

Jenks, Chris, Allison James and Alan Prout, *Theorizing Childhood* (Cambridge: Polity Press, 1998). Sociologists working with ideas of childhood as construction (see also previous works by these authors).

Notes

1. See for examples of more extensive accounts of the precarious 'academic' status of children's literature: Peter Hunt, 'Criticism and Children's Literature', in his *Criticism, Theory, and Children's Literature* (Oxford: Basil Blackwell, 1991), pp. 5–16; Roderick McGillis, 'Beginnings', in his *The Nimble Reader. Literary Theory and Children's Literature* (New York: Twayne Publishers, 1996), pp. 1–26.
2. Roger D. Sell, ed., *Children's Literature as Communication: The ChiLPA project*, series: Studies in Narrative, volume 2, series ed.: Michael Bamberg (Amsterdam/ Philadelphia: John Benjamins Publishing Company, 2002), p. 2 (emphasis Sell).
3. Jacqueline Rose, *The Case of Peter Pan or The Impossibility of Children's Fiction*, series: Language, Discourse, Society, series eds.: Stephen Heath and Colin MacCabe (Basingstoke: Macmillan, 1984), p. 154.
4. Peter Hunt, *Criticism, Theory, and Children's Literature* (Oxford: Basil Blackwell, 1991), p. 1.
5. Hunt, *Criticism, Theory, and Children's Literature*, p. 1, quoting from: Anita Moss, 'Structuralism and its critics', *Children's Literature Association Quarterly*, 6(1), Spring 1981, 25.
6. Hunt, *Criticism, Theory, and Children's Literature*, p. 1.
7. Hunt, *Criticism, Theory, and Children's Literature*, p. 2 (emphasis mine).
8. Hunt, *Criticism, Theory, and Children's Literature*, p. 5, quoting from: Aidan Chambers, *Booktalk: Occasional writing on literature and children* (London: Bodley Head, 1985).
9. McGillis, *The Nimble Reader*, pp. 16–17 (emphasis mine).
10. Fran Claggett, 'Foreword', in: Lissa Paul, *Reading Otherways* (Portland, Maine: Calendar Islands Publishers, 1998), pp. 3–4, p. 3.
11. John Stephens, 'Children's Literature, Text and Theory: What are we interested in now?', *Papers: Explorations into Children's Literature*, 10(2) August 2000, 12–21, 12 (first published in: Susan Clancy with David Gilbey (eds), *Something to Crow About: New Perspectives in Literature for Young People* (Wagga Wagga: Charles Sturt University, 1999)).
12. David Rudd, *Enid Blyton and the Mystery of Children's Literature* (Basingstoke: Macmillan – now Palgrave Macmillan, 2000), p. 6.

22   *Children's Literature*

13. Sell, ed., *Children's Literature as Communication: The ChiLPA project*, p. 24 (emphasis mine).
14. Hunt, *Criticism, Theory, and Children's Literature*, p. 7.
15. Quintilian, *Institutes of Oratory or: Education of an Orator, in 12 Books*, trans. John Selby Watson (London: George Bell and Sons, 1903), p. 117. For a more extensive discussion of classical writings on children, education, and children's books see: 'On Knowing the Child: Stories of Origin and Hierarchical Systems', in my *Children's Literature: Criticism and the Fictional Child* (Oxford: Clarendon Press, 1994), pp. 37–68.
16. This is also the argument formulated first of all by Jacqueline Rose in *The Case of Peter Pan or The Impossibility of Children's Fiction*.
17. I will not include here any further analysis of Peter Hunt's arguments, or of the well-known work of Barbara Wall in her book *The Narrator's Voice: The Dilemma of Children's Fiction* (Basingstoke: Macmillan – now Palgrave Macmillan, 1991), as I have discussed these before extensively in: 'On Not Knowing the Child: Children's Literature Criticism and Adult Literary Theory', in my *Children's Literature: Criticism and the Fictional Child*, pp. 131–64.
18. To give just one example: John Stephens himself lists, in his 1999 article surveying the state of children's literature criticism ('Children's Literature, Text and Theory': see above), as included in the 'steady trickle of notable books which attempt to place children's literature within the context of those modern literary and cultural theories', 'in particular, Hunt, 1991; Wall, 1991; Stephens, 1992; Nodelman, 1994/1996; McGillis, 1996; Nikolajeva, 1996)', while, in a footnote, he also adds Jacqueline Rose's *The Case of Peter Pan* and Zohar Shavit's *Poetics of Children's Literature* (Athens, Georgia: University of Georgia Press, 1986).
19. See Sue Walsh, 'Child/Animal: It's the "Real" Thing', in *The Yearbook of English Studies*, Special Section 'Children in Literature', ed. by Karín Lesnik-Oberstein, vol. 32 (Leeds: MHRA, 2002), 152–62, and ' "Irony? – But Children don't get it do they?" The Idea of Appropriate Language for the Child in Narratives for Children', in *Children's Literature Association Quarterly*, for the special issue on 'Narrative Theories and Practices in Children's and Young Adult Literature', 28(1), 2003, 26–36.
20. McGillis, *The Nimble Reader*, p. 21.
21. McGillis, *The Nimble Reader*, p. 21.
22. McGillis, *The Nimble Reader*, pp. 23–4.
23. McGillis, *The Nimble Reader*, p. 24.
24. McGillis, *The Nimble Reader*, p. 24.
25. McGillis, *The Nimble Reader*, p. 26.
26. McGillis, *The Nimble Reader*, p. 24.
27. McGillis, *The Nimble Reader*, pp. 18–19.
28. McGillis, *The Nimble Reader*, p. 19.
29. McGillis, *The Nimble Reader*, pp. 19–20.
30. McGillis, *The Nimble Reader*, p. 40.
31. McGillis, *The Nimble Reader*, p. 38.
32. McGillis, *The Nimble Reader*, p. 24.
33. McGillis, *The Nimble Reader*, p. 128.
34. McGillis, *The Nimble Reader*, p. 124.
35. McGillis, *The Nimble Reader*, p. 123.
36. McGillis, *The Nimble Reader*, p. 124.
37. McGillis, *The Nimble Reader*, p. 124.

38. McGillis, *The Nimble Reader*, p. 166.
39. Stephens, 'Children's Literature, Text and Theory', 12–13.
40. McGillis, *The Nimble Reader*, p. 206.
41. Rudd, *Enid Blyton and the Mystery of Children's Literature*, p. 6, quoting from: Brian W. Alderson, 'The Irrelevance of children to the children's book reviewer', *Children's Book News*, 4(1), 1969, 10.
42. Rudd, *Enid Blyton and the Mystery of Children's Literature*, p. 4.
43. Rudd, *Enid Blyton and the Mystery of Children's Literature*, p. 6
44. Rudd, *Enid Blyton and the Mystery of Children's Literature*, p. 11.
45. Rudd, *Enid Blyton and the Mystery of Children's Literature*, p. 12.
46. Rudd, *Enid Blyton and the Mystery of Children's Literature*, pp. 13–14.
47. Rudd, *Enid Blyton and the Mystery of Children's Literature*, p. 14.
48. Rudd, *Enid Blyton and the Mystery of Children's Literature*, p. 14.
49. Perry Nodelman, 'Decoding the Images: Illustration and Picture Books', in: Peter Hunt, ed., *Understanding Children's Literature: Key Essays from the Routledge Companion Encyclopedia to Children's Literature* (London: Routledge, 1999), pp. 69–81, p. 77.
50. Rudd, *Enid Blyton and the Mystery of Children's Literature*, p. 12.
51. Perry Nodelman, 'The Hidden Meaning and the Inner Tale: Deconstruction and the Interpretation of Fairy Tales', *Children's Literature Association Quarterly*, 15(3) Fall 1990, 143–8, 147.
52. I will not consider Nodelman's position with regard to the construction of the child further here, as Sue Walsh has already done so extensively in her article 'Child/Animal: It's the "Real" Thing' (see above for reference), as well as also having considered there further the positions on constructivism of John Stephens and Roderick McGillis.
53. Rudd, *Enid Blyton and the Mystery of Children's Literature*, p. 17.
54. Rudd makes clear his concern to include in his interviews children from differing social, class and ethnic backgrounds, but this, in fact, confirms, rather than disrupts, that *despite* such differences, the category of 'childhood' is seen by him to unite them all. My argument here is related to the problem, as I see it, that many children's literature critics quote Jacqueline Rose's work approvingly primarily in relation to her pointing out that

    the very idea of speaking to *all* children serves to close off a set of cultural divisions, divisions in which not only children, but we ourselves, are necessarily caught. There is no children's book market which does not, on closer scrutiny, crumble under just such a set of divisions – of class, culture, and literacy – divisions which undermine any generalised concept of the child. (*The Case of Peter Pan*, p. 7)

    They read Rose here merely as stating the obvious: that children come from different backgrounds. But this is not my reading of Rose: instead, as in my argument in relation to Rudd's selection of his interviewees, her fundamental point here seems to me to be that the very category of 'childhood' itself is disrupted by these divisions (as are all 'generalised concept[s]' of identity, therefore). In other words, that there are ultimately, in philosophical terms, no 'children' who can be seen as divided by cultural divisions. For a more extensive discussion of the way I read children's literature critics' understanding of Rose, see my article: 'The Psychopathology of Everyday Children's Literature Criticism', in: *Cultural Critique*, 45, Autumn 2000, 222–42.

55. Rudd, *Enid Blyton and the Mystery of Children's Literature*, p. 17.
56. Rudd, *Enid Blyton and the Mystery of Children's Literature*, pp. 11–12.
57. Rudd, *Enid Blyton and the Mystery of Children's Literature*, p. 31.
58. Rudd, *Enid Blyton and the Mystery of Children's Literature*, p. 50.
59. Rudd, *Enid Blyton and the Mystery of Children's Literature*, p. 87.
60. Rudd, *Enid Blyton and the Mystery of Children's Literature*, p. 102.
61. Nicolas Tucker, *The Child and the Book: A Psychological and Literary Exploration* (Cambridge: Cambridge University Press, 1990 (orig. pub. 1981)), p. 2.
62. Rudd, *Enid Blyton and the Mystery of Children's Literature*, p. 203.
63. For a similarly self-contradictory statement about 'adult-centredness' see: Rudd, *Enid Blyton and the Mystery of Children's Literature*, p. 104. The idea incidentally that the problem with children's literature is that adults act as 'colonizers' of the child is again attributed frequently to Jacqueline Rose. As I argued before, however, to my reading, unlike those children's literature critics, Rose is not arguing merely that adults impose on or oppress children, who should be released from such imposition, but that the production of an identity such as 'childhood' is *always*, inevitably, on behalf of the group so defined by others.
64. For a more extensive discussion of issues around 'authorship', see Sue Walsh's chapter in this volume.
65. Rudd, *Enid Blyton and the Mystery of Children's Literature*, p. 167.
66. Rudd, *Enid Blyton and the Mystery of Children's Literature*, pp. 12–13.
67. For a classic discussion of the range of definitions and uses literary criticism makes of psychoanalysis, including those such as Rudd's here, see: Shoshana Felman, 'Turning the Screw of Interpretation' in: Shoshana Felman, ed., *Literature and Psychoanalysis: The Question of Reading Otherwise*, Yale French Studies, 55/56 (1977), 94–207.
68. Rudd, *Enid Blyton and the Mystery of Children's Literature*, pp. 189 and 195.
69. Rudd, *Enid Blyton and the Mystery of Children's Literature*, pp. 203, 204 and 205.
70. Rudd, *Enid Blyton and the Mystery of Children's Literature*, p. 203.
71. Rose, *The Case of Peter Pan*, pp. 1 and 10.
72. Rose, *The Case of Peter Pan*, p. 8.
73. Hunt, *Criticism, Theory, and Children's Literature*, p. 172.
74. See: Patrick Casement, *On Learning from the Patient* (London: Tavistock Publications, 1985). For a more extensive discussion of the ways I draw parallels between some forms of psychoanalytic psychotherapy and ideas about literary criticism, see: 'The Reading Child and Other Children: The Psychoanalytic Child and Psychoanalytic Space', in my *Children's Literature: Criticism and the Fictional Child* (Oxford: Clarendon Press, 1994), pp. 165–225.

2
Author and Authorship. Effigies of Effie: On Kipling's Biographies

Sue Walsh

The purpose of this chapter is to analyse the consequences of an historical tendency in children's literature criticism to look to accounts of the life of the author to explain and account for the fiction. In these critical narratives childhood is seen as something that is elusive and yet retrievable through the literature that is characterized either as a writing of, or a response to, the actuality of the author's own childhood, and/or as an account of the author's relationship with his/her own children.

I will suggest that such biographically informed narratives have a tendency to limit the interpretation of children's literature to this supposed personal story, the uncovering of which is seen to be the purpose of the criticism. In this way, the fiction becomes a kind of mystery to be unravelled in order to discover the 'true' childhood already existing 'behind' the story. So while this chapter will focus on how ideas about authorship and biography are mobilized in the criticism of Rudyard Kipling's literature for children, what I hope to develop, by using Kipling criticism as a sort of case study, is an analysis that will prove to be relevant to children's literature criticism in a much broader sense, and not only to children's literature criticism, but to any criticism that relies on, or bases itself in ideas about the author's life, intentions and/or unconscious motivations.

Kipling would seem to be a useful choice in elaborating the questions and problems around ideas of authorial intention, if only because of what Sandra Kemp refers to as 'the continuing fascination with the details and events of Kipling's life'.[1] This fascination has repeatedly expressed itself in Kipling criticism as a drawing of correspondences between the work and the life. This is particularly marked in the relatively few discussions of Kipling's *Just So Stories* (1902)[2] and is most clearly expressed in reference to a group of tales that I will henceforward refer to as the 'Taffy' stories. These stories comprise two tales found in the standard editions of the *Just So Stories*: 'How the First Letter Was Written'[3] and 'How the Alphabet Was Made',[4] and a third, 'The Tabu Tale',[5] sometimes referred to as the 'missing' or 'lost' Just So Story.[6] What might be said to justify the grouping together of these stories is that they all feature and revolve around the relationship between a 'Neolithic' father, Tegumai Bopsulai, and his daughter Taffimai Metallumai ('Taffy'). Each of the stories is also elaborated around the implications and consequences of language and the use of signs. In this, the 'Taffy' stories follow through, in what could be said to be a metafictional way, the language games that can be read as a feature of the *Just So Stories* as a collection. However, although critics frequently refer to the way the *Just So Stories* play with language this is usually characterized as a species of mimicry of what seems to be constituted as child-like exuberance and playfulness.[7] In their treatment of the 'Taffy' stories, critics (and not many give more than cursory attention to them) often seem compelled to assume the texts' origins in the 'real' of Kipling's life (whichever account is given of it). Angus Wilson for example, writes in *The Strange Ride of Rudyard Kipling* that 'when the stories of private man's advancement begin, we are in the land of Tegumai and Taffy, of Kipling and his own children, and sentimental whimsicality takes over'.[8] Here then the connection between fictional characters and the author's life is simply asserted as fact. Likewise, in his award winning essay 'Kipling's "Just-So" Partner: The Dead Child as Collaborator and Muse', even U.C. Knoepflmacher identifies the three 'Taffy' stories as those in which Kipling 'allowed himself the luxury of a more direct expression of his feelings [... in which] The joy and loss of a father [...] could [...] be ascribed to a Neolithic man'.[9] Thus the stories become primarily, it seems, personal tales of Kipling's relationship with his children, and particularly with his first child Josephine, whose early death in 1899 tends to function in the criticism as an absence or a kind of mystery (since it is unwritten even in Kipling's autobiography, as I will explain below) to which the stories must then in some way refer. As a result of this, the play with language, though noted, recedes into the background, or is attributed significance *only* when it is bound in with this personal and biographical narrative.

According to Lisa Lewis's efforts to establish the dates of composition for the 'Taffy' stories, 'The Tabu Tale' appears to have been written first, though presumably altered later since it is narrated parenthetically as following on from the other two – '(You remember how Taffy and Tegumai made up the Alphabet? That was why she and the Head Chief were rather friends)'.[10] The date of writing that Lewis arrives at, 1898, is the year before Josephine's death; however, the bibliographical information has its problematic aspects. For where dates of first publication can be verified, dates of writing are rather more slippery. Lisa Lewis refers for this information to C.E. Carrington's notes from Carrie Kipling's diaries. Thus the information does not come in any sense directly from the author, and this raises the question of which conditions would have to be fulfilled for us to be satisfied that the information did come from an indisputable and *author*itative source, since Kipling's own autobiography, *Something of Myself*,[11] has been variously described by biographers and critics as 'tantalizing' and 'unsatisfactory',[12] 'unreliable',[13] 'inaccurate',[14] 'maddening',[15] 'cryptic',[16] 'idiosyncratic'[17] and 'muted'.[18] It also brings me to question what it is, as far as these critics and biographers are concerned, that the autobiography ought to be supplying but apparently is not? I read the charge that *Something of Myself* is inaccurate as depending upon the notion that it is somehow possible for an autobiography to be written that produces *the* 'truth'. Indeed I am arguing that this statement of inaccuracy goes so far as to imply that in the absence of an adequate rendering of the truth from the author, the job of the biographer is to produce that very truth in his stead. By contrast J.M.S. Tompkins argues that the problem is rather that *Something of Myself* is inaccurate in the sense that it does not conform to the standard for autobiography of the day:

> In his autobiographical sketch, *Something of Myself*, he conformed to the standards of his youth, though the pattern of autobiography and the expectations of readers had changed around him. It has been called evasive. [...] But it is entirely in harmony with the autobiographical utterances of many Victorian gentlemen who were authors. [...] By the side of these books [the autobiographies of Trollope, Walter Besant and C.G. Leland], indeed, his will appear normal. [...] What is remarkable about *Something of Myself* is the survival of this accepted form, unaltered by contemporary pressures, some fifty years beyond its time. [...] To this generation, eager for psychological evidence, often more interested in what is suppressed than in what has been selected for expression, *Something of Myself* appears defiant and uncommunicative enough.[19]

Tompkins's assessment of *Something of Myself* addresses autobiography as a literary form, as a construction rather than the repository of 'truth'. Nevertheless, even she refers to Kipling's autobiography as a 'sketch' and is thus not as far from the exasperation expressed by those such as Hilton Brown as she might at first appear. This exasperation – 'It is true that towards the end of his long life he set down his autobiography, but a more tantalizing work than *Something of Myself* with its odd stresses and maddening omissions can rarely have been penned'[20] – is apparently levelled at the text because it does not supply all that it ostensibly purported to. One telling statement of what is held to be missing from the autobiography is made by Lord Birkenhead in his biography of Kipling. Birkenhead writes of *Something of Myself*:

> We have already observed Kipling's reticence, and it is nowhere better exhibited than in this cautious, tantalizing work. Vividly written, eminently readable, it yet masks every intimate detail of his past. We have already seen that he felt adverse events so strongly that he could not bear to think about them, preferring to suppress them. He was thus denied the release from grief which many authors obtain through their writings. The reader will search this baffling work in vain for any reference to

the Vermont Tragedy, to the deaths of Josephine and John, [...] These
memories were excised from his mind by a surgical cut.[21]

Here, in this quotation that equates the text of *Something of Myself* with the
mind of Kipling the man, as though an event not mentioned in the text
indicates a loss of memory on his part, it appears that what the autobiography is expected to provide is the man – complete. And what is specifically
understood as the mark of completeness here is the emotion that
Birkenhead claims is 'suppressed'. The lack of reference in the autobiography to certain specific events is held to be a 'masking' of them by that which
is presumably a large part of the raison d'être of the biography, Kipling's
'eminently readable' and 'vivid' writing. Thus Birkenhead's biography writes
its reading of what is not there: 'he felt adverse events so strongly that he
could not bear to think about them'. As such it conforms to Tompkins's
assessment (which was published 18 years previously) of biographies and
criticism 'more interested in what is suppressed than in what has been
selected for expression'.[22]

Returning now to Lisa Lewis's attempts to establish the original dates for the
writing of 'The Tabu Tale' it transpires that Lewis's information, while not
coming directly from Kipling, cannot even be said to come directly from his
wife. Carrie Kipling's diaries were later destroyed, and the only access to them
is through Carrington's notes[23] so we are inevitably tied to his interpretation
of them and what constitutes the important information in them. What is
more, the notes themselves are rather ambiguous, for example Lisa Lewis
derives her date for the writing of 'The Tabu Tale' from the following: 'CK
recorded that a children's story "modelled on the totem tales" was written
11 Oct. 1898. In *SOM*, p. 123, RK mentions a visit to the native American col-
lections in the Smithsonian, Washington, DC.'[24] This is not exactly conclusive.

The bibliographical research is not the only way in which Lewis invokes
the author and his intentions or unconscious motivations, she also attempts
to define the text of the *Just So Stories* by categorizing it in terms of a specific
genre within children's literature. The tales are identified as 'stories of fantasy
animals',[25] and thus marked out as one of a series of classics within a genre
that includes the work of Beatrix Potter (1902), Kenneth Grahame (1908)
and Kipling's earlier *Jungle Books* (1894, 1895). Lewis does not really attempt
to do anything critically with this construction of a genre, there is no discussion of what it means to identify a text as 'fantasy' and distinguish it
particularly as an 'animal' fantasy. However, she does explain the emergence
of this genre by referring to the supposed 'real' personal histories of the
authors involved. She writes: 'All three writers invent for their creatures
imaginary worlds of great lyrical charm, as if to compensate for their own
lonely or unhappy childhoods.'[26] Thus Lewis constructs the works of Potter,
Grahame and Kipling as being generated by a set of specific 'real' circumstances, and as being created in order precisely to escape from those 'real'

circumstances. This has been and continues to be a frequent move in children's literature criticism, which, in this way, treats the text as the production of an author who is, by implication, in a state of arrested development. Gillian Avery alludes to this tendency in her contribution to John Gross's *Rudyard Kipling: The Man, His Work and His World*:

> It is often asserted that the best children's books come from authors who are not writing deliberately with children in mind, but for themselves. It is also said that the best children's authors are those who have their own childhood in mind, or who still retain in some respects a child-like outlook.[27]

This kind of reading of the children's author can be found in Michael Woods's 'The Blyton Line' which is reproduced as an appendix to Enid Blyton's biography: '[Enid Blyton] was, I am sure, really a child at heart, a person who never developed emotionally beyond the basic infantile level'.[28] It also pervades Humphrey Carpenter's *Secret Gardens*; for instance, Carpenter writes of J.M. Barrie, that 'As an adult he would enthral children by becoming a child himself.'[29] Yet another example can be found in Barbara Wall's *The Narrator's Voice*: 'To write for girls, Alcott became herself a girl again',[30] and to bring us back to Kipling again, we find Peter Hunt writing that with *Puck of Pook's Hill* 'Kipling seems, almost, to be looking through children's eyes and seeing the nonsense that passes for adult logic'.[31]

An additional strategy employed by Lisa Lewis to stabilize the text of the *Just So Stories* is an appeal to the notion of audience; thus she 'reveals' the identities of various specific children Kipling is supposed to have tried the stories out on. These include Marjorie Balestier (Kipling's niece), Angela Thirkell (daughter of one of Kipling's cousins), his children, Josephine, Elsie and John, and his American publisher's son Nelson Doubleday. Peter Hunt follows Lewis in this, declaring of the *Just So Stories* that 'Here [Kipling] is directly addressing specific children (his own, and their cousins), and the book appears to be a remarkable transcription of actual oral performances, complete with incantations and very local jokes.'[32] However, if we are to take this kind of approach, surely as important in considering the question of audience is the fact that nearly all of the *Just So Stories*, save 'How the Alphabet Was Made', were published in magazines or journals (largely *St Nicholas Magazine* or the *Ladies Home Journal*) prior to their collection in one volume, and therefore would presumably must have been written with their editors and audiences in mind. How might the interpretation be altered, for instance, by considering Kipling as a professional writer? Alongside this, there remains the question of the construction in the *Just So Stories* of a text for general consumption.[33]

It is around this question of audience, I would argue, that the critical accounts of the 'Taffy' stories become even more problematic. As I have noted, the tendency in the accounts of these stories that I have come across is to identify 'Taffy' with Josephine. One of the ways in which this link between the fictional character and Kipling's daughter is made is through 'Effie', the child figure constructed as audience in the 'uncollected' preface to the *Just So Stories*.[34] The fact that these fictional characters have different names is elided, 'Taffy' and 'Effie' are identified with each other, and this then serves the purpose of a biographically informed critical narrative which in turn goes on to suggest 'Effie' as the pet-name of Kipling's daughter Josephine, who died of influenza at the age of six in 1899.[35] Lisa Lewis's notes to the preface inform us that it was 'published with the first story in *SN* [*St Nicholas Magazine*], XXV/2 (December 1897), 89, under the title 'The "'Just-So' Stories"'; it was never collected.'[36] Lewis's assumption that Josephine was the 'real-life model' for Taffy is most clear in her assertion that 'her portrait in "The Tabu Tale" combines with some contemporary evidence to suggest a highly strung, over-active child'.[37] This concern to characterize the 'Taffy' stories as being primarily about the author's relationship with his dead daughter (writing as therapy) is most vigorously pursued in U.C. Knoepflmacher's article entitled 'Kipling's "Just-So" Partner: The Dead Child as Collaborator and Muse', to which I will devote more detailed discussion later in this chapter.

The assumption of the Taffy–Josephine connection is so prevalent in the criticism that exists (and perhaps less surprisingly, in the biographies) that it cannot be ignored. As such, it constitutes a problem for a different reading of the 'Taffy' stories, the biographical readings shaping all subsequent readings, and exerting control (almost in the form of a veto) on what may and may not be said about the texts. Any departure from this persistent association of the text with the putative life would therefore seem to demand justification and explanation, but such a justification inevitably carries with it the dangers of reinstating, through re-stating, precisely the reading that is being challenged.

However, the inadequacy of biographical readings is well illustrated in the previously mentioned quotation from Lisa Lewis: 'her portrait in "The Tabu Tale" combines with some contemporary evidence to suggest a highly strung, over-active child'.[38] It is not even clear here which text has the authority. Is Taffy based on Josephine? Or is it that Josephine is based on Taffy? While Lewis makes the claim that the character of Taffy is based on the 'real-life' Josephine, what we are given is a description of Josephine that claims authority by its reference to the fictional Taffy. This illustrates a general problem with biographical readings which assert the primacy of the life as 'truth', but go on to construct that life by reference to a variety of texts including those that are elsewhere acknowledged as fictional. Something similar occurs in M. Daphne Kutzer's discussion of Kipling in *Empire's Children*, where an India affirmed as 'complex and contradictory' is seen as being the reason for, and/or the explanation of, the character of Kipling's writing. But where does this notion of India come from?

Kipling was born in India, a complex and contradictory country of jungle and desert, mountain and plain, drought and monsoon; a country populated by a bewildering number of ethnicities and religions, languages and customs; [...] that such a country spawned as contradictory and at times confounding a writer as Kipling is not surprising.[39]

This India is an India Kutzer reads from the work of Kipling, and yet it here becomes the reality of India and becomes, after the manner of a self-fulfilling prophecy, the explanation and the causation of the Kipling who writes that India. Likewise, in *The Narrator's Voice*, Barbara Wall claims that the *Just So Stories* were 'first told to [Kipling's] daughter Josephine ("the daughter that was all to me," who died in 1899 at the age of six)'.[40] In this, Wall could be said to be following Carrington and Birkenhead, both of whom quote from the 'Merrow Down' poems that follow 'How the First Letter Was Written' and 'How the Alphabet Was Made' in their chapters on the death of Josephine. Carrington uses an edited version of the poems as a kind of preface to the chapter and makes no further reference to them. Birkenhead, on the other hand, introduces the poem (again an edited version of the two that appear in the *Just So Stories*, sandwiched together) with: 'It is not in his letters, but in such works as *They* and "Merrow Down" that we shall find the intensity of Kipling's passion and dereliction', and goes on to claim that 'two years later, and wandering about the countryside, he could not look at Merrow Down or any part of the Surrey landscape without thinking of the dead child'.[41] But Wall's quotation is a misquotation, substituting a 'me' for a 'him' (and I shall argue later for the importance of attending to personal pronouns), deriving as it does from the poem that follows 'How the Alphabet Was Made', which attributes the sentiment to Tegumai in respect of Taffy. Here again then the decision has already been made that Taffy is, to all intents and purposes, Josephine. Thus a line from a poem treating of fictional characters is quoted as though it were a line in a personal letter, or a diary perhaps.

In addition to this tendency to read the fiction through an idea of the life (and the life according to an interpretation of the fiction), which in turn seems to result in a lack of attention being given to the specificity of the literary texts, the biographical and autobiographical material is not dealt with as scrupulously as one might hope. For example, Kutzer writes:

In his autobiography, Kipling said that the tales in *Puck of Pook's Hill* 'had to be a sort of balance to, as well [as] a seal upon, some aspects of my "Imperialistic" output in the past'. They are a balance in the sense that they provide a historical perspective to the British Empire and that they show Britain's own experiences as a colonized nation, as well as her rise to imperial power. They are a seal in that they present his imperial beliefs more overtly than in many other works, and in that they are stories meant for children, [...][42]

There are two problems with this. First, if we refer to Kipling's autobiography it would appear that this statement pertains not to *Puck of Pook's Hill* but to *Rewards and Fairies*.[43] Second, Kutzer quotes from *Something of Myself* and then explicates the quotation, and accounts for it, by, among other things, asserting that these Kipling stories were intended for children. This is done in a manner which, given the proximity of the quotation from *Something of Myself*, suggests that the claim is one endorsed by Kipling's autobiography. However, the sentence in which the line that Kutzer quotes is embedded is rather more complex, and reads as follows:

> Yet, since the tales had to be read by children, before people realized that they were meant for grown-ups; and since they had to be a sort of balance to, as well as a seal upon, some aspects of my 'Imperialistic' output in the past, I worked the material in three or four overlaid tints and textures, which might or might not reveal themselves according to the shifting light of sex, youth, and experience.[44]

I am not here claiming that the Kipling autobiography has the last word on how *Rewards and Fairies* should be read: my argument as I have formulated it means that I cannot ascribe to Kipling's writing on his own writing any particular authority over and above his status as another reader of the Kipling texts. I merely draw attention to the way in which the autobiography is used here to endow Kutzer's claims with authority. Not only is this particular instance misleading in its use of the autobiography, but also more generally it draws attention to the necessarily selective nature of critical uses of biographical and autobiographical material.

Reading the *Just So Stories* through Kipling biography involves the use of other people's interpretations of texts (letters, diaries, other texts from the period, texts written about the period by writers who have examined historical texts, and the literary texts themselves), in order to produce yet another. Most importantly and problematically, the biographical approach has a tendency to circumscribe what may be written about with reference to the text. U.C. Knoepflmacher for instance writes:

> In 'How the First Letter Was Written,' 'How the Alphabet Was Made,' and 'The Tabu Tale,' [Kipling] allowed himself the luxury of transforming Effie into Taffy, a best beloved child he deposited in the safe haven of a prehistoric past. The joy and loss of a father, who was not a Briton or an Indian, or even an American, which he might well have been, could thus be ascribed to a Neolithic man who was 'not a Jute or an Angle, or even a Dravidian, which he might well have been, Best Beloved, but never mind why' (*Just So Stories* ...).[45]

By this process of relating the text back to the life as it is supposed to have been, the 'Taffy' stories become stories about grief at the loss of a daughter, or at the very least stories with a compensatory purpose. My argument is that it is only through recourse to the Kipling biographies that this carries weight as an interpretation. The 'translation' of Jutes, Angles and Dravidians into Britons, Indians and Americans is not only a sleight of hand, it also elides the way the opening passage of 'How the First Letter Was Written' asserts Tegumai's identity as Neolithic on the one hand through his difference from Jutes, Angles and Dravidians, and on the other hand through the equation of Neolithic with 'primitive', which in turn is associated with not being able to read or write. Part of the interest for me, of this opening section of 'How the First Letter Was Written', is the way it constructs *in* writing a time that is supposed to be *before* writing, and the way it plays with questions of knowledge and its lack:

> Once upon a most early time was a Neolithic man. He was not a Jute or an Angle, or even a Dravidian, which he might well have been, Best Beloved, but never mind why. He was a Primitive, and he lived cavily in a Cave, and he wore very few clothes, and he couldn't read and he couldn't write and he didn't want to, and except when he was hungry he was quite happy.[46]

As I have already observed, one of the ways Knoepflmacher and Lewis assert and establish a link between Josephine and Taffy is through the 'Effie' of the 'uncollected' preface to the *Just So Stories*:

> All the Blue Skalallatoot stories are morning tales (I do not know why, but that is what Effie says). All the stories about Orvin Sylvester Woodsey, the left-over New England fairy who did not think it well-seen to fly, and who used patent labour-saving devices instead of charms, are afternoon stories because they were generally told in the shade of the woods. You could alter and change these tales as much as you pleased; but in the evening there were stories meant to put Effie to sleep, and you were not allowed to alter those by one single word. They had to be told just so; or Effie would wake up and put back the missing sentence. So at last they came to be like charms, all three of them, – the whale tale, the camel tale, and the rhinoceros tale. Of course little people are not alike, but I think that if you catch some Effie rather tired and rather sleepy, and if you begin in a low voice and tell the tales precisely as I have written them down, you will find that that Effie will presently curl up and go to sleep.[47]

Knoepflmacher reads the child figure here as referring in a straightforward manner to Kipling's daughter, taking 'Effie' as a pet-name abbreviation of Josephine, this passage is then interpreted as Kipling's account of telling the original 'Just-So' stories to his daughter. What is obscured in the effort to make the 'uncollected' preface correspond to Kipling's life, is the detail of the text itself. Let us note for example the way the personal pronoun 'you' is used here. On the one hand the second person plural seems to *stand in* for 'I' in a way that raises the question as to why 'you' rather than 'I' is employed here; on the other hand 'you' is also used to interpellate a reader: 'but I think if *you* catch some Effie rather tired [...] and if *you* begin in a low voice'. Secondly, since 'I' *is* used, in parentheses and also towards the end of the passage, there is after all a distinction operating in the text between 'I' and 'you', and the question then becomes, what is that distinction?

Furthermore, I would give attention to the way 'Effie' on the one hand appears to refer to a specific child, and then later to some idea of a 'general' child.[48] With the caveat in place, that 'little people are not alike', Effie nevertheless becomes 'some Effie' and 'that Effie'. Yet another distinction the preface makes is between reading and telling. Reading becomes something that is done quietly and telling is done aloud, and while the preface acknowledges the written-ness of the text, it suggests that 'you' '*tell* the tales precisely as I have *written* them down'. Thus the preface constructs a narrative about and around the reading and writing of the texts, about authors and readers where the distinctions between them shift. The reader *tells* tales that are *written*, and the audience is in the end potentially the *writer* of the tale, and what is more, one who writes in her sleep:[49] 'They had to be told just so; or Effie would wake up and put back the missing sentence.' This rather complicates the notion of a 'real' historical and knowable audience that both Lisa Lewis and U.C. Knoepflmacher resort to in order to explain the 'Taffy' stories. To demand that the preface refer to the supposed 'real' of Kipling's life outside the text seems necessarily to lead to the text's specificity being overlooked.[50] Lewis notes for instance that 'all that survives' [*sic*] of the Blue Skalallatoot stories 'is a map and a letter (*KJ* (March 1968), 6–8). Of the Orvin Silvester [*sic*] Woodsey stories nothing is known.'[51] It is possible of course that these stories *never* existed in the sense that Lewis means, other than as a construction by the preface, of a type of story different from those that have to be 'just-so'. In any case, if we are to pursue the idea that the preface is equivalent to an authoritative and indisputable pronouncement about how the text came into being (that is to say, a statement about the truth of the text's origins guaranteed in some way by the author's signature), then what are we to make of the following excerpt from the preface to *The Jungle Book*?

The demands made by a work of this nature upon the generosity of specialists are very numerous, and the editor would be wanting in all title to the generous treatment he has received were he not willing to make the fullest possible acknowledgement of his indebtedness.

His thanks are due in the first place to the scholarly and accomplished Bahadur Shah, baggage elephant 174 on the Indian register, who, with his amiable sister Pudmini, most courteously supplied the history of

'Toomai of the Elephants' and much of the information contained in 'Her Majesty's Servants'.[52]

This is read by most critics as obviously fictional in a way that the preface to the *Just So Stories* is not. Daniel Karlin, in his notes to the Penguin Classics edition of *The Jungle Books* twice uses the word 'facetious' in reference to it,[53] while Roger Lancelyn Green, though he goes on to claim that 'the acknowledgements […] contain some germ of truth', notes that 'As Kipling expresses his gratitude in this preface to an elephant, a wolf, a mongoose and a bird, it is usually dismissed as a mere skit on the usual "Prefatory acknowledgements" contained in most scholarly biographies or studies.'[54] Similarly, W.W. Robson informs us that the preface 'is of course a parody of a scholarly Editor',[55] and Tess Cosslett refers to it as 'very tongue-in-cheek'.[56] The preface to *The Jungle Book* is labelled as obviously fictional by the critics because they read it as using a language of parody or of 'skit', in other words a language that is perceived to be at one remove from the 'real', whereas the 'uncollected' preface to the *Just So Stories* fits in with the critics' preconceptions of the 'real'. For them, elephants do not provide the kind of information claimed, whereas 'Effies' do. By this account the child ('Effie') can speak for itself and is not written. For these critics, the preface to *The Jungle Book* foregrounds its own written-ness in ways that the 'uncollected' preface to the *Just So Stories* does not, but I would argue that the greatest problem with the assumption that the *Just So Stories* preface refers to a 'real' world out there that is supposed not to be textual, is that to approach it as a transparent window on 'reality' is to miss its *own* constructions of its written-ness as I have sketched them out above.

Another reason for re-examining the proposed link between Josephine–'Effie' and 'Taffy' is the preface's specificity as to which stories it refers to: that is, the first three tales that are collected in the *Just So Stories*.[57] It was published in 1897, four years before the initial publication of 'How the First Letter was Written' and almost a year before the suggested date of writing for 'The Tabu Tale'. More to the point, the 'Taffy' stories are not mentioned in the preface, and indeed, if we are to be guided by the bibliographical detail, the preface, as Lewis notes, remained uncollected. U.C. Knoepflmacher circumvents this problem by asserting that the absence of the preface from the collected *Just So Stories* is further evidence that the stories constitute an expression of loss, and that the 'Taffy' stories in particular function as therapy: 'the introductory paragraph of 1897 had also become undesirable for another, more painful, reason: after Effie's death and Kipling's months of convalescence, the personal origins of the three animal tales obviously needed to be obscured'.[58] Thus what is in the text is read exclusively as evidence for the therapy theory, and what is absent from the text is likewise mobilized to that end; Knoepflmacher, like Lord Birkenhead before him, has it both ways. Everything in his reading has been derived from a narrative that has already been constructed about the life of the author.[59] The dead Josephine weighs down on the interpretative possibilities of the text. Everything founders in the face of the 'real', and even more so in the face of death as the ultimate 'reality' as it is constructed by Knoepflmacher's text.

Because he argues that the 'Taffy' stories are *about* Kipling's relationship with his dead daughter Josephine, first identified in the figure of Effie in the 'uncollected' preface and then in the figure of Taffy, Knoepflmacher's biographical reading leads him to foreground 'death' in his account of the *Just So Stories*, and particularly in his reading of the 'Taffy' stories. In his analysis, both the text of the *Just So Stories*, and writing in general, have a contradictory relationship to the idea of death that is also produced therein. Parts of 'How the Alphabet Was Made' are described as being 'elegy' and 'perilously close to a ritual mourning',[60] while 'The Tabu Tale', it is said, 'hints at an impassable gulf between child and grownup'.[61] I read this 'impassable gulf' as being linked to the 'separation between adult and child, but also [...] between the sexes and between the living and the dead'[62] that Knoepflmacher on the other hand sees the *Just So Stories* as countering.

However, the gaps and separations that Knoepflmacher's analysis seeks to present as healed or covered over by the Kipling texts, have to be asserted *a priori*. Indeed, one of the initial assumptions on which the rest of Knoepflmacher's text is predicated is that there exists a 'child-self' and an 'adult-self' which are separable and distinguishable as different from each other and which are defined by their respective 'child-ness' and 'adult-ness'. On the other hand, however, child and adult selves are not thought of as being necessarily located within, or determined by, '*the* child' or '*the* adult' as defined in Knoepflmacher's text, since a 'child-self' can apparently be expressed by an adult author – though interestingly, not the other way round. This leaves the question of what it is that determines the identity of these selves *as* child or adult, a question that is not addressed by Knoepflmacher's celebration of the *Just So Stories* as a work that 'animates a child-self imbedded in all grownup psyches and yet also recognizable as a juvenile Other'.[63] Here, the child is that which is associated with an idea of the 'real' which is also preserved, and apparently unproblematically retrieved, by memory: both the 'real' ' "Effie" or Josephine' (of whom an 'empirical' knowledge, as opposed to memory only, is also claimed)[64] and/or 'the writer's own childhood'.[65] 'Death' meanwhile, is precisely the lost 'real' child, the 'really' dead Josephine. If 'death', 'child' and the 'real' seem conflated here in my analysis of Knoepflmacher's 'Kipling's "Just-So" Partner', that is because they are produced as more or less interchangeable terms in the article: 'The child – and childhood – he had now twice lost could therefore be recaptured once again, kept alive through the agency of an undying fictional other who was his personal Best Beloved as well as a universal Every-child.'[66] So, in contradistinction to what is suggested by

Knoepflmacher's quotation from Brian Alderson which implicitly produces writing as 'dead' and 'public' as opposed to ' "these stories [which] originated in the living – and private – exchange between a teller and a listener" (Alderson …)',[67] here writing is what 'keeps alive' (but it should be borne in mind that this is a writing that is defined in oral terms as having 'listeners'[68] rather than readers).

These are not by any means the only meanings revolving around 'death' in this text however. In the following description of the final illustration to 'The Tabu Tale' Knoepflmacher produces a number of other associations:

> Whereas the floating Taffy looks reposed and free, surrounded by blank space, Tegumai seems crowded and cramped into an awkward position. He is in the act of slaying Death, yet the child who seems to ascend toward the godlike Chief has entered a stillness that somehow belongs to a different order of reality.[69]

A constellation of words that Knoepflmacher's text associates with death such as 'repose', 'free[dom]', 'blank[ness]', 'space', 'ascen[sion]' and 'godlike' also draw 'stillness' into their orbit where death is also figured as 'enter[ing] a stillness that somehow belongs to a different order of *reality*'.[70] Earlier in the piece however, Knoepflmacher has implied that it is Taffy's mastering of 'codes'[71] and signs that enables her to avoid death, and in particular it is her mastery of the 'still Tabu' sign that is supposed to preserve her from it.[72] Earlier too, Knoepflmacher has described Taffy and her father as 'artificer[s]'[73] and the Head Chief as 'a far more powerful artist figure',[74] and in one of his renderings of 'The Tabu Tale' the following account is given:

> Yet the creation of this alternative father figure, who clearly prefers Taffy to Tegumai and whose hatchet would have killed the wolf even if Tegumai had faltered, also suggests that Taffy has approached a phase of existence in which more than a childlike 'Daddy' is needed to help her master the art of stillness.[75]

Again there is the ambiguous 'phase of existence' that recalls the 'different order of reality' referred to above, especially when the alternative father figure is read as 'godlike' also. What then is 'stillness' in Knoepflmacher's text? On the one hand it is associated with 'codes' and signs, art and storytelling; and on the other it is associated with death. 'The art of stillness' can here be read as the art of death, a reading that throws into relief the Knoepflmacher text's ambivalence with respect to the 'Art [that …] survives artists young and old'[76] and to that very writing that is claimed to be 'designed to counter not only the separation between adult and child, but also gaps between the sexes and between the living and the dead'.[77]

Knoepflmacher writes:

> By celebrating the child's adaptability and its gradual mastery of verbal and
> visual signs, Kipling could also partake in a transformative process of obvi-
> ous therapeutic value to himself. He had previously transferred to Effie his
> memories of a self-centered little rajah by becoming her paternal playmate.
> It now remained for him to take the more difficult step of rechanneling his
> deep emotional attachment by transferring it to maturing children as
> bright as she had been. To do so, he required a new set of listeners – the
> Effigies of Effie, as it were – Elsie and John Kipling, the many girls and boys
> he continued to befriend, and all those faceless children he could charm
> and help to grow beyond the age at which Effie's life had stopped. The
> child – and childhood – he had now twice lost could therefore be recap-
> tured once again, kept alive through the agency of an undying fictional
> Other who was his personal Best Beloved as well as a universal Every-child.[78]

Here, that which is to *capture* and produce the 'undying' and the 'fictional' –
which has already been associated by Knoepflmacher with 'stillness' – is
described in terms of change, transformation and movement. The dead child
(fixed), is re-captured (re-fixed) kept alive (fixed as changeable) through
the undying (changeless) and fictional (fashioned/manufactured/artificial).
Furthermore, the 'memories' that have elsewhere been appealed to in order
to stabilize a claim to the 'real' are here produced as subject to transferral and
alteration. Most curiously of all, in a text which is so keen to emphasize the
'real' purchase of the 'real child' Effie/Josephine, there is the paradoxical
transformation of children who according to Knoepflmacher's terms must
likewise be 'real' – Elsie and John – into 'effigies': still models of the 'original'
Effie. In the idea of the 'effigy' death and stillness are brought together in an
uneasy and ambivalent relationship to an opposition, alternately asserted
and denied, between the 'real' and the 'artificial'.

The supposed transferral of the stories from 'private' and oral to 'public'
and written is also replete with difficulties for Knoepflmacher's text in which
the effigy, by being an imitation of the 'real' Effie, is both a tribute to and
a betrayal of her, since writing, as it publicizes the 'real', in doing so, also
corrupts, exposes and simplifies it. Thus Knoepflmacher's text, as already
observed, on the one hand implicitly associates the public and written stories with death, while on the other hand it finds its most ominous hint of
mortality in what is characterized as the residue of the 'private' tale, that
which is unfathomable[79] in the illustrations and their captions:

> ['The Tabu Tale'] hints at an impassable gulf between child and grown-
> up. The joyous traffic of the other tales no longer seems possible in a
> narrative that makes the sharing of 'meanings and signs' difficult for both
> kinds of readers.[80]

One such 'group' of illustrations singled out as such by Knoepflmacher are the 'T's that he reads as indicative of the importance of an idea of distinct yet conjoined identities to the whole of the *Just So Stories* and that he sees as particularly prominent in the 'Taffy' sequence 'where it comes to signify the bond between the father–daughter letter-makers whose first names begin with the same consonant *T*'.[81] This apparently certain and fixed meaning of the 'T' in 'How the Alphabet Was Made' is rendered ambiguous and therefore interpretable in the hieroglyph that opens 'The Tabu Tale'. This figure is discussed by Knoepflmacher in a footnote to his essay in which he worries over establishing its meanings, and analyses it as an 'example of the difficulties posed by what has become a private symbology'.[82] Knoepflmacher here isolates the 'T' as something that is fundamentally indeterminable and yet goes to great lengths to tease out the personal meanings he assumes the other 'T's in a number of the *Just So Stories* to have.[83] He also assumes that the 'T' should have a meaning that is ultimately located elsewhere than the text itself and that is in the end recoverable, though with difficulty, through a combination of attention to the letter's repeated appearances in the *Just So Stories*, and an excavation of Kipling's personal life:

> With a curved bottom bar as long as its straight top bar, this letter can be read as a *T* even if it is inverted. But why? To capture the dual *T* alliterations of 'Tabu/Tale' and 'Taffy/Tegumai'? And why are six black Chinese letters that have no phonetic relation to a *T* placed inside the white letter? Were the outer four thinner signs – the simplest of which resembles the T-shape of the daggers and axe drawn for the earlier stories – chosen because they belonged to a more ancient Chinese alphabet that was carved on bones? Were the inner, fatter ones chosen as more modern representations of continuity and life?[84]

Nevertheless, the 'T' is recognizable to Knoepflmacher as a 'T' because of what follows – '[T]HE most important thing about Tegumai Bopsulai and his dear daughter, Taffimai Metallumai, was the Tabus of Tegumai, which were all Bopsulai'[85] – and yet what he does not address is the possibility of the figure's function as something which does not have a meaning in and of itself, but which precisely functions as that which only attains meaning through its juxtaposition with the rest of the text. While Knoepflmacher reads the hieroglyph as uniquely ambiguous, the implication is that it is 'death' that lies at the heart of this ambiguity, and it is therefore also 'death' that is after all *fathomed* by Knoepflmacher through his excavation of the 'life', despite the claim that 'Kipling here encodes private meanings he neither wants or expects his readers to fathom':[86]

> Moreover, *J* and *K*, Josephine Kipling's initials, are no longer in their proper sequential order [...] 'JLK' are the initials of the jovial father-artist, [...]

Yet the separation of *J* and *K* by the broken silver spear of the letter *L* also suggests a generational discontinuity: Collaboration Lost. *L* may well stand for Love, transfixed by a spear, but it also stands for Loss. [...] This record of a collaboration comes perilously close to a ritual of mourning.[87]

Here then in Knoepflmacher's reading of the 'Taffy' stories, which is reliant on his production of Kipling's biography, the hieroglyph that opens 'The Tabu Tale' ultimately has its meaning determined as the *ultimate* meaning by reference to that biography. What is lost in this account is any serious analysis of how the 'Taffy' stories may be read as discussing ideas about language, where 'the fine old easy, understandable Alphabet – A, B, C, D, E, and the rest of 'em'[88] is both claimed and undermined as that which enables us to 'always say exactly what we mean without any mistakes'.[89] Returning once more to the opening sentence of 'The Tabu Tale' – '[T]HE most important thing about Tegumai Bopsulai and his dear daughter, Taffimai Metallumai, was the Tabus of Tegumai, which were all Bopsulai'[90] – I would note that there are a number of words in it which, since they function as proper names but as proper names that do not always refer to the same thing, produce language as slippery and not fixable. For instance, 'Tegumai' refers both to Taffy's father and to the tribe, and Bopsulai which is part of Tegumai's name, also functions in another, not fully determinable way, when it is used to describe the 'Tabus of Tegumai', or rather it is determinable as indeterminable. Furthermore 'Tabu', like the 'nonsense' words, is capitalized here, thus suggesting a link between them which can be understood in the light of the 'Head Chief's explanation that meaning is not inherent to 'Tabu', that it only has meaning negatively, in that its meaning only seems to come about in the instance of a prohibition being transgressed: 'Tabu doesn't mean anything till you break it, O Only Daughter of Tegumai; but when you break it, it means sticks and stinging-nettles and fine, freehand, tribal patterns drawn on your back with the cutty edges of mussel-shells.'[91] Nevertheless, despite the indeterminacy of its meaning, Tabu is 'the most important thing'[92] about Taffy and her father; it is produced as their defining characteristic.

The problem with Knoepflmacher's analysis lies in the implied relationship of language to the 'real' that it subscribes to, which means that it does not and cannot question the ontological reality of the themes produced by Knoepflmacher's readings. For instance, the 'effigy' is, in his text, a figure that is used to assert the claim of that 'real relation' and yet according to my reading, it also problematizes it, since, while it is supposed to represent that which is already there, *as* re-presentation it is already necessarily constituted as lacking in that it is *not* the real. But the 'Taffy' stories, as I read them, in contrast to Knoepflmacher's text, constantly throw into question this presumed relation of the 'word' to the 'real'.

My argument has been that biographical readings tend to detract from the reading of the literary text except as a species of allegory, where the text becomes *really* about something located elsewhere, in the 'life' of the author, where the 'life' is understood not as a production of the interpretation of texts but as a reality which is re-presented by the literary text. This reading of language as having direct relation to the 'real' is not unique to children's literature criticism, although, as Karín Lesnik-Oberstein argues in her introduction to this collection, there are reasons why it is particularly prevalent in children's literature criticism. Nevertheless, as I suggested in my opening paragraph, this chapter is also concerned to acknowledge that critical works dealing with literature that is not designated as 'for' children also wrestle with some of the problems around ideas of authorship that I have discussed earlier. Even in a critical text that explicitly engages with and addresses a problem it diagnoses as 'the unspoken yet persistent gravitational pull of authorial intention',[93] that 'gravitational pull' continues to make itself felt. Though Peter Morey's *Fictions of India: Narrative and Power* announces that it 'is not interested in authorial intention'[94] it nevertheless goes on to claim not only that 'Kipling does not seek a constant authoritative and authorial stand point',[95] but also that Kipling's short stories reveal a 'technique' and a 'strategy' which is 'designed' to achieve certain effects, for example the alienation of the reader.[96] This, notwithstanding the earlier disclaimer, reinstates an author with an intention that can be determined and analysed. Indeed, the argument in *Fictions of India*, is that Kipling's short stories about India come in two kinds: 'straight allegories'[97] in a Gothic tradition 'used to impose a consoling, one might say conservative, ending on what had appeared to be a wilful and radical text'[98] and stories 'where the supernatural remains undiluted'[99] and 'not so easily assimilable'[100] or as 'reducible to the level of imperialist morality plays [... but] exhibit[ing] a disconcerting "life" of their own in that no imposed resolution is adequate to erase contradiction'.[101] What is striking here is the way in which the stories that are read as 'conservative' are regarded as being so because of Kipling's success in maintaining authorial control, while those that are read as 'subversive' are claimed to be so as a result of Kipling's lack of success at 'polic[ing] the[ir] potential interpretative possibilities'.[102] Indeed, for the 'subversive' texts to be recognized as such, it is necessary that they be *read* ' "against the grain of [their] intended meaning",'[103] implying rather that these stories, which, unlike the others, are claimed to be somehow independent of their author, do after all apparently betray their author's intentions even while they fly in the face of them. What is also not clear is what justifies the assumption that the 'conservative' tales are the product of Kipling's intentions while the 'subversiveness' of the others is held to have nothing to do with authorial intention.

The problem of the author as a revenant, in criticism that would seem to want to resist resorting to claims about authorial intention to account for a text, is not unique to Kipling criticism and can be seen to be operative in a number of works of children's literature criticism not specifically concerned with Kipling, nor even with author-based analysis.[104] As I have shown, the author recurs in words or claims which may not seem to be to do with ideas of authorship, but which implicitly invoke them: words such as 'design', 'technique' and 'strategy'.

Another example of the way in which the author creeps back into criticism that claims to have other priorities can be found in Maria Nikolajeva's recent article on narrative theory and children's literature criticism.[105] In it Nikolajeva claims that 'Narratology is expressly not concerned with the major objects of investigation in children's literature research: social context, the author's intentions, or the reader.'[106] Indeed, for Nikolajeva, a narratological approach to children's literature is precisely constituted by its *difference* from 'conventional approaches' with their socio-historical, biographical, psychoanalytic, etc. concerns,[107] and by its interest rather in ' "What constitutes a narrative?" and "What elements is a narrative made of?".'[108] However, this is expressed as an interest in 'all features in a narrative that make it a narrative, including *composition* (plot, temporal structure), characterization (narrative *devices used by* writers *to* reveal a character), and perspective (voice and point of view)'.[109] Thus, ideas of authorial intention are cleaved to once again even in assertions that claim to leave them behind. As I understand it here, 'composition', while it can mean 'a work of art', also means 'the *act* of putting something together', which brings with it an idea of the 'actor' or author doing the composing. However, I base this reading of Nikolajeva's use of 'composition' also on what follows: 'devices used by writers to…', since it could be objected that my own usage of 'construction' and/or 'production' is subject to the same limitations. However, I would argue that 'construction' lends itself more to being read as being about 'interpretation', as in: 'they put a generous construction on his behaviour'; while 'production', with its associations with industry and collaborative output, is even more distanced from the idea of the singular author and his intentions.[110]

Furthermore, having stated that as a narratologist she is not interested in either authorial intention or the reader, Nikolajeva goes on to assert that 'One of the essential characteristics of children's literature is the cognitive gap between the adult writer and the child reader'[111] and that 'For a narratologist, the essential questions are "How are characters constructed *by* authors?" and "How are they revealed *for* readers?".'[112] The inconsistency of Nikolajeva's argument comes even more clearly to the fore in her discussion of characterization where she claims that 'characters in children's stories have been employed by authors as mouthpieces and bearers of certain ideals and opinions'[113] and repeatedly returns to the notion of authorial intention by discussing 'devices' – such as defamiliarization – as 'allowing authors'[114] to achieve certain ends and to 'manipulate the reader'[115] into interpreting the text in particular, presumably intended, ways.

Self-contradictory criticism such as this, I would argue, is the result of espousing certain ideas without fully working through the implications of those ideas. For example, Nikolajeva gets into a significant tangle over the ontological status of literary characters since on the one hand she makes the by now uncontroversial claim that 'Literary characters do not exist outside their texts',[116] while at the same time suggesting precisely that kind of connection with such statements as 'Not even a long description can *necessarily* convey all the shades of a person's feelings'[117] and questions like 'Can an adult writer render a child's state of mind without sounding false?'.[118] If we take the first statement about literary characters seriously this last question does not seem to make sense, a literary character does not correspond to a child outside the text, but the child within the text could presumably have its state of mind rendered without seeming inauthentic if that was consistent with the idea of childhood being produced therein.

The problems that I read in Nikolajeva's analysis are precisely rooted, as I suggested in the case of Knoepflmacher's article, in questions of an ontological nature. That is to say that they derive, whether they will or no, from a notion of language as reflecting the world rather than constitutive of it. This can clearly be seen in Nikolajeva's suggestion that 'Most classical children's novels present events chronologically, the way they happened. This structure is considered suitable for children, because especially very young children may have problems reconstructing the actual flow of events unless they are rendered chronologically.'[119] Such a statement relies on the notion that the 'events' 'actually' happened, and did so in a sense independent of their telling. And this way of approaching the text precisely produces the severing of form from content whose 'mutual dependence' Nikolajeva claims to want to elucidate 'by combining purely narratological studies with other theories and methods'.[120]

Following the notion that different theories and methodologies can simply be combined seems to result in a kind of theoretical cherry-picking which, however, dispenses with the logic that produces those very cherries. Similar inconsistencies to those in Nikolajeva's article can also be found in Roderick McGillis's *The Nimble Reader*.[121] There we can read on the one hand that 'Language does not simply state truths; it creates them'[122] and that 'We find our existence in language; we do not create our language out of the world we exist in',[123] while on the other hand McGillis argues that the setting for *Winnie-the-Pooh* could *not* be 'anywhere at all'[124] because 'The south and central regions of England are precisely appropriate because of their domestic and pastoral qualities. Sussex, Berkshire, Shropshire, and Somerset, for example, with their rolling downs and peaceful woodlands, perfectly complement the Hundred Acre Wood's unthreatening landscape.'[125] Once again then here is a reality that takes precedence over language after all, because it *exists*, and is there waiting to be described. 'The south and central regions of England' simply *are* 'domestic', 'pastoral' and 'peaceful'. To bring us full circle, I would suggest that this bears comparison with Lisa Lewis's attempt to fix the *Just So Stories* geographically by enumerating the extent of Kipling's travels and claiming his identification [*sic*] with 'aspects of all these places'.[126] Lewis ends up conceding that '[Kipling] could never be said to belong to any of them in the sense that (say) Hardy belonged to Wessex',[127] but this concession still mobilizes the notion that Hardy's Wessex is a 'reflection' of his experience of a specific place and time rather than a construction produced by the Hardy novels. Bound up then with the belief in the 'life' of the author as source and origin of the text is a conception of language as reflective rather than constitutive of reality.

Further reading

On the wider issues pertaining to authorship see the following classic texts:

Roland Barthes, 'The Death of the Author' in *Modern Criticism and Theory: A Reader*, second edition, ed. by David Lodge, revised and expanded by Nigel Wood (London and New York: Longman, 2000), pp. 146–50.

Michel Foucault, 'What is an Author?' in *Modern Criticism and Theory: A Reader*, second edition, ed. by David Lodge, revised and expanded by Nigel Wood (London and New York: Longman, 2000), pp. 174–87.

For a working out of some of the issues in relation to children's literature, its criticism and ideas about childhood, see also:

Karín Lesnik-Oberstein, '*Holiday House*: Grist to *The Mill on the Floss*, or Childhood as Text', in *The Yearbook of English Studies*, Special Section 'Children in Literature', ed. by Karín Lesnik-Oberstein, volume 32 (Leeds: MHRA, 2002), pp. 78–94.

For further discussion of ideas about the status of the authorial preface see:

Gérard Genette, *Paratexts: Thresholds of Interpretation*, ed. by Richard Macksey and Michael Sprinker, trans. by Jane E. Lewin (Cambridge: Cambridge University Press, 1997).

And on interpretation 'no longer turned toward the origin' see:

Jacques Derrida, *Writing and Difference*, trans. Alan Bass (Chicago: University of Chicago Press, 1978).

Jacques Derrida, 'Plato's Pharmacy', in *Dissemination*, trans. Barbara Johnson (London: Athlone Press, 1981), pp. 61–171.

Notes

1. Sandra Kemp, 'The archive on which the sun never sets: Rudyard Kipling', *History of the Human Sciences*, volume 11, number 4, 1998, 33–48, 33.
2. Rudyard Kipling, *Just So Stories*, [1902], Oxford World's Classics, ed. Lisa Lewis (Oxford: Oxford University Press, 1998).
3. Rudyard Kipling, 'How the First Letter Was Written', *Just So Stories*, Oxford World's Classics, ed. Lisa Lewis (Oxford: Oxford University Press, 1998), pp. 91–107. It was first published in *Ladies Home Journal*, December 1901 (see Lisa Lewis's 'Explanatory Notes' to the Oxford World's Classics edition of the *Just So Stories*, p. 231). See also James McG. Stewart, *Rudyard Kipling: A Bibliographical Catalogue*, ed. A.W. Yeats (Toronto: Dalhousie University Press and University of Toronto Press, 1959), p. 219.
4. Rudyard Kipling, 'How the Alphabet Was Made', *Just So Stories*, Oxford World's Classics, ed. Lisa Lewis (Oxford: Oxford University Press, 1998), pp. 109–28. There was no previous publication of this story before its inclusion in the first edition of

the *Just So Stories* (see Lisa Lewis's 'Explanatory Notes' to the Oxford World's Classics edition of the *Just So Stories*, p. 232).

5. Rudyard Kipling, 'Appendix A: The Tabu Tale', *Just So Stories*, Oxford World's Classics, ed. Lisa Lewis (Oxford: Oxford University Press, 1998), pp. 189–211. First published in *Collier's Weekly*, 29 August 1903, and in *Windsor Magazine*, September 1903. 'The Tabu Tale' appeared in the first American edition of the *Just So Stories* in 1903 (volume 20 of Scribner's Outward Bound edition). The story was not published in England until 1938 in volume 16 of the Sussex edition of Kipling's work (again, see Lewis, 'Explanatory Notes', p. 236 and also Stewart, *Rudyard Kipling: A Bibliographical Catalogue*, pp. 216–17 and 220).

6. Roger Lancelyn Green, *Kipling and the Children* (London: Elek Books, 1965), pp. 172 and 180.

7. The words 'play' and 'playful' come up again and again in relation to the *Just So Stories*, though this playfulness is not really given much account of beyond Barbara Wall's explanation that 'the words are designed to amuse and entertain without much informing' (*The Narrator's Voice* (Basingstoke: Macmillan – now Palgrave Macmillan, 1991), p. 130), or Celia Catlett Anderson's suggestion that '[Kipling's] intention was to convey his own love of language' ('Kipling's Mowgli and Just So Stories: The Vine of Fact and Fantasy', *Touchstones: Reflections on the Best in Children's Literature*, volume 1, ed. Perry Nodelman (West Lafayette: Children's Literature Association Publishers, 1985) pp. 113–22, p. 115).

8. Angus Wilson, *The Strange Ride of Rudyard Kipling* (London: Granada Publishing/Panther Books, 1979), p. 307.

9. U.C. Knoepflmacher, 'Kipling's "Just-So" Partner: The Dead Child as Collaborator and Muse', *Children's Literature*, volume 25, ed. Elizabeth Lennox Keyser (New Haven and London: Yale University Press, 1997), 24–49, 30. Hailed as the best article of the year by the Children's Literature Association in 1997.

10. Kipling, 'The Tabu Tale', p. 196.

11. Rudyard Kipling, *Something of Myself* (London: Macmillan, 1937).

12. Lord Birkenhead, *Rudyard Kipling* (London: Weidenfeld & Nicholson, 1978), p. 35.

13. Charles Carrington, *Rudyard Kipling: His Life and Work* (London: Macmillan, 1955), p. 188.

14. Philip Mason, *Kipling: The Glass, the Shadow and the Fire* (London: Jonathan Cape, 1975), p. 32.

15. Hamilton Brown, *Rudyard Kipling: A New Appreciation* (London: Hamish Hamilton, 1945), p. 19.

16. John A. McClure, *Kipling and Conrad: The Colonial Fiction* (Cambridge, MA and London: Harvard University Press, 1981), p. 15.

17. Andrew Rutherford, 'Select Bibliography', *Just So Stories*, by Rudyard Kipling, Oxford World's Classics, ed. Lisa Lewis (Oxford: Oxford University Press, 1998), pp. xliv–xlvii, p. xlv.

18. Andrew Lycett, *Rudyard Kipling* (London: Phoenix/Orion Books, 2000), p. 82.

19. J.M.S. Tompkins, *The Art of Rudyard Kipling* (London: Methuen, 1959), pp. 229–30.

20. Brown, *Rudyard Kipling: A New Appreciation*, p. 19.

21. Birkenhead, *Rudyard Kipling*, p. 353.

22. Tompkins, *The Art of Rudyard Kipling*, p. 230.

23. There are also notes made by Douglas Rees, Lord Birkenhead's assistant, which are in the Kipling archive at Sussex University, but the point remains the same, and in this case Lewis informs us that she is referring to Carrington's notes.

24. Lisa Lewis, 'Explanatory Notes', *Just So Stories*, by Rudyard Kipling, pp. 219–37, p. 236.

25. Lisa Lewis, 'Introduction', *Just So Stories*, by Rudyard Kipling, pp. xv–xlii, p. xv.
26. Lewis, 'Introduction', p. xv. Peter Hunt makes a similar claim with respect to Kipling's *Stalky and Co.*, but interestingly he *contrasts* it with the *Just So Stories* as being 'writing for children as therapy for the adult. Kipling may be exorcising part of his own unhappy childhood'. Peter Hunt, *Children's Literature*, series: Blackwell Guides to Literature, series ed.: Jonathan Wordsworth (Oxford: Blackwell, 2001), p. 83.
27. Gillian Avery, 'The Children's Writer', *Rudyard Kipling: The Man, His Work and His World*, ed. John Gross (London: Weidenfeld & Nicholson, 1972), pp. 113–18, p. 117.
28. Michael Woods, 'The Blyton Line', in *Enid Blyton*, by Barbara Stoney (London: Hodder & Stoughton, 1974), pp. 216–20, p. 219.
29. Humphrey Carpenter, *Secret Gardens: A Study of the Golden Age of Children's Literature* (London: Allen & Unwin, 1985), p. 172.
30. Barbara Wall, *The Narrator's Voice* (Basingstoke: Macmillan – now Palgrave Macmillan, 1991), p. 90.
31. Hunt, *Children's Literature*, p. 210.
32. Hunt, *Children's Literature*, p. 82. Indeed this seems, for the critics, to be one of the prime markers for a supposed difference between the *Just So Stories* and *The Jungle Books*: the *Just So Stories* are repeatedly thought to be 'private' and hence the critics cannot quite account for their popularity 'now'. Barbara Wall writes:

    > Although they are now the most popular of Kipling's stories for children, they bear all the marks of having been written for a particular child. They are full of private and family jokes and of local references, and take their value not from their plots – [...] but from the brilliance of the telling. (Wall, *The Narrator's Voice*, p. 129)

    This issue of the supposedly private nature of the *Just So Stories* is one that I will address in more detail in my extended discussion of U.C. Knoepflmacher's 'Kipling's "Just-So" Partner', later in this chapter.
33. In reference to this question of 'audience' I would also like to draw attention to Sandra Kemp's assessment of the implications of Ann Parry's study of 'the late Victorian Press', which suggests a high degree of '"control" exercised over [Kipling's] stories by contemporary journal reviewers [which] sets limits upon Kipling's writings from which they are not yet free.' Kemp, 'The archive on which the sun never sets: Rudyard Kipling', p. 41.
34. Rudyard Kipling, 'Author's Preface (Uncollected)', *Just So Stories*, Oxford World's Classics, ed. Lisa Lewis (Oxford: Oxford University Press, 1998), p. 1.
35. It is interesting to note that while Andrew Lycett's biography of Kipling mentions three different pet-names for Josephine – 'Bo', 'Bips' and 'Flat Curls' – it provides no such account of 'Effie', and 'Ettie' is recorded as Elsie's pet-name. See Lycett, *Rudyard Kipling*, p. 357, and the photographs of 'The Kipling children at The Rock House, Torquay in early 1897 (Bo is Josephine and Ettie Elsie)'. The photographs are inset between pages 434 and 435.
36. Lewis, 'Explanatory Notes', p. 219.
37. Lewis, 'Introduction', p. xix.
38. Lewis, 'Introduction', p. xix.
39. M. Daphne Kutzer, *Empire's Children: Empire and Imperialism in Classic British Children's Books* (New York and London: Garland Publishing, Inc. a member of the Taylor & Francis Group, 2000), p. 14.

40. Wall, *The Narrator's Voice*, p. 129.
41. Birkenhead, *Rudyard Kipling*, p. 200, contained in chapter XIII entitled 'American Tragedy', pp. 194–203. The corresponding section in the Carrington biography is chapter XII, 'Last Visit to the United States', pp. 283–95, the edited 'Merrow Down' poems appear on pp. 281–2 after a photograph on p. 281 captioned 'The young family, 1898: Caroline Kipling with John, Elsie, and Josephine'. Andrew Lycett also makes the 'Merrow Down'–Josephine connection in his biography of Kipling, in which he writes: 'memories of [Josephine] frolicking on the River Wey were affectionately recorded in [Kipling's] poem "Merrow Down".' Lycett, *Rudyard Kipling*, p. 427. The verses which follow 'How the First Letter Was Written' and 'How the Alphabet Was Made' first appeared together under the title 'Merrow Down' in Kipling's *Songs from Books* published by Macmillan in 1913. See Stewart, *Rudyard Kipling: A Bibliographical Catalogue*, p. 290.
42. Kutzer, *Empire's Children*, p. 40.
43. The paragraph in Kipling's *Something of Myself*, which comes immediately before this passage quoted by Kutzer reads: 'I embarked on *Rewards and Fairies* – the second book – in two minds' and continues, in the paragraph containing the line Kutzer quotes, with 'My doubt cleared itself with the first tale, "Cold Iron"' (Kipling, *Something of Myself*, p. 142). This also clears *my* doubts since 'Cold Iron' is indeed the first story in *Rewards and Fairies*.
44. Kipling, *Something of Myself*, p. 142.
45. Knoepflmacher, 'Kipling's "Just-So" Partner: The Dead Child as Collaborator and Muse', 30.
46. Kipling, 'How the First Letter Was Written', p. 91. For a more elaborated discussion of ideas about oral and written language in children's literature and its criticism, and for my analysis of these ideas in relation to 'How the First Letter Was Written' see my ' "Irony? – But Children Don't Get It, Do They?" The Idea of Appropriate Language in Narratives for Children', *Children's Literature Association Quarterly*, volume 28, number 1, 2003, 26–36.
47. Kipling, 'Author's Preface (Uncollected)', p. 1.
48. Some sense of this is close to being acknowledged by Knoepflmacher who remarks on the similarities between the way 'Effie' is constructed here and the way an idea of a general child audience is constructed in a Kipling letter to the editor of *St Nicholas Magazine*:

    > He can thus do more than compose 'slick' stories *about* children for 'a Wee Willie Winkie' audience of adults; instead, he can directly address 'a People a good deal more important and discriminating – a peculiar People with the strongest views on what they like and dislike' (21 Feb. 1892, cited by Wright ...). This sincere respect for the child's acuity was retained when a few years later he considered the interests of the precocious Effie.

    Knoepflmacher, 'Kipling's "Just-So" Partner: The Dead Child as Collaborator and Muse', 26. Knoepflmacher also refers to 'Effie' as 'a universal Every-child' on p. 31.
49. With thanks to Tony Pringle for this observation.
50. A different argument for resisting a biographical reading is made by J.M.S. Tompkins in her preface to *The Art of Rudyard Kipling*. She writes that in 'criticism that proceeds from, or to, "the man" [...] The works are raided to find support for some conception of the writer's personality, and since the writer's personality is not to be equated exactly with that of the man, the works are thrown out of perspective

and much in them is ignored and undervalued'. Tompkins, *The Art of Rudyard Kipling*, p. x.

51. Lewis, 'Explanatory notes', p. 219. The map and 'The Blue Skalallatoot Letter', dated 26 August 1911, can be found, as Lewis indicates here, in the *Kipling Journal* volume 165, March 1968, 6–8.
52. Rudyard Kipling, *The Jungle Book* (London: Macmillan, 1972), p. v.
53. Daniel Karlin, 'Notes', *The Jungle Books*, by Rudyard Kipling, Penguin Classics, ed. Daniel Karlin, pp. 345–84, p. 348.
54. Green, *Kipling and the Children*, p. 126.
55. W.W. Robson, 'Explanatory Notes', *The Jungle Books*, by Rudyard Kipling, Oxford World's Classics, ed. W.W. Robson (Oxford: Oxford University Press, 1992), pp. 352–73, p. 352.
56. Tess Cosslett, 'Child's Place in Nature: Talking Animals in Victorian Children's Fiction', *Nineteenth Century Contexts*, volume 23, number 4, 2002, 475–95, 487.
57. These stories are: 'How the Whale got his Throat', 'How the Camel got his Hump' and 'How the Rhinoceros got his Skin', *Just So Stories*, Oxford World's Classics, ed. by Lisa Lewis, pp. 3–12, pp. 13–22, pp. 23–31.
58. Knoepflmacher, 'Kipling's "Just-So" Partner: The Dead Child as Collaborator and Muse', 30.
59. This reading of the *Just So Stories* through a predetermined narrative of Kipling's life can also be found operating in a recent BBC radio adaptation of the stories, in which a selection is linked narratively by equating Kipling the author with the narrator of the *Just So Stories*. The radio version begins and ends with Kipling finishing the writing of the *Just So Stories*. Likewise Josephine is equated with the 'Best Beloved'. At the beginning, the actor playing Kipling is heard to say 'So. Finished. Just so, my Best Beloved. I have caught your stories on the page' and at the end he says 'Finished, just so, Josephine …' (Classic Serial: *Just So Stories*, BBC Radio 4, dramatized by Nandita Gosh, scheduled at 3pm on Sunday 24 November 2002). Furthermore, Josephine and 'Taffy' are played by the same child-actor, and it is indicative that 'Taffy' is not even mentioned as a character in the cast list published in the *Radio Times*. Is it simply to be understood that Josephine and 'Taffy' are one and the same? Interestingly this is not the case with Kipling and 'Tegumai' who are played by two different actors (*Radio Times*, 23–29 November 2002, p. 139).
60. Knoepflmacher, 'Kipling's "Just-So" Partner: The Dead Child as Collaborator and Muse', 42.
61. Knoepflmacher, 'Kipling's "Just-So" Partner', 46.
62. Knoepflmacher, 'Kipling's "Just-So" Partner', 25.
63. Knoepflmacher, 'Kipling's "Just-So" Partner', 24.
64. Knoepflmacher, 'Kipling's "Just-So" Partner', 26.
65. Knoepflmacher, 'Kipling's "Just-So" Partner', 25.
66. Knoepflmacher, 'Kipling's "Just-So" Partner', 31.
67. Knoepflmacher, 'Kipling's "Just-So" Partner', 27.
68. Knoepflmacher, 'Kipling's "Just-So" Partner', 31.
69. Knoepflmacher, 'Kipling's "Just-So" Partner', 46.
70. Knoepflmacher, 'Kipling's "Just-So" Partner', 46 (emphasis mine).
71. Knoepflmacher, 'Kipling's "Just-So" Partner', 44.
72. Knoepflmacher, 'Kipling's "Just-So" Partner', 44.
73. Knoepflmacher, 'Kipling's "Just-So" Partner', 40.
74. Knoepflmacher, 'Kipling's "Just-So" Partner', 44–5.
75. Knoepflmacher, 'Kipling's "Just-So" Partner', 45.

76. Knoepflmacher, 'Kipling's "Just-So" Partner', 42–3.
77. Knoepflmacher, 'Kipling's "Just-So" Partner', 25.
78. Knoepflmacher, 'Kipling's "Just-So" Partner', 30–1.
79. Knoepflmacher, 'Kipling's "Just-So" Partner', 42.
80. Knoepflmacher, 'Kipling's "Just-So" Partner', 46.
81. Knoepflmacher, 'Kipling's "Just-So" Partner', 34.
82. Knoepflmacher, 'Kipling's "Just-So" Partner', 48.
83. Describing the capital 'T' that opens 'How the Alphabet Was Made', Knoepflmacher writes:

> Kipling places his initials 'R K' beneath the cutting edge of the axe, and now draws the head of a young chick at the very end of the handle. Adult and child, therefore, now seem farther apart than they were in the capital *T* of the Armadillo story. And yet it is the chick handle that gives the edge of the blade its velocity and power, just as, in the story, it is Taffy who will empower her father as an artificer.
>
> [...]
>
> Just as Taffy begot the individual letters her father then worked into this fuller construct, so is Effie implicitly credited as the begetter of a mode her father perfected after her death. (Knoepflmacher, 'Kipling's "Just-So" Partner', 39–40, 41)

84. Knoepflmacher, 'Kipling's "Just-So" Partner', 48–9.
85. Kipling, 'The Tabu Tale', p. 189.
86. Knoepflmacher, 'Kipling's "Just-So" Partner', 42.
87. Knoepflmacher, 'Kipling's "Just-So" Partner', 42.
88. Kipling, 'How the Alphabet Was Made', p. 123.
89. Kipling, 'How the First Letter Was Written', p. 106.
90. Kipling, 'The Tabu Tale', p. 189.
91. Kipling, 'The Tabu Tale', p. 193.
92. Kipling, 'The Tabu Tale', p. 189.
93. Peter Morey, *Fictions of India: Narrative and Power* (Edinburgh: Edinburgh University Press, 2000), p. 9.
94. Morey, *Fictions of India*, p. 10.
95. Morey, *Fictions of India*, p. 23.
96. Morey, *Fictions of India*, p. 23.
97. Morey, *Fictions of India*, p. 29.
98. Morey, *Fictions of India*, p. 27.
99. Morey, *Fictions of India*, p. 28.
100. Morey, *Fictions of India*, p. 27.
101. Morey, *Fictions of India*, p. 29.
102. Morey, *Fictions of India*, p. 27.
103. Morey, quoting Pierre Macherey, *Fictions of India*, p. 29.
104. In her introductory chapter for this volume Karín Lesnik-Oberstein analyses how 'the author' becomes again, notwithstanding avowals to the contrary, a determining factor in David Rudd's *Enid Blyton and the Mystery of Children's Literature* (Basingstoke: Palgrave Macmillan, 2000).
105. Maria Nikolajeva, 'Beyond the Grammar of Story, or How Can Children's Literature Criticism Benefit from Narrative Theory?', *Children's Literature Association Quarterly*, volume 28, number 1, 2003, 5–16.
106. Nikolajeva, 'Beyond the Grammar of Story', 6.

107. Nikolajeva, 'Beyond the Grammar of Story', 5.
108. Nikolajeva, 'Beyond the Grammar of Story', 6.
109. Nikolajeva, 'Beyond the Grammar of Story', 6 (emphases mine).
110. See *The Concise Oxford Dictionary of Current English*, eighth edition, ed. R.E. Allen (London and New York: BCA by arrangement with Oxford University Press, 1991) and *The Oxford English Dictionary*, second edition, prepared by J.A. Simpson and E.S.C. Weiner (Oxford: Clarendon Press, 1989).
111. Nikolajeva, 'Beyond the Grammar of Story', 6.
112. Nikolajeva, 'Beyond the Grammar of Story', 8 (emphases mine).
113. Nikolajeva, 'Beyond the Grammar of Story', 8.
114. Nikolajeva, 'Beyond the Grammar of Story', 9.
115. Nikolajeva, 'Beyond the Grammar of Story', 10.
116. Nikolajeva, 'Beyond the Grammar of Story', 9.
117. Nikolajeva, 'Beyond the Grammar of Story', 10 (emphasis mine).
118. Nikolajeva, 'Beyond the Grammar of Story', 11.
119. Nikolajeva, 'Beyond the Grammar of Story', 12.
120. Nikolajeva, 'Beyond the Grammar of Story', 14.
121. Roderick McGillis, *The Nimble Reader: Literary Theory and Children's Literature* (New York: Twayne Publishers, 1996).
122. McGillis, *The Nimble Reader*, p. 19.
123. McGillis, *The Nimble Reader*, p. 172.
124. McGillis, quoting Rebecca Lukens, *The Nimble Reader*, p. 34.
125. McGillis, *The Nimble Reader*, p. 35.
126. Lewis, 'Introduction', pp. xv–xvi.
127. Lewis, 'Introduction', p. xvi.

3
Victorian Childhood. Reading Beyond the 'Innocent Title': *Home Thoughts and Home Scenes*

Christine Sutphin

Those of us who are fascinated by the past often begin with what Stephen Greenblatt calls 'a desire to speak with the dead'.[1] The results of this desire are complex, however, because the more we read and study the artifacts of the past and what others have said about them, the more difficult it is to make generalizations. Postmodern ideas about history have complicated what can be said about a text or a time period. Indeed 'time period' has been shown to be a convenient construction, and the images and ideas associated with such constructions have been called into question. Greenblatt argues that the English Renaissance was not a time of great stability and power for England as later scholars have imagined, and many feminist critics point out that it was hardly a 'renaissance' for women writers, a phenomenon they see happening to varying degrees in the eighteenth, nineteenth and twentieth centuries.

Like the English Renaissance, the Victorian period is a convenient construction created by post-Victorians for our own purposes. Some historians argue that much of what we think of as 'Victorian' was invented by those we now think of as 'Modernist', most notably by Lytton Strachey's debunking of respected Victorian figures in *Eminent Victorians*[2] and Virginia Woolf's witty hyperbole about Victorian stuffiness and feminine sacrifice.[3] The Modernists, the argument goes, needed to believe that the Victorians were naïve, conservative, and sexually repressed in order to create their own sense of sophistication and liberation. They were so successful in creating their version of the Victorians that it is still with us, still enabling us to congratulate ourselves on our advanced technology as well as our advanced views.[4] It should be noted, however, that 'revisionist' history, which attempts to set the record straight or to complicate it more productively, is just as much a construction as the version against which it argues. As John Kucich and Dianne F. Sadoff note in their introduction to *Victorian Afterlife*, 'the post-modern conviction [is] that history is always already discursive, and, in that sense, always changing'.[5] They quote Dominick LaCapra who 'defines the historical project as a " 'dialogic[al]' exchange both with the past and with others inquiring into it" '.[6] Given those assumptions, the following inquiry acknowledges that both 'Victorian' and 'twentieth century' are necessarily constructions with which we try to make sense of the past and the present. And this 'making sense' is always part of a rhetorical project. As John McGowan puts it, 'the Victorians as a group characterized by certain shared features do not exist except insofar as they are produced in that similarity by a discourse that has aims on its audience'.[7] Even as we acknowledge our rhetorical aims, however, we are still looking for knowledge about the past, and as Fredric Jameson has argued, 'we are not at liberty to construct any historical narrative at all'.[8] Our sources and the narratives we construct about them will constitute a kind of truth – even if a 'truth' is not understood as final and forever. We are looking for more complex, nuanced truths because, provisionally, they fill in a blank, correct what becomes in turn defined as an exaggeration or imbalance, or usefully call into question concepts we have previously taken for granted.

One of the major contributions of new historicist, cultural and feminist theory has been to 'denaturalize' what seems natural and self-evident. So Michel Foucault famously argued that sexuality, often thought of as natural and ahistorical, does indeed have a history,[9] while feminist critics of various stamps have argued that human gender roles are not natural but socially constructed.[10] This essay examines some of the versions of 'home' and 'childhood' in Victorian texts and how these versions might be read by a post-Victorian audience. Looking at how two texts in particular, mid-Victorian and late twentieth century, interact with a nearly identical set of illustrations, I hope to illuminate how we might productively examine assumptions about how home and childhood were constructed in the middle decades of the nineteenth century.

Home Thoughts and Home Scenes, a volume of poems about childhood by women poets well known in their day – including Dora Greenwell, Jean Ingelow, and Dinah Mulock Craik – with engravings by Arthur Boyd Houghton, appeared in 1865.[11] It was advertised as a gift book for Christmas,[12] and a reader giving it a cursory glance today might see it as conventionally sweet and quaint. However, with careful study the pictures can be read to reveal a more complex, not altogether cheerful construction of childhood and home. Commenting briefly on this collection, Paul Goldman in *Victorian Illustration* writes that

> the drawings of the children show them as heavy visaged, frequently frightened and rarely carefree. They seem to hint at a real unease at the centre of the Victorian psyche, and although ostensibly about children, the work … is definitely a far more complex and disturbing volume than the innocent title might suggest. The poetry, all by leading women poets … is also overdue for reevaluation.[13]

Goldman's comment indicates an increasing tendency in criticism that emphasizes the disturbing, contradictory qualities in literature and art, qualities more likely to interest today's academic audiences than those of sweetness and light. Children's literature might seem an unlikely field for the study of psychic unease. In 1893, Mary Louisa Molesworth, a successful writer for children, argued that children's literature cannot be free of conflict and pain:

> But underlying the sad things, and the wrong things, and the perplexing things ... there must be a belief in the brighter side – in goodness, happiness and beauty – as the real background after all. And anyone who does not feel ... that this 'optimism' is well-founded, had better leave writing for children alone.[14]

Admittedly, children's books of the present era often deal overtly with painful and difficult subjects, but there is still a prevailing expectation that children's books will suggest solutions to problems and offer comfort in distressing situations.[15] It could be argued that readers expect resolution and eventual comfort especially in Victorian works for or about children, where didacticism seems more obvious to them and that these readers would otherwise not be so compelled by disturbance and dis-ease. These expectations allow us to agree with Goldman that *Home Thoughts and Home Scenes* is an 'innocent title' and that works 'about children' will be simple and reassuring. Disturbance and dis-ease seem an intrusion in such a vision of the Victorian world of childhood because, however sophisticated we may be, we may associate idyllic images with that 'world'. Before analysing *Home Thoughts and Home Scenes*, it is useful to examine Victorian ideologies about childhood and home as they are available to us in literary and popular culture.

Perhaps the most widespread of these images appear today in popular culture through greeting cards and decorative commodities, but Victorian literature and art often offer less idealized, more dangerous constructions. Readers need only recall a few canonical texts, such as *Jane Eyre* (1847) and *Oliver Twist* (1837–39) in which institutions and the people representing them terrorize and oppress children. Any generalizations about idyllic Victorian childhoods have also been complicated by the growing attention paid to working-class children,[16] and canons have expanded to include more works dealing specifically with class oppression. For example, the latest edition of *The Norton Anthology of British Literature* includes Elizabeth Barrett Browning's (until recently uncanonical) plea for child factory workers, 'The Cry of the Children'.[17]

Paintings that represent oppressed and dying children are less well known today as they are certainly not likely to be marketable on calendars and greeting cards, but an examination of these paintings suggests that sweet sentimentality is not the only response to these conditions. Frank Holl's *Doubtful*

Hope (1875),[18] for example, shows a grief-stricken working-class mother, holding a dangerously ill infant and waiting for the medicine in which she appears to put little faith. While this picture might be calculated to tug at the heartstrings, it is a far cry from depicting children carried off by angels.

Studies of Victorian childhood typically discuss evangelicals' and romantics' conflicting constructions of the child.[19] The evangelical view was that children were tainted by original sin and must be closely controlled in order to save their souls. Those influenced by Rousseau[20] subscribed to a more romantic view of childhood and saw children as innocent and spontaneous. Most scholars agree that evangelical ideology held firmer sway in the early years of the century while the romantic gradually gained influence, yet both existed at the same time to varying degrees.[21] Publishing her memoirs in 1972 Sylvia McCurdy (b. 1876) says, 'So much is written about the harsh treatment and narrow existence of Victorian children that a Victorian child who passed and remembers a very happy childhood, owes it to her parents, teachers and domestics to say a few words in their defense.'[22] In 1978, David Grylls assumed that the current stereotype of Victorian families was that they were 'strict', with 'despotic' fathers and 'deferential' mothers and included a strong dose of corporal punishment and hypocrisy.[23] Yet the 1980s saw a revival of interest in Victorian 'style' that reproduced and emphasized positive images of the family, an interest that continues to this day.

Popular culture does sometimes use images of dour Victorian families for humorous purposes. However, idealized happy depictions are far more ubiquitous, taking at face value the clichés of joyful 'young lambs' and 'young birds' in Barrett Browning's opening verses of 'The Cry of the Children', clichés which one could argue have the rhetorical purpose of contrasting a romantic, middle-class Victorian view of childhood with the lot of the young factory workers Barrett Browning wishes to champion. The poem implies that all children should have the blissful childhood represented by her anthropomorphic versions of young animals and that middle-class children already live this ideal.

Like Barrett Browning, John Ruskin is aware of the exploitation of children and presents innocence as their birthright. In an 1884 lecture discussing the history of paintings and illustrations, he asserts that 'in England [depicting the 'immortal beauty of children'] was long repressed by the terrible action of our wealth, compelling our painters to represent the children of the poor as in wickedness or misery'.[24] Tracing a 'reaction' in literature through Burns, Mitford, Wordsworth, and Dickens and in public sentiment as evidenced by protest movements, he argues that 'at last [in art] ... you have the radiance and innocence of reinstated infant divinity showered again among the flowers of English meadows by Mrs. Allingham and Kate Greenaway'.[25] Ruskin's language, like that of Barrett Browning's poem, suggests that 'radiance and innocence' should be the qualities of childhood regardless of social class. In fact, Ruskin praises Greenaway for depicting a pre-industrial age which is classless and utopian;[26] childhood is thus linked with the pastoral.

While Ruskin denounced commodity culture, the images of beautiful children that he championed were profitable and became objects of exchange. Because images considered pleasant were more popular in the Victorian age than those considered disturbing, more are available for popular consumption today. Thus, they can tell us something about attitudes towards childhood, but whether children experienced their own childhoods as radiant, innocent, and pastoral or not – or reconstructed them as such when they looked back on them – is not the domain of either Victorian or twentieth-century commodity culture, which is in the business of selling pretty pictures.

Constructions of childhood are inseparable from constructions of home, and like our ideas about Victorian childhood, which become complex with investigation, the Victorian version of 'home' is equally contested. That Victorians revered home is certainly one of the truisms accepted by several studies of the period. Throughout the century, writers often associated home with the sacred. J.A. Froude's fictional skeptic in *The Nemesis of Faith* (1849), links the desire for home and childhood with childlike religious faith:

> ... God has given us each our own Paradise, our own old childhood, over which the old glories linger – to which our own hearts cling, as all we have ever known of Heaven upon earth. ... [E]arth's weary wayfarers ... [and] poor speculators ... turn back in thought ... to that old time of peace – that village church – that child faith – which, once lost, is never gained again. ...[27]

Perhaps the most famous paean to home is John Ruskin's (published in 1865, the same year as *Home Thoughts*), worth quoting at length:

> This is the true nature of home – it is the place of Peace; the shelter, not only from all injury, but from all terror, doubt, and division. In so far as it is not this, it is not home; so far as the anxieties of the outer life penetrate into it, and the inconsistently-minded, unknown, unloved, or hostile society of the outer world is allowed by either husband or wife to cross the threshold, it ceases to be home. ... But so far as it is a sacred place, a vestal temple, a temple of the hearth watched over by Household Gods ... so far it vindicates the name, and fulfills the praise, of home.[28]

Although, in the above passage, husband and wife seem equally responsible, it becomes clear that constructing home is women's mission:

> And wherever a true wife comes, this home is always round her. The stars only may be over her head; the glowworm in the night-cold grass may be the only fire at her foot, but home is yet wherever she is. ...[29]

As many critics have pointed out, Ruskin intended this passage to signify, not that people did not need material houses as long as they had 'true wives' – but that middle-class women should move outside the literal walls of their houses, carrying their spiritual sense of home into the wider world in order to reform it. But whether writers conceived of home in limited or liberal terms, it is almost impossible to read about the sacred character of home without finding reference to a cult of true womanhood. Sarah Stickney Ellis's conduct books for women published in the 1830s and 1840s continually refer to the 'sacred' and 'holy' duties of parents, but particularly mothers.[30] As late as 1884 John W. Burgon argues 'it is in the sweet sanctities of domestic life, – in home duties – in whatever belongs to and makes the happiness of *Home*, that Woman is taught by the SPIRIT to find scope for her activity ...'.[31] Many reformers of Victorian working-class life – even if they might be skeptical of Ruskin's vision of stars and glowworms – assumed that improvements could not be made as long as women worked outside the home; for example, Peter Gaskell argues, 'No great step can be made till she is snatched from unremitting toil, and made what Nature meant she should be – the centre of a system of social delights.'[32] That the domestic world was not free of 'unremitting toil' (much of it shouldered by servants in middle and upper-class homes) was evident from even a superficial perusal of Mrs Beeton's *Household Management*.[33] Yet Beeton's emphasis on the social and psychological benefits of an efficiently run home helped to create and strengthen the cult of domesticity in which women, especially mothers, were in large part considered responsible for creating both 'childhood' and 'home'.

As in other areas, Victorian discourses are not in agreement about home. After all, the domestic sphere in literary works is not always free from strife. Jane Eyre's first 'home' is not benign; Helen Huntington's home is depressing and corrupting in Anne Brontë's *The Tenant of Wildfell Hall* (1848); oppression, violence, and rebellion characterize much of the home life in Emily Brontë's *Wuthering Heights* (1847). Nor do the Brontës have a corner on domestic conflict. Maggie Tulliver in George Eliot's *The Mill on the Floss* (1860), for all the narrator's talk of the nostalgic power of home influence and memories, has a difficult childhood; Dickens's Pip in *Great Expectations* (1860–61) is at the mercy of his angry sister. The three Brontë novels mentioned do finally create an image of home as peaceful and loving, but their domestic troubles may be more memorable. Maggie and Pip never achieve the Victorian middle-class ideal of home. Female characters often are presented as inadequate nurturers and moral exemplars. It is worth observing, however, that much of the worst distress literary children experience is not at the hands of their own parents.[34] A notable exception, Samuel Butler's somewhat autobiographical novel *The Way of All Flesh*, was not published until 1903 after Butler and all his family were dead.

Literature is not life, but unmediated life is not available to us: all our knowledge of Victorian life comes from texts or from objects that we interpret as if they were texts. Various discourses – autobiographies, letters, law records, essays, photographs, illustrations – attest to domestic unrest and suggest that home was an ideal rather than a lived reality for many people. Perhaps Victorian readers read Mrs Beeton – and even Ellis and Ruskin – much as readers today pour over the pages documenting the modern cult of domesticity in *Martha Stewart Living* (1990–present). Probably few people – especially those of scarce to moderate means – believe their lives could be so ordered, clean, cheerful, and beautiful, but it is a compelling narrative. Moreover, texts constitute the available cultural narratives, actually creating our perceptions of 'reality'. If we cannot imagine living the pristine life, we imagine – at least fitfully – that others do, or that we could too if only we were more organized, determined, and talented. Victorian women were often encouraged to believe that if their home lives were not faultless it was because they themselves were lacking in managerial and angelic qualities that other, more successful women, possessed. It could be argued that today's cult of domesticity is more materialistic than spiritual, that no one expects wives and mothers to be angels in the house.[35] But the ideal of mothers as the patient, compassionate primary caretakers of children, responsible for creating a sense of home is still very much with us. 'Home' still carries connotations of peace, belonging, and privacy.

Homes do not need to be entirely orderly or free of conflict in order to be happy, however, or to be remembered as happy by adults.[36] Texts – such as those by Ellis, Froude, and Ruskin – may have helped to shape those 'memories'. Certainly a volume called *Home Thoughts and Home Scenes*, comprised of poems about childhood by women poets and illustrated with 'home scenes' (usually middle-class with a few prosperous rural working-class examples), might suggest to many readers an idea of childhood as a happier, less complicated time.

In fact, the note to readers at the beginning of the book demonstrates that adults are considered a major audience for *Home Thoughts*:

> In preparing for publication this series of Pictures of Home Scenes, it has been felt that the theme chosen was certain to excite wide and general interest.
>
> The children's little world of cloud and sunshine is, and always will be, sure to awaken near and living memories, even in the minds of the oldest. How well Mr. HOUGHTON has accomplished the task committed to his care, and how vividly pourtrayed these tenderest of human sympathies, his Pictures abundantly testify.
>
> In the literary portion of the work, the lady authors, no less than the artist, have been animated by the spirit expressed in Schiller's beautiful line,
>
> 'There lies deep meaning oft in childish play'.[37]

That images of childhood evoke the 'tenderest of human sympathies' and 'deep meaning' is significant for, as Claudia Nelson argues, '[a] major function of childhood in the mid- to late-nineteenth century was to serve ... as a kind of spiritual palate cleanser – a dose of innocence and purity protecting adult men, in particular, from the moral dubiousness of the public sphere'.[38] Nelson goes on to describe how

> [i]llustrations and greeting cards, paintings and photographs, verses and novels and advertisements, offered up children for adult consumption. [These] children share certain important characteristics: they are depicted as infantile, with large heads or rosebud mouths or lisps, and thus as innocent; as vulnerable, in need of adult protection; as trusting, perceiving only the good in the world.[39]

Home Thoughts does not depict children as uniformly innocent and vulnerable, but it is instructive that some of the poems and illustrations might be seen in the terms Nelson describes. And many of the poems' personas are adults who appear to be speaking to an adult audience.

Some of the poems and pictures appear to conform to conventional ideology about the innocence of childhood, the sacred peace of home, and women's mission. 'The Music of Childhood' by Jean Ingelow[40] is a study in nostalgic longing for a happier time and its companion illustration of little girls in the woods is conventionally pretty.[41] Occasionally, sweet poems and illustrations contain an 'outsider' or non-participant, but without any obviously disturbing qualities. One example is a reverential poem by Dinah Mulock Craik called 'Grandpapa',[42] accompanied by a picture of a young mother and children with a grandfather.[43] One child in the upper left portion of the picture does not appear to be paying attention to the exhortation to 'Let everyone honour grandpapa' but is not overtly resisting it either. More suggestive is 'The Queen of Hearts' by L.T.W. (Mrs Tom Taylor) which goes into raptures over a new baby, emphasizing conventional ideas about gender and motherhood: 'Happy mother! closer, nearer, / Revel in that velvet kiss – / Take your fill – for nothing dearer / Life can offer you than this.'[44] The picture is dominated by a mother lovingly holding and gazing at her baby while an older child seems equally devoted to the newest arrival (Figure 3.1).[45] The poem asks 'From the nursery to the kitchen, / From the parlour to the hall, / With her tyranny bewitching, / Is she not the Queen of all?' The assumed answer is 'yes', but at the bottom of the picture a toddler lies on the floor, apparently asleep and unnoticed by the group in the middle. Displaced as the center of attention, the child looks rather like a discarded doll. At any rate, he or she is not worshiping baby. The contrast is marked between this kind of domestic scene and that depicted in the frontispiece for Sarah Stickney Ellis's *The Women of England* (Figure 3.2).[46]

Figure 3.1   Illustration for 'The Queen of Hearts', Houghton

Obvious disjunctions between poem and picture are rare in *Home Thoughts*, however. One notable example occurs with Dora Greenwell's 'Child Among the Rocks', which – although it contains 'heavy cliffs' and 'winds that wail' – resolves in the idea that 'Childhood's realm ... / Lies ... ever hidden, safe and sweet, / Warm 'mid sheltering rocks that guard and love it.'[47] Houghton ironically illustrates this poem with a round-faced little girl, terrified of a crab.[48] In Taylor's 'The Baby Brigade' children playing soldier are encouraged by a 'smiling' old soldier who 'loves to drill his Baby Brigade',[49] but in the illustration the old soldier regards the children grimly

Figure 3.2 Frontispiece from 'The Women of England' by W. Wetherhead and T. Allem[?]

from the background suggesting neither joy nor vitality but instead a contrast between soldiering and play, old age and youth.[50]

Most interesting, however, are a set of poems and illustrations that work together to 'hint at a real unease at the center of the Victorian psyche'.[51] In one scene from 'innocent childhood' a group of children are shown in the nursery (Figure 3.3).[52] One little boy is trying to saw off a doll's head, while a little girl pushes on *his* head, trying to get him to stop. Another boy above and behind her is squirting the back of her head with ink or water. The poem accompanying the illustration is 'Law and Justice' by Jean Ingelow:

> Now, this is Mary Queen of Scots!
> Push all her curls away;
> For we have heard about her plots,
>   And she must die today.
>
> What's this? *I must not hurt her so;*
> *You love her dearly still;*
> *You think she will be good* – Oh no!
>   I say she never will.

Figure 3.3   Illustration depicting 'Law and Justice', Houghton

> My own new saw, and made of steel!
> Oh silly child to cry;
> She's only wood; she cannot feel;
>   And, look, her eyes are dry.
>
> Her cheeks are bright with rosy spots;
> I know she cares for none –
> Besides, she's Mary Queen of Scots,
>   And so it MUST be done.[53]

Ingelow's vision of the power politics of the nursery is both amusing and disturbing. The juvenile male logic is ridiculous, but it determines what happens in the nursery where little girls in training for motherhood cannot save their dolls. In spite of the poem's finality, the illustration shows the little girl resisting, even as she's attacked by another boy, suggesting that she may lose in the power struggle but continue to resist the logic.[54]

'Unease at the center' is more obvious in an eerie picture in which a doctor, mother, and five children gather around a child the mother is holding on her lap (Figure 3.4).[55] The doctor is taking the child's pulse. The child's expression looks anguished, but also 'frozen'. The poem is Dinah Mulock

Figure 3.4   Illustration for 'A Sick Child', Houghton

Craik's 'A Sick Child':

> How the trembling children gather round,
>   Startled out of sleep, and scared and crying!
>   'Is our merry little sister dying?
> Will they come and put her underground
>
> As they did poor baby that May day?
>   Or will shining angels stoop and take her
>   On their snow-white wings to heaven, and make her
> Sit among the stars, as fair as they?
>
> 'But she'll have no mother there to kiss!
>   We are sorely frightened', say the children,
>   'Thinking of this death, so strange bewildering:
> Tell us, only tell us what death is?'
>
> Ah, we cannot, any more than you!
>   We are also children of our Father;
>   And we only know that He will gather
> All His own, and keep them safely too.
>
> So this death as sweet as sleep is made:
>   For where'er we go, we go together,
>   Father, mother, children – He knows whither.
> Since He takes us, we are not afraid.
>
> Whether little sister lives or dies,
>   Mother knows her safe, and stills all weeping;
>   Christ, who once said 'Lazarus is *sleeping*',
> Will awake us all in Paradise.[56]

By late twentieth-/early twenty-first-century standards, this poem might be considered sentimental and morbid and its consolation facile. But it works intertextually with the illustration to convey a sense of suspense and powerlessness with regard to death, a frequent occurrence in Victorian texts, even those dealing with upper- and middle-class children. Certainly, the child – highlighted in the center of the picture – looks stricken by an 'unease' that could be fatal. David Grylls argues that the rate of childhood death alone cannot account for the increased number of child deaths in Victorian literature since children were then living longer than they had at any previous time. He attributes the rise in literary mortality to a desire to win sympathy for children, especially if they died as a result of 'social injustice', and to the promotion of a 'vindication' of Christian faith, which became increasingly 'pathetic and decorative'.[57] In 'A Sick Child' there is no suggestion of neglect, either social or parental, but there certainly is an assertion of religious faith. Readers do not know, however, whether the anxiously questioning children, who have already lost one sibling, are convinced. That they already know the rhetoric of 'pathetic and decorative' death is illustrated by their references to 'shining angels' and 'sit[ing] among the stars'. Since these lofty images do not comfort them, perhaps the homely metaphors of sleeping and waking are more effective. But the poem only offers the comfort rather than showing the children being comforted. The speaker may be addressing adults too, although the ostensible audience is children. The poem may be read both as a comfort and as an exhortation to mothers to 'still all weeping' in order to provide an example of faith to children.

That poems about childhood are vehicles for adult reflection rather than expressions of children's views or values[58] is evidenced by Jennett Humphreys's 'The Chair Railway'. In the foreground of Houghton's engraving, five children are playing the game of the poem's title (Figure 3.5).[59] A

Figure 3.5   Illustration for 'The Chair Railway', Houghton

close look at the picture reveals a woman in the upper right corner with her head in her hands, expressing weariness and dejection. 'The Chair Railway' not only accounts for this woman in the background, but – readers discover – speaks in her voice:

> The Chair Railway
>
> Gesture, clatter,
> Whistle, chatter,
> Chairs in position, passengers placed;
> Progress shouted,
> Late ones scouted,
> No heed that they implore.
>
> Noise, appearance,
> Pomp of clearance,
> Terminals sighted, course to run traced;
> Signals waving,
> Tunnels braving;
> – All feigned! But would ye more? –
>
> Clamour, hurry,
> Boasting, flurry,
> Hope to proceed on vehemence based;
> Skill assuming,
> Strength presuming,
> Advance so sure in store.
>
> No step gaining,
> Naught attaining,
> Stir and commotion, all of it, waste;
> Train unmoving,
> Weakness proving,
> Held fast to the floor!
>
> No acquirement,
> All requirement! –
> Naught but bluster, blazon, and haste;
> Outcry failing,
> Unavailing!
> – Ah me! Have I done more?[60]

Without the poem, it might be easier to miss the woman in the picture and concentrate only on the children, or to see the children as providing only a contrast to the woman. With the poem, however, the pictured children's stolid immobility is more noticeable. Only one child who peers around a chair at the viewer looks very playful. The children seem to be taking their game seriously, providing a strong analogy to the woman's reflections. If the woman is the children's mother, both picture and poem undercut the ideal of the angelic matron as moral center of the home, example and instructor of her children. If the woman is a governess or nursemaid, the mother's absence is disturbing – is she ill or dead? too busy? uncaring? – and comments on the difficulty of women working for money in private homes even when the duties involved those supposedly natural to women.

It is not known who arranged the pairs of poems and pictures, and space restrictions preclude an analysis of the effects created by their sequence, but it is worth discussing the placement of the final poem and illustration. *Home Thoughts* contains some more or less reassuring poems, such as 'Cradle Song',[61] or 'Going to Bed',[62] which might have created a fairly happy ending. However, whoever arranged the poems chose to end with Caroline Norton's 'Crippled Jane':

> They said she might recover, if we sent her down to the sea,
> But that is for rich men's children, and we knew it could not be:
> So she lived at home in the Lincolnshire Fens, and we saw her, day by day,
> Grow pale, and stunted, and crooked; till her last chance died away.
> And now *I'm* dying; and often, when you thought that I moaned in pain,
> I was moaning a prayer to heaven, and thinking of Crippled Jane.
> Folks will be kind to Johnny; his temper is merry and light;
> With so much love in his honest eyes, and a sturdy sense of right.
> And no one could quarrel with Susan; so pious and meek and mild,
> And nearly as wise as a woman, for all she looks such a child!
> But Jane will be weird and wayward; fierce and cunning, and hard;
> She won't believe she's a burden, be thankful and win regard. –
> God have mercy upon her! God be her guard, and guide;
> How will strangers bear with her, when, at times, even *I* felt tried?
> When the ugly smile of pleasure goes over her sallow face,
> And the feeling of health for an hour, quickens her languid pace;
> When with dwarfish strength she rises, and plucks with a selfish hand,
> The busiest person near her, to lead her out on the land:
> Or when she sits in some corner; no one's companion, or care,
> Huddled up in some darksome passage, or crouched on a step of the stair
> While far off the children are playing, and the birds singing loud in the sky,
> And she looks through the cloud of her headache, to scowl at the passers-by.
> I die – God have pity upon her! – how happy rich men must be –
> For they said she might have recovered – if we sent her down to the sea.[63]

Houghton's engraving shows a woman and child sitting on steps while other children walk by them (Figure 3.6).[64] The woman appears to be sleeping; the child is crouched, peering through the railing at the other children, her

Figure 3.6 Illustration for 'Crippled Jane', Houghton

crutch lying on the step below her. Jane is far from perfect; her illness has not made her pious and long-suffering in the tradition of *Jane Eyre*'s Helen Burns. Others are not inspired by her example. The poem also includes class issues because the speaker believes, rightly or wrongly, that a rich person's child might have been saved. One reading of *Home Thoughts'* ending leads to a reflection on the kind of 'home' Jane will have now. Unlike Barrett Browning's 'The Cry of the Children' and much overtly didactic literature of the period, it does not ask for reform, but it hints that at least the fortunate should think of the unfortunate and be more charitable.

Home Thoughts' ending may support Molesworth's contention that 'writing *about* children is by no means the same thing as writing *for* them'.[65] In fact, *Home Thoughts* was advertised with 'gift books' in one column, while 'juvenile books' were listed in another. Whatever the intended audience, the book's ending refuses to conform to Molesworth's dictum that writing for children should show that 'goodness, happiness, and beauty [are] the real background after all';[66] like much writing *about* childhood, it refuses to produce childhood as blissful and innocent.

The poems and pictures I have described here are compelling when we try to construct a Victorian context around them and see contradictions between Victorian ideals and Victorian dis-ease. We may assume – sometimes wrongly – that this kind of analysis is more sophisticated than any of which Victorian writers would have been capable. Consequently, when Victorian images appear in popular culture in the late twentieth and twenty-first centuries, they are often taken at face value or assumed to be 'innocent'. Such is certainly the case with *Victoria* (1987/88–2003), a magazine that popularized Victorian culture at the same time that it erased from it all vestiges of dirt, poverty, or oppression. Letters to the editor of *Victoria* often commented on how readers valued the magazine as an escape from modern life to a kinder, gentler world.[67] Whether they sincerely believed that the Victorian world was as it was portrayed in the magazine is doubtful, but the rhetoric of the pictures and articles themselves encouraged readers to think of Victorian times as simpler, more gracious, and more refined. Particularly significant to the present discussion is an article on nineteenth-century children's books, showing a number of illustrations.[68] The copy mentions that some pictures were hand colored by women and children, but – in keeping with the magazine's focus – does not mention that these workers earned barely enough to survive and were often poisoned by lead paint. It might be said that *Victoria* presents the Victorian world as a fantasy 'childhood' to which world-weary Technical Age readers can retreat temporarily, just as world-weary Industrial Age readers used an ideal of childhood to promote faith in innocence and beauty.

The ideological uses of *Victoria* are particularly relevant to an analysis of Fred Cody's *Make-Believe Summer: A Victorian Idyll* (1980) which appropriates most of Houghton's engravings from *Home Thoughts*, rearranges them, and includes a few more from other sources in order to tell a different story.[69]

While Cody's interpretation of the engravings cannot be representative of all twentieth-century attitudes towards Victorian childhood, his book is a rare opportunity to analyse an example of how the twentieth century has constructed and commodified images of childhood from the Victorian period. Not only are Houghton's illustrations and Cody's story strangely at odds, but Cody's remarks in the introduction about his intentions (and Houghton's) are contradictory. He shows no interest in the poems, but thinks the engravings have

> an appeal as a charming depiction of middle-class Victorian life, [though] there are other – and possibly more compelling – reasons for their appearance a century later. ... [Houghton's] was a view of childhood that was not unclouded and, although his love of children is always evident, there is also present the 'dark and mysterious' Goya-like quality in his work of which van Gogh wrote. The joy and vivacity of childhood are here, but so are the moments of introspective moodiness. ... His domestic scenes record a memory of what was apparently a happy childhood, but they reflect the shadows in his early life as well. It is these hints of the 'other' side of childhood that impart to the pictures a curiously contemporary feeling.
>
> Hence this book. The object has been to allow the pictures to tell the story of the children and their idyllic summer on an English farm. This, I believe, approaches the original aim of the artist; the matching of pictures and poems in their earlier appearance merely followed the publishing practice of the time. The engravings appear here with a modest and unobtrusive text close to the spirit and feeling of the present-day children's picture book. In this form, it is hoped the reader will now be encouraged to see in them the ... perceptiveness, sensitivity and originality, which make them an extraordinarily evocative view of childhood in their own time and in ours.[70]

Cody's idea that Houghton's work 'hints at the "other" side of childhood' is curiously at odds with his next statement that the pictures represent an 'idyllic summer', which is closer to the author's intention. It's as if Cody is freeing the illustrations from the implicitly obtrusive text of *Home Thoughts*, where the 'matching' of pictures to text inhibits the artist, and *allowing* them to tell the story they were originally meant to tell. Yet that story, as told by Cody, is extremely sunny, glossing quickly over the 'other side of childhood'. Every potentially bad experience or emotionally scarring event is made to work out simply and easily. The story begins with the death of the father of a middle-class English family living in America. The mother brings her three daughters home to England where the two girls past infancy find their new surroundings both pleasant and strange – but not too strange. Nearly every depiction of anxiety or sadness in the illustrations is ignored or easily resolved in the text.

Cody's story registers the terror of the little girl confronted with a crab, but she is quickly rescued by her cousin John.[71] The text accompanying the nursery execution scene is

> Next morning our cousins welcomed us! I finally rescued my doll from Tom's saw, but I didn't escape the spray from Peter's squirt gun.[72]

Both saw and squirt gun are innocuous here, given the rescue of the doll, in a sharp contrast to the Victorian nursery of 'Law and Justice' where dolls are not saved. The frightening sick child illustration is explained as

> Beth had a terrible stomach-ache that evening from eating the jam. So the doctor came over, gave her some dreadful medicine, and she was sent to bed to get well.[73]

Unlike the patient in 'A Sick Child', this child's recovery is assured. No matter that the subject of the illustration looks stricken by something worse than indigestion.

Even more significant perhaps is Cody's handling of 'The Chair Railway' illustration: 'Playing train was something new for us – we had never had so many chairs'.[74] This kind of persona may strike us as more like Robert Louis Stevenson's in *A Child's Garden of Verses* (1885), particularly 'A Good Play', in which the speaker and Tom 'built a ship upon the stairs / All made of the back-bedroom chairs'.[75] Stevenson uses a child speaker who comments on the significance of the experience at hand, rather than an adult speaker who extrapolates from childhood play to adult experience. This choice of speaker makes his poem less didactic than many in *Home Thoughts*, and it could be argued that Cody, attempting to appeal to twentieth-century readers, also wishes to avoid didacticism. However, while the child speaker in Stevenson's poem might be seen as naïve, nothing can be assumed to be missing from the poem because the poem itself constructs the child as interpreter of the world. Cody's use of the child's perspective leaves the weary or despairing woman in Houghton's picture unaccounted for. If we think of the pictures and words operating intertextually, this particular part of Cody's book represents, not an erasure of disturbance, but an attempt to ignore it. One could argue that his choice to narrate in the child's voice means that his naïve narrator can be constructed as largely unconscious of adult problems, and that his point is precisely that the children are unaware of their mother's (?) state of mind. However, this strategy disregards the more troubled aspects of childhood Cody says Houghton's engravings depict.

Most tellingly, Cody's story ends with the picture that accompanies 'The Baby Brigade' with the narrator telling how their new stepfather draws pictures of them, of which this one is their favorite:

> [T]he old farmer who never tired of staring at the Yankee children, and ...
> Rufus, our pet raven, who often flew down to peck at crumbs around our
> feet ... might represent all that seemed difficult and strange about that first
> summer in England. ... Our time of make-believe had passed. We were
> stepping forward now into the real happiness of our future life together.[76]

Home Thoughts, as we have seen, ends with 'Crippled Jane', and if Cody were
going to cut any illustration, it might well be this one. However, he includes
it about halfway through the volume with the text

> As the days became warmer, we trooped out into the fields and woods.
> Bessie, who had a wooden leg, watched us enviously. Later in the summer
> we grew to be good friends.[77]

Bessie never appears again in the story, but here the text does not either
erase or completely ignore a disturbing element. Instead, it accounts for
Jane/Bessie, swiftly undercutting her disability and envy. This strategy
suggests that, again, reassurance is thought to be of paramount importance
in appealing to a twentieth-century audience reading about Victorian childhood. Ironically, then, the twentieth-century text ends happily, while the
Victorian one ends with sadness and powerlessness.

That Cody recognizes the disturbing elements of the illustrations in his
introduction but undercuts them in his story suggests that his perception of
'childhood in [Victorians'] times and in ours' actually requires de-emphasizing
somber moods and subjects. His erasure of the poetry is less easy to interpret. Perhaps Cody thinks the poems are saccharine or moralistic and does
not read them as speaking to the 'other side of childhood'. Or perhaps he
does recognize their less than consistently happy tone and thinks them
inappropriate for children. It seems reasonable to assume that, in addition
to parents who would purchase the book for their children, Cody's audience
includes people interested in twentieth-century Victoriana, such as the
readers of *Victoria* magazine. In any case, Cody's reworking of Houghton
allows me to read a twentieth-century construction of the 'Victorian' as pre-
cluding the 'dark and mysterious' qualities of childhood, while claiming for
the present those 'dark and mysterious' qualities that I see in Houghton's
engravings. Cody seems conscious of this tension in his use of the term
'idyll', a form which traditionally creates a fictionalized pastoral world for
readers who consider themselves more sophisticated. The difficulty lies in
assuming that Victorian poets and readers were incapable of seeing the
engravings as anything other than pastoral, innocent, or simple, while
claiming for the present the ability to read 'beyond' these Victorians to a
more sophisticated and complex 'truth'.

Further reading

Armstrong, Isobel and Joseph Bristow, with Cath Sharrock, eds, *Nineteenth-Century Women Poets* (Oxford: Oxford University Press, 1996).
Houghton, Arthur Boyd, *Arthur Boyd Houghton: A Selection From His Work in Black and White* (London: Kegan Paul, Trench, Trubner, 1896).
Leighton, Angela, *Victorian Women Poets: Writing Against the Heart* (Charlottesville and London: University of Virginia Press, 1992).
Leighton, Angela and Margaret Reynolds, eds, *Victorian Women Poets: An Anthology* (Oxford, UK and Cambridge, USA: Blackwell, 1995).
Mermin, Dorothy, *Godiva's Ride: Women of Letters in England, 1830–1880* (Bloomington: Indiana University Press, 1993).

Notes

1. Stephen Greenblatt, *Shakespearean Negotiation* (Berkeley: University of California Press, 1988), p. 1.
2. Lytton Strachey, *Eminent Victorians* (New York: Putnam, 1918).
3. Virginia Woolf, *Orlando* (Oxford: Oxford University Press, 1992, orig. pub. 1928), chapter 5, pp. 217–50 and 'Professions for Women' in: *Collected Essays* (New York: Harcourt, Brace, and World, 1967, orig. pub. 1925), vol. 2, pp. 284–9.
4. As early as 1963 E.P. Thompson in *The Making of the English Working Class* (Harmondsworth: Penguin, 1980, orig. pub. 1963) was concerned with 'rescu[ing]' the obscure and stereotyped in Victorian history 'from the enormous condescension of posterity' (p. 12). For revisions of Victorian sexuality, see Michael Mason, *The Making of Victorian Sexuality* (Oxford: Oxford University Press, 1994) and *The Making of Victorian Sexual Attitudes* (Oxford: Oxford University Press, 1994). See also Elizabeth Langland's debunking of the Victorian middle-class angel stereotype in *Nobody's Angels: Middle-Class Women and Domestic Ideology in Victorian Culture* (Ithaca, NY: Cornell University Press, 1995). Good discussions of the construction of the Victorian period include John McGowan, 'Modernity and Culture, the Victorians and Cultural Studies' in: John Kucich and Dianne F. Sadoff, eds, *Victorian Afterlife: Postmodern Culture Rewrites the Nineteenth Century* (Minneapolis: University of Minnesota Press), pp. 3–28, and Simon Joyce, 'The Victorians in the Rearview Mirror' in: Christine Krueger, ed., *Functions of Victorian Culture at the Present Time* (Athens, OH: Ohio University Press, 2002), pp. 3–17, the latter arguing that 'anti-Victorian sentiment…began much earlier' than the Bloomsbury Modernists (p. 7). For a popular, but well documented, summary of the argument against Victorian stereotypes, see Matthew Sweet, *Inventing the Victorians* (New York: St Martin's Press – now Palgrave Macmillan, 2001).
5. John Kucich and Dianne F. Sadoff, 'Introduction: Histories of the Present', in: *Victorian Afterlife*, pp. ix–xxx, p. xxvi.
6. Dominick LaCapra, *History and Criticism* (Ithaca, NY: Cornell University Press, 1985), p. 9. Quoted in Kucich and Sadoff (see note 4 above), p. xxvi.
7. McGowan, 'Modernity and Culture', p. 23.
8. Frederic Jameson, 'Imaginary and Symbolic in Lacan: Marxism, Psychoanalytic Criticism, and the Problem of the Subject', *Yale French Studies*, 55–56 (1977), 338–95, 388.
9. Michel Foucault, *The History of Sexuality* (New York: Pantheon, 1978).

10. Studies that denaturalize gender roles are too numerous to mention, but see Elizabeth Langland, *Nobody's Angels* and Tricia Lootens, *Lost Saints: Silence, Gender, and Victorian Literary Canonization* (Charlottesville and London: University of Virginia Press, 1996).

11. *Home Thoughts and Home Scenes*, original poems by Jean Ingelow, Dora Greenwell, Mrs Tom Taylor, the Hon. Mrs Norton, Amelia B. Edwards, Jennett Humphreys, and the author of 'John Halifax, Gentleman' [Dinah Mulock Craik], illustrated by Arthur Boyd Houghton (London: Routledge, Warne and Routledge, 1865). Poems in this text are numbered with Roman numerals and engravings with Arabic numerals and will be so indicated in subsequent references.

12. See the full page advertisement for George Routledge & Sons headed 'For Christmas Presents & New Year's Gifts' in *The Reader*, 23 December, 1865.

13. Paul Goldman, *Victorian Illustration: The Pre-Raphaelites, the Idyllic School, and the High Victorians* (Brookfield, VT: Ashgate, 1996), p. 128.

14. Mary Louisa Molesworth, 'On the Art of Writing Fiction for Children' in: Lance Salway, ed., *A Peculiar Gift: Nineteenth Century Writings on Books for Children* (Harmondsworth: Kestral (Penguin), 1976), pp. 340–6, p. 342 (first published in: *Atalanta* 6 (May 1893), 583–6).

15. Colin McGeorge notes that by the 1970s, ' "death itself had reentered children's books" as one of a number of issues – including divorce, illness, and teenage sexuality – that children might be helped to come to terms with through literature' ('Death and Violence in Some Victorian School Reading Books', *Children's Literature in Education*, 29 (1998): 109–17, 109, quoting from: Maxine Walker, 'Last Rites for Young Readers', *Children's Literature in Education*, 9 (1978), 188–97, 192). Twentieth-century readers have certainly been disturbed by some nineteenth-century children's texts. Perhaps the most notorious is Mary Sherwood's *The History of the Fairchild Family* (New York: Garland, 1818, 1842, 1847, 1977) which is full of awful warnings against disobedience and crime, most notably in the scene in which the father takes his children to see a corpse on a gibbet. Mary F. Thwaite argues that nevertheless the Fairchild children feel 'secure and happy', knowing that their parents have their best interests at heart (*From Primer to Pleasure in Reading* (Boston: Horn Book, 1972), p. 65). That later readers did not feel as 'secure and happy' is evidenced by the expurgated editions that appeared around the turn of the century. Some nineteenth-century writers, such as Richard Henry Horne argued that some literature was inappropriate for children: nursery rhymes and tales 'are full of horrors and other alarming things, most improper for children to read' (see his 'A Witch in the Nursery' in: *A Peculiar Gift* (note 14 above), pp. 173–94, p. 186, first published in: *Household Words* 78 (Sept. 1851, 601–9). Yet some children may have enjoyed the 'horrors'. Kate Rathbone remembers a reprint of Elizabeth Turner's *The Daisy and the Cowslip: Cautionary Stories in Verse for Children* : 'Now we had the whole thing with every sadistic detail, and how we revelled [sic] in it, and the delightful woodcuts' (p. 26). (These stories were originally published in separate volumes: *The Daisy: Or, Cautionary Stories in Verse, Adapted to the Ideas of Children from Four to Eight Years Old* (London: Printed for J. Harris, 1807) and *The Cowslip, Or, More Cautionary Stories in Verse* (London: Printed for J. Harris, 1811)). Perhaps Rathbone would have agreed with F.J. Harvey Darton who writes that these stories 'fascinate one almost obscenely, like a murder-trial' (*Children's Books in England: Five Centuries of Social Life* (London: Cambridge, 1982), 1932, p. 189).

16. See Eric Hopkins, *Childhood Transformed: Working-class Children in Nineteenth-Century England* (Manchester and New York: Manchester University Press, 1994)

and Thomas E. Jordan, *Victorian Childhood: Themes and Variations* (Albany: State University of New York, 1987).

17. Elizabeth Barrett Browning, 'The Cry of the Children' in: M.H. Abrams, ed., *The Norton Anthology of English Literature*, 7th edn (New York: Norton, 2000), pp. 1174–8.

18. Frank Holl, *Doubtful Hope* (1875) in: Susan P. Casteras, *Victorian Childhood: Paintings from the 'Forbes' Magazine Collection* (New York: Abrams, 1986), plate 7, pp. 20–1. For another collection of Victorian paintings of children, see Richard O'Neill, *The Art of Victorian Childhood: A Compilation of Work from the Bridgeman Art Library* (New York: Smithmark, 1996).

19. See Darton, *Children's Books in England*; David Grylls, *Guardians and Angels: Parents and Children in Nineteen-Century Literature* (London and Boston: Faber and Faber, 1978); Thomas E. Jordan, *Victorian Childhood: Percy Muir, English Children's Books 1600–1900* (New York: Praeger, 1954); Dieter Petzhold, 'A Race Apart: Children in Late Victorian and Edwardian Children's Books', *Children's Literature Association Quarterly*, 17 (Fall 1992): 33–6; Mary F. Thwaite, *From Primer to Pleasure*.

20. Jean-Jacques Rousseau, *Émile* (Harmondsworth: Penguin, 1991, orig. pub. 1762).

21. Sara Stickney Ellis, writing in 1843, approved of well-controlled children, but deplored as inhumane and ineffectual the practices of 'some fifty years ago, [which brought] up children under a mistaken notion of rooting out evil…of breaking the natural will…by constant mortification' (*The Mothers of England: Their Influence and Responsibility* (London: Fisher, 1843), pp. 151–2).

22. Sylvia McCurdy, *Sylvia: A Victorian Childhood* (Lavenham, Suffolk, England: Eastland Press, 1972), p. 69.

23. Grylls, *Guardians and Angels*, p. 11.

24. John Ruskin, 'Fairy Land: Mrs. Allingham and Kate Greenaway' in: *The Art of England: Lectures Given in Oxford* (New York: Garland, 1979, orig. pub. 1884), pp. 117–57, p. 139.

25. Ruskin, 'Fairy Land', p. 140.

26. Ruskin, 'Fairy Land', pp. 152–4.

27. J.A. Froude, *The Nemesis of Faith* (London: Chapman, 2nd edn 1849), p. 106.

28. John Ruskin, *Sesame and Lilies* in: *The Works of John Ruskin* (London: Allen, 1903–12, 1865), vol. 18, p. 122.

29. Ruskin, *Sesame*, p. 122.

30. See, for example, *The Mothers of England: Their Influence and Responsibility*, pp. 57, 252, 292, 312. To do her justice, Ellis says that fulfilling a woman's sacred domestic duties is not easy, although she does believe women are naturally fitted for such duties.

31. John W. Burgon, *To Educate Young Women Like Young Men – A Thing Inexpedient and Immodest, A Sermon* (Oxford: Oxford University Press, 1884), p. 17.

32. Peter Gaskell, *The Manufacturing Population of England* (New York: Arno, 1972, orig. pub. 1833), pp. 166–7.

33. Isabella Mary Beeton, *The Book of Household Management* (New York: Farrar, Straus, Giroux, 1969, orig. pub. 1861).

34. Mary Louisa Molesworth argues that 'parental mistakes and failings should surely be avoided when writing *for* the tender little ones' (p. 343), and apparently Victorian writers generally agreed. David Grylls points out that most Victorian books for children completely 'ignore' '[p]arent–child discord' (p. 100) while books for adults increasingly criticize parents; in addition to Butler's *The Way of All Flesh* (1903), Grylls cites Dickens's *Hard Times* (1854) and *Dombey and Son*

(1846–48) and Meredith's *The Ordeal of Richard Feverel* (1859). Blocking and ineffectual parents had been a staple of fiction and drama for a long time, but Victorian literature produced more pointed criticism (p. 42). See especially his nuanced analysis of parents in Dickens, pp. 132–52. I would still argue, however, that much Victorian criticism is deflected from biological parents to parental figures.

35. See Coventry Patmore's poem *The Angel in the House* (London: Haggerston Press with Boston College, 1988, orig. pub. 1854–56) and Virginia Woolf's influential interpretation and critique of the domestic angel in 'Professions for Women' (see note 3 above). For a detailed analysis of the nineteenth-century domestic angel, see Tricia Lootens, *Lost Saints*.
36. Victorian memoirs and autobiographies provide a range of versions of childhood (as well as wide variations in style and willingness or ability to analyse). For examples, see Maude Ballington Booth (1865–1948), *A Rector's Daughter in England: Memories of Childhood and Girlhood* (Metairie, Louisiana: Volunteers of America, 1994); Thomas Edward Lewis (1863–1952), *Blue Ribbon Days: A Tale of Victorian Childhood, Apprenticeship, Love and Marriage in Shropshire*, Geoffrey T. Eddy, ed. (Shropshire: Shropshire Books, 1992); Emily Lutyens (1874–1964), *A Blessed Girl: Memoirs of a Victorian Girlhood Chronicled in an Exchange of Letters 1887–1896* (Philadelphia and New York: Lippincott, 1954); Edmund Gosse (1849–1928), *Father and Son* (New York: Penguin, 1986, orig. pub. 1907); Sylvia McCurdy (1876–?) (see note 22 above); E.M. Bengough (1869–?), 'Memories of my Victorian Childhood at the Ridge, Wotton-under-Edge' in Geoffrey Masefield, ed., *Wotton–under-Edge: A Century of Change* (Gloucester: Alan Sutton, 1980), pp. 91–6; John Stewart Mill (1806–1873), *The Autobiography of John Stewart Mill* (New York: Columbia University Press, 1966, 1873); J.R. Mortimer (1825–1911), *A Victorian Boyhood on the Wolds*, J.D. Hicks, ed. (North Humberside, England: East Yorkshire Local History Society, 1978) and Kate Rathbone (1861–1948), *The Dales: Growing Up in a Victorian Family*, ed. Bob and Harlan Walker (Birmingham, England: printed by Northstep, 1989).
37. 'Advertisement', *Home Thoughts and Home Scenes* [p. 2].
38. Claudia Nelson, 'Growing Up: Childhood' in: Herbert F. Tucker, ed., *A Companion to Victorian Literature & Culture* (Oxford and Malden, MA: Blackwell, 1999), p. 79.
39. Nelson, p. 80.
40. Jean Ingelow, 'The Music of Childhood' in: *Home Thoughts and Home Scenes*, no. I.
41. A.B. Houghton, 'Untitled' in: *Home Thoughts*, no. 1.
42. Dinah Mulock Craik, 'Grandpapa' in: *Home Thoughts*, no. XIX.
43. Houghton, 'Untitled', in: *Home Thoughts*, no. 19.
44. L.T.W. [Mrs Tom Taylor], 'The Queen of Hearts' in: *Home Thoughts*, no. XXV.
45. Houghton, 'Untitled, in: *Home Thoughts*, no. 25.
46. S.S. Ellis, 'The Women of England: Their Duties, Domestic Influence, and Social Obligations' in: *The Select Works of Mrs. Ellis* (New York: Langley, 1844, orig. pub. 1838).
47. Dora Greenwell, 'Child Among the Rocks' in: *Home Thoughts*, no. IV.
48. Houghton, 'Untitled' in: *Home Thoughts*, no. 4.
49. Taylor, 'The Baby Brigade' in: *Home Thoughts*, no. VI.
50. Houghton, 'Untitled' in: *Home Thoughts*, no. 6.
51. Goldman, p. 128.
52. Houghton, 'Untitled' in: *Home Thoughts*, no. 7.
53. Ingelow, 'Law and Justice' in: *Home Thoughts*, no. VII.

54. That gender may not be an entirely determining factor here is suggested by Maude Booth's description of her own and her sister Florrie's doll executions: 'On glorious occasions when all grown people were out of the way, we enacted such historic scenes as the executions of Mary, Queen of Scots and Lady Jane Gray, or Joan of Arc being burned at the stake. ... One of my wildest fights with my eldest sister [Annie] came after I had stolen one of her treasured dolls and condemned it to the axe on our "Tower Hill"' (pp. 22–3). However, Booth says Florrie had always wanted to be a boy and trained them both in 'Spartan' exercises (pp. 10, 21–2).
55. Houghton, 'Untitled' in: *Home Thoughts*, no. 31.
56. Craik, 'A Sick Child' in: *Home Thoughts*, no. XXXI.
57. Grylls, pp. 40–2.
58. The line between poems for children and poems about them is a contested one. See Alexander Hay Japp, 'Children and Children's Books' in: *A Peculiar Gift: Nineteenth Century Writings on Books for Children* (Harmondsworth: Kestral (Penguin)), 1976, pp. 195–205, first published in: *The Contemporary Review*, May 11, 1869; Darton, *Children's Books in England*, pp. 176–98; 243–5; 274–6; 313–15); Molesworth, 'On the Art of Writing', p. 342, and Muir, *English Children's Books*, p. 119.
59. Houghton, 'Untitled' in: *Home Thoughts*, no. 15.
60. Jennett Humphreys, 'The Chair Railway' in: *Home Thoughts*, no. XV.
61. Taylor, 'Cradle Song' in: *Home Thoughts*, no. XXXIII.
62. Greenwell, 'Going to Bed' in: *Home Thoughts*, no. XXXIV.
63. Caroline Norton, 'Crippled Jane' in: *Home Thoughts*, no. XXXV.
64. Houghton, 'Untitled' in: *Home Thoughts*, no. 35.
65. Molesworth, 'On the Art of Writing', p. 342.
66. Molesworth, 'On the Art of Writing', p. 342.
67. For examples of letters praising *Victoria* for providing an escape to the Victorian era or readers' childhoods, see the 'Dear Friends' section of Winter 1987/88 (Dianne Svec, p. 4), Summer 1988 (Sharon Glover, Gayle Warrington, p. 4) December 1988 (Marilyn Oliver, p. 10) and April 1989 (Mrs Dale Carter Andrews, p. 14). See also Miriam Bailin's 'The New Victorians' in: Christine Krueger, ed., *Functions of Victorian Culture at the Present Time* (Athens: Ohio University Press, 2002) pp. 37–46, in which she argues that in *Victoria* the past is 'retrievable because it exists in a space that is neither history nor lived experience but rather a neutral "timelessness" of imputed essences – enduring friendship, the magic of childhood, the romance of moneyed leisure' (p. 38). In addition, readers commend the promotion of 'womanliness' and 'femininity' in issues for Winter 1987/88 (Dianne Svec, Donna Street Warner, p. 4), Summer 1988 (Mrs Robert Mathes, p. 6), December 1988 (Melinda J. Hofelder, p. 10).
68. 'A Love of Childhood', *Victoria* 3 (April 1989), pp. 114–17.
69. Cody uses 28 of the 35 illustrations in *Home Thoughts* and adds five of Houghton's engravings from other sources. I have been able to identify the source of only one of these: *Kiss Me* (Cody, [p. 20]) appeared in *Good Words* (1863, p. 636), accompanying a poem entitled 'Childhood'; see *Introduction and Check-List of the Artist's Work*, Paul Hogarth, ed. (Chatham: Mackay, 1975), plate 21 [p. 54]).
70. Fred Cody, *Make-Believe Summer: A Victorian Idyll*, illustrations by Arthur Boyd Houghton (New York: A & W, 1980) [pp. 3–4].
71. Cody, *Make-Believe Summer* [p. 57].
72. Cody, *Make-Believe Summer* [p. 13].

73. Cody, *Make-Believe Summer* [p. 26].
74. Cody, *Make-Believe Summer* [p. 20].
75. Robert Louis Stevenson, *A Child's Garden of Verses* (New York: Gramercy, 1985, orig. pub. 1885), p. 17.
76. Cody, *Make-Believe Summer* [p. 80].
77. Cody, *Make-Believe Summer* [p. 34].

4

Reading. *The Swiss Family Robinson* as Virtual Reality[1]

J. Hillis Miller

When I was a child, I did not want to know that *The Swiss Family Robinson* had an author who had made it all up. I thought the words on the page were a true report of events at a place that actually existed somewhere – somewhere else. Those words gave me magical access to this independently existing reality. I was offended and deeply troubled when my mother pointed out the name of the author on the title page and told me the work was a fiction. It was the beginning of the disillusionment that has, I suppose, along with the remnants of mystified enchantment, made me a literary critic. I hasten to add that I make no claims for the accuracy of this memory. How would one verify or disprove that what I remember is what really happened? My mother is long dead, and no other verifying witness can be called. Whatever there is of the autobiographical in this essay is as much a construction after the fact as any other autobiography.[2] I only claim that this is what I remember now. After all, you have only my word even for my testimony of the present effect on me of re-reading *The Swiss Family Robinson*.

I have recently reread *The Swiss Family Robinson*, some 65 years after my last reading, to see what I make of it now. I must confess that I have been as enchanted, or almost, as I remember myself being at my first reading, at about the age of ten. I can still see that tree house in my mind's eye, the one the family Robinson builds after being shipwrecked. I have rediscovered again that wonderful, safely uninhabited, tropical island, teeming with every sort of bird, beast, fish, tree and plant. I can still see the fully developed farm the Robinson family constructs, with a winter house and a summer house, farm buildings, fields of potatoes, rice, cassava, vegetable and flower gardens, fruit trees, fences, aqueducts, all sorts of domesticated animals multiplying like anything – ducks, geese, ostriches, cattle, pigs, pigeons, dogs, a tame jackal, tame flamingos (!), and so on. You name it, they have got it in abundance – plenty of sugar, salt, flour, rice, utensils, even farm machinery. I still rejoice in the decision the father, mother, and two of the children make at the end to stay in their colony of

'New Switzerland', even when they are rescued and could go back to 'civilization.'

I think I know now, however, just why I found *The Swiss Family Robinson* so enchanting. One of my earliest memories is of being carried in a 'pack basket' on my father's back on a camping trip with the rest of my family and another family to the Adirondack Mountains in northern New York State. Camping out was for me magical in the same way that reading *The Swiss Family Robinson* was magical. Equipped with no more than you could carry on your back, you could 'set up camp', cut some fragrant balsam boughs for bedding, make a camp fire for cooking and heat, and, in short, create a whole new domestic world in the wilderness. I can still remember the pleasure of falling asleep in the open-fronted lean-to with the other children, wrapped in my blanket (no sleeping bags then), smelling the balsam, and listening to the murmur of the adults' voices as they sat talking by the dying campfire. *The Swiss Family Robinson* is a hyperbolic version of that pleasure. It is a deep satisfaction of the nest-making instinct. The family creates, out of the materials at hand (plus a few things saved from the wreck, of course!), a new world, a metaworld. In this creation of a culture, *The Swiss Family Robinson* is a marvelous allegory of what every literary work does. Within the story the family creates a new realm, with hard work and ingenuity. The reader of the book creates within his or her imagination a new realm. This is a virtual reality that for the time seems, or seemed to me at any rate, more real, and certainly more worthy to be lived in, than the 'real world'.

So much for what might be called the *allegro* reading, the reading I spontaneously performed as a child. A slow, suspicious, *lento* reading produces something very different. Almost 65 years of training and professional practice have made me unable to suspend my habits of critical reading. I would certainly not have been able to perform the *lento* reading at the age of ten, nor would I have wanted to, as my resistance to my mother's bad news about the work's fictitious quality indicates.

This factitious, fabricated quality is rubbed in, unnecessarily, it seems to me, by a gratuitous disclaimer on the verso of the title page of one paperback copy of *The Swiss Family Robinson* I have procured: 'This is a work of fiction. All the characters and events portrayed in this book are fictitious, and any resemblance to real people or events is purely coincidental.'[3] Why bother to say that? Who but an innocent child of ten, such as I was, would think *The Swiss Family Robinson* is anything but a work of fiction? Who in the world would think at this late date of suing Tor Books for giving away secrets about real people in a book first published, in the original German version, in 1812? Moreover, the disclaimer, it happens, as is so often the case, is a lie. The father, mother, and four sons of the Swiss Family Robinson are closely modeled, so scholars and the author's son, Johann Rudolf Wyss, say, on the family of the author, Johann David Wyss. Wyss was a Swiss clergyman and sometime Army Chaplain. He lived from 1743 to 1818.

Ernst, the second son in the story, is, for example, modeled on Wyss's son, Johann Rudolf.

I was right in one way at least. *The Swiss Family Robinson*, as English readers know it today, has no single author. It is a composite work, as well as being a translation. It began as improvised evening stories that the Reverend Wyss told to his four sons. These new stories were a follow-up to reading Defoe's *Robinson Crusoe* aloud to them in the evening. Wyss, though of large girth, was an avid hunter, fisherman, and outdoorsman, a genuine Swiss. He also had read many travel books (Captain Cook's *Voyages*, Lord Anson's circumnavigation of 1748, and many others). He knew a lot of natural history, much of it clearly from books with illustrations – of kangaroos, flamingos, platypuses, and so on.

Wyss was also a true son of the Enlightenment. The stories were a pleasurable way to teach his sons natural history and what might be called 'woodsy lore', for example how to build a rustic bridge, or how to calculate the height of a tree from the ground, or how to cure an animal hide. His goal, Wyss said, was 'to awaken the curiosity of my sons by interesting observations, to leave time for the activity of their imagination, and then to correct any error they might fall into'.[4] Wyss wrote down many of the episodes of the endlessly extendable story in a bulky manuscript of 841 pages. Johann Rudolf Wyss, the author's second son, was a philosophy professor in Berne, a folklorist, and author of the Swiss national anthem. With his father's approval, he revised and organized the manuscript for publication, under his own (Johann Rudolf's) name, in 1812. It was called *Der Schweizerische Robinson; oder, Der schiffbruchige Schweizerprediger und seine Familie (The Swiss Family Robinson; or, the Shipwrecked Swiss Clergyman and His Family).*

That is not the end of the story, however. A French translation by one Mme la Baronne Isabelle de Montolieu, with a new ending, was published in 1814. Another French translation, by Mme Elise Volart, with yet new material, followed. The first English translation, *The Family Robinson Crusoe*, was made by Mary Jane Godwin, with more new material. It was published by M.J. Godwin and Co. in 1814. Mary Jane Godwin may have used the first French translation rather than the German original. She was the wife of the political philosopher, novelist, and educationist, William Godwin. The book was part of William Godwin's children's book project, 'the Juvenile Library'. The preface, which sounds as if it might have been written by William Godwin himself, is actually Johann Rudolf Wyss's explanation of how he came to make a publishable book out of his father's detached manuscripts. Nevertheless, the preface is, as Jason Wohlstadter has observed,[5] a good expression of William Godwin's anti-Rousseauistic claim that children can be taught much natural history, geography, and other useful things by books like *The Family Robinson Crusoe*.

Many new English versions followed. New episodes continued to be added, and abbreviated versions were produced. The concluding episode of the rescue of Jenny Montrose, the castaway English girl, is missing from the earliest versions, for example the Godwin one. The story is in principle endless, like a television soap opera. It always invites the interpolation or extrapolation of yet another episode, the encounter with yet another exotic animal, tree, or bird. The English version by W.H.G. Kingston (1889) has tended to become standard for English readers. I have no knowledge of which version I read, since the book has not survived among the books from my childhood. I do, however, have my old copy of *Alice in Wonderland* and *Through the Looking-Glass*, with the Tenniel illustrations. I taught myself to read that book at the age of five or six. I was tired of depending on my mother to read the book to me. Though neither I nor my mother knew it, this was in defiance of a stern prohibition expressed in the preface to the Godwin translation of what the Godwins called the *The Family Robinson Crusoe*: 'In reality, it is very rarely, and perhaps never, proper that children should read by themselves; few indeed are the individuals in those tender years that are not either too indolent, too lively, or too capricious to employ themselves usefully upon this species of occupation.'[6]

What is most interesting, to me, in this publication history is the way reader after reader has been so taken by the virtual reality *The Swiss Family Robinson* reveals that he or she feels authorized to extend the original with new episodes. It seems as if, once you are inside this alternative world, you can explore and record even those parts of it Wyss did not happen to write down, so powerful is the reader's persuasion of its independent existence.

The Swiss Family Robinson can be thought of as standing in a midpoint, historically, between *Robinson Crusoe*, and such a twentieth-century 'Robinsoniad' as J.M. Coetzee's *Foe* (1987). This historical placement must not be misunderstood. I do not see the three works as dots on a line representing some all-inclusive, ineluctable, historical progression from the time of George I, for *Crusoe*, to the period of romanticism, for *The Swiss Family Robinson*, to our own times for *Foe*. No doubt these books are of their own times. Much in them can be explained by their historical placement. They can, however, hardly be said to be 'typical' of their times and places. Each of these works is atypical. It is not typical of anything but itself.

Is any work, moreover, really 'typical of its period'? *The Swiss Family Robinson*, for example, is coeval with German romanticism and German idealist philosophy. It is contemporary with the Schlegel brothers, with Hegel, Hölderlin, and Novalis in Germany, not to speak of Goethe's *Elective Affinities* (1809). *The Swiss Family Robinson* is also coeval with English romanticism, with Wordsworth, Coleridge, Keats, and Shelley in England, along with Jane Austen. Connecting Wyss's work with these worthies in a search for similarities does not get one very far. Coetzee's work has its own unique stamp. It is not just 'post-modernist'. Each of these works fits a definition of a literary work as incomparable, singular, strange. None is satisfactorily explicable either by its historical placement or by its author's biography.

One intellectual context, however, is useful for understanding *The Swiss Family Robinson*. It is no accident that William Godwin's wife made the first English translation of it. William Godwin was, among other things, an educational theorist. As Jason Wohlstadter has shown in detail, Godwin was deeply influenced by Jean-Jacques Rousseau's *Émile*, though he differed from Rousseau on some points. Godwin wrote theories of childhood education. He also wrote and published children's books, for example his own *Fables Ancient and Modern* (1805). The latter was brought out under the pseudonym of 'Edward Baldwin'. The Godwins must have seen in Wyss's novel a confirmation of their theories. Like Rousseau, and like Godwin, Wyss evidently believed that the best way to learn is not from books but directly from nature. The children in *The Swiss Family Robinson*, Émile-like, learn about kangaroos, sharks, whales, great bustards, jackals, lions, rubber trees, cassava, and so on, not from books but through direct encounter with these beasts and plants. The irony of course is that Johann David Wyss was teaching his children about these things through words and pictures, not through things. The reader of *The Swiss Family Robinson* also learns through reading, not through direct encounters with nature. Wyss had presumably never seen a live platypus in his life.

As opposed to the ironic undercutting of himself by *Robinson Crusoe*'s first person narrator, the first person narrator of *The Swiss Family Robinson*, the father, is without regrets or self-irony. He is, on the contrary, rather self-congratulatory and self-approving. No doubts exist about the identity of the characters in Wyss's story. They have fixed personalities from the beginning. These personalities are carefully labeled: Fritz's courage and level-headedness as the eldest, Ernst's laziness and bookish thoughtfulness in the next oldest son, then the impetuous and somewhat foolhardy Jack, and last, the youngest, the naïve but game Franz.

Wyss's motive seems to have been partly to write a book that would correct *Robinson Crusoe*, just as Coetzee's *Foe* was quite overtly to do in our own epoch. *The Swiss Family Robinson* is the most famous and best of the 'Robinsoniads' that followed the original in the eighteenth and early nineteenth centuries. The two adjectives in the title, 'Swiss' and 'family' identify what is being corrected. In place of Robinson Crusoe's isolated self-reliance, it puts the 'family values' of loving interdependence and cooperation, along with the pieties of nationalism. *The Swiss Family Robinson* is unashamedly sexist and patriarchal. The father is explicitly referred to with the latter adjective. The long-suffering mother is kept in her place, cheerfully performing endless household chores. She has no given name. She is just 'die Mütter', or sometimes she is called by the diminutive 'Mütterchen'. Any other females are conspicuously absent, until the climactic episode of Jenny Montrose, added later. These boys can go it alone, without any women around, except the mother, who sews, cooks, and washes. Girls may like *The Swiss Family Robinson*, but it is not a 'girl's book', unless all that housework done by the mother can be seen as useful instructions about a woman's lot.

In place of Crusoe's faithful/faithless, ironically undercut, English Puritanism, *The Swiss Family Robinson* puts a Swiss Protestantism that is never disobeyed or questioned. That Protestantism stresses piety, hard work, and collective effort rather than individual self-help. A great deal of praying punctuates *The Swiss Family Robinson*. That is something I had entirely forgotten from my first reading, perhaps because my father too was a clergyman, a Baptist minister. We had grace before meals and were taught to say prayers before going to sleep. It probably seemed natural enough to me that there is a lot of praying in this book. The difference from *Robinson Crusoe* is that in *The Swiss Family Robinson* religion is much more nominal, taken for granted, incorporated in everyday behavior. Defoe's *Robinson Crusoe* is, among other things, a fictive Puritan conversion narrative, modeled on real seventeenth-century ones. A Puritan Protestant interpretation of experience is deeply inwrought in *Robinson Crusoe*. It is much harder to miss or pass over than the routine praying in *The Swiss Family Robinson*. An example is a lengthy reflection by Crusoe about the 'secret intimations of Providence' that have led him to make right decisions when the wrong would have been disastrous: 'certainly they are a proof of the converse of spirits, and the secret communication between those embody'd and those unembody'd; and such a proof as can never be withstood', and so on.[7]

The ultimate message of *Robinson Crusoe*, however, is ambiguous. While Crusoe is camping out for 28 years, two months, and 19 days on his desert island and having his conversion experience, the slave-worked sugar and tobacco plantation he has left behind in 'the Brazils' is flourishing. Crusoe ends his life a rich man, whereas Coetzee's Cruso dies in Susan's arms on the way back to England after they are rescued. Defoe's Crusoe's wealth is another example of Providence's care for him. He also maintains possession of the island he had lived on alone for so many years. He colonizes it successfully. This endpoint is a spectacular example of 'religion and the rise of capitalism', to borrow the title of a famous book by R.H. Tawney. It also anticipates the ending of *The Swiss Family Robinson*. In the latter book too a permanent colony is established.

Both *Robinson Crusoe* and *The Swiss Family Robinson* are episodic and open-ended, promising further adventures that might be told. Defoe did publish *The Farther Adventures of Robinson Crusoe* a few months after the publication of *Robinson Crusoe* in 1719. *The Serious Reflections ... of Robinson Crusoe* appeared in 1720. *Robinson Crusoe*, however, has a plot. It has a narrative goal toward which the whole story moves. *The Swiss Family Robinson*, on the contrary, is endlessly episodic. In each episode, each one probably corresponding to a single evening's improvisation in the original oral version, the family confronts some new problem. They then learn something about science or natural history from it, for example how to make a kayak, or pemmican, or what a kangaroo is, and how to kill and skin one. They then wait for the next adventure. No reason can be given for these ever to end. The ending in the family's rescue seems more or less accidental and unmotivated.

The central purpose of *The Swiss Family Robinson* is to teach natural history. One by one the animals, birds, and fish the family encounters are named out of the storehouse of Father Robinson's knowledge, just as Adam named all the animals, in *Genesis*. God is praised for his benevolence and wisdom in creating all these living things. The bones of whales and birds, for example, are said to be hollow to make the creatures lighter: 'The bones of birds are also hollow, for the same reason, and in all this we see conspicuously the wisdom and goodness of the great Creator.'[8] The tamed creatures are given pet names by the children, Hurricane for the ostrich, Fangs and Coco for two tame jackals, Knips for the tame monkey, Storm for the buffalo bull they make into a beast of burden, Lightfoot for the 'onager', and so on. All this naming firmly incorporates these creatures into civilized society.

The Swiss Family Robinson's episodes recount the gradual taming of a wilderness. The island is transformed into a thriving domain of farms, houses, gardens, fields, and pens. Wild animals that are encountered must either be shot or tamed, sometimes some of each. An example is the encounter with a troop of monkeys, one of whom becomes a pet after they shoot the mother. The ostrich encounter, the kangaroo encounter, and the eagle encounter tell the same story with different materials. I had forgotten how much murdering of innocent wildlife exists in this novel. The instinct, or learned behavior, of the father and his four sons, when some animal or bird or fish appears before them, is to shoot it or to spear it. Fish are for catching and eating. Animals and birds are for shooting and eating, if they are edible. Reading the book again after so long, I found all this mayhem shocking, offensive to my green piety. Emphasis, however, is placed on killing animals cleanly, so they do not suffer long, and on not killing them unnecessarily, though a lot of that occurs anyhow.

The ideology of hunting and using guns in *The Swiss Family Robinson* is more or less the same as the one I was taught by my Virginia farm-bred father, grandfathers, and uncles, except that an irresponsibly small amount of safety instruction is given in Wyss's novel. By 'ideology' here and throughout this essay I do not mean a consciously promulgated doctrine. I mean a taken-for-granted local set of socially shared convictions that is incorrectly assumed to be natural and universal.[9] I too, like the Robinson boys, was taught to kill only for food, not for sheer sport, though I could not bring myself to kill anything now, unless I was starving to death. My ideology was different, however. I was also taught: 'Don't ever point a gun at yourself or at another person'; 'Assume every gun is loaded, even if you have unloaded it yourself 15 minutes ago'; 'Don't leave loaded guns around the house'; 'Store ammunition separately, in a locked place.' My father showed me a hole in the paneling of the living room in my Grandfather Miller's farmhouse. It had been made, he said, by a bullet from a supposedly unloaded gun. The Robinson boys are taught none of this. At least the reader is not told that they are. They wander around, often on their own, hyperbolically trigger-happy, blasting away at anything that moves.

What is the function of all this violence? The violence of killing in chapter after chapter of *The Swiss Family Robinson* enacts, in however muted and covert a way, that drama of sacrificial violence Nietzsche saw as essential to all art. In many chapters the Swiss family encounters some strange and threatening animal, bird, or fish: sharks, buffaloes, elephants, walruses, ostriches, jackals, lions, a tiger, a ferocious hyena. In each case the creature, or more than one among many of them, is shot, identified, skinned, or taken home to be eaten, or stuffed for the museum, in a somewhat comic enactment of the progress of enlightened civilization.

One killing, however, is not enough. The threatening outside of civilization's small enclosure has to be confronted again and again in different forms. Fear of the outside, which *The Swiss Family Robinson* both generated and appeased in me as a child, has to be faced down again and again, potentially ad infinitum. If a superabundance of food in various forms is present for the Robinsons, so also is an inexhaustible supply of wild and dangerous things. All these demand to be killed or tamed, but no hope exists of ever coming to the end of them.

This mechanism of the arousal of fear and its always partial appeasement may explain why reading a single literary work is never enough. The person who is hooked on reading always needs one more virtual reality. No one of them ever fully succeeds in doing its work. Habitual readers of mystery stories will know what I mean. They will also know that this arousal of fear, and its always only partial appeasement, are intensely pleasurable. Mystery stories give great pleasure, but they do not wholly satisfy. You always need to read another. Another murder always remains to be solved, perhaps one committed unwittingly by yourself, as Oedipus killed Laius without knowing Laius was his father. Children's books too arouse fear in order to appease it. The appeasement, however, is never total, and so the demand for yet another story always continues.

The wildness of *The Swiss Family Robinson*, the endless proliferation of its episodes, and the excessive killing that occurs within it, are matched by the irrationality of Crusoe's self-condemnation in *Robinson Crusoe*. This is a spiritual violence that runs through the book. That self-accusation condemns traits that make Crusoe in the end a rich imperialist, living off slave labor. The wildness of *The Swiss Family Robinson* is matched also by the wild illogic of dreams in the 'Alice' books. Freud said we dream in order not to wake up. Some dreams, however, are so violent and so terrifying that they do wake us up. The silent center that may be a roar, hidden in the heart of every story, is Coetzee's version of literature's irrationality. *Foe* explicitly names that silent center, Literature's wildness, source of the intense pleasure it gives, both allows us to keep dreaming within the ideological constants of the culture to which we belong and, at the same time, wakes us up from what James Joyce, notoriously, called 'the nightmare of history'.

Fortunately, for the Swiss family if not for the creatures already on their island when they arrive, a great store of powder and shot, along with many other essentials of Swiss farm civilization, have been saved from the wreck: a cow, a donkey, a pig, ducks, chickens, fruit trees, knives, guns, a Bible of course, a good many other books, and so on. This is because, according to the 'Introduction' to the Godwin version, their ship was bound for Tahiti, with plans to go on to Port Jackson, now Sydney, Australia, to settle there.[10] It was loaded with the materials necessary for setting up a farm. In Coetzee's *Foe*, on the contrary, 'Cruso' has swum ashore with nothing saved but a single knife, whereas Crusoe, in Defoe's novel, salvages all sorts of useful things from *his* wreck. The account of the library saved from the ship in *The Swiss Family Robinson* is a more or less overt indication of its 'sources': 'Besides a variety of books of voyages, travels, divinity, and natural history (several containing fine colored illustrations), there were histories and scientific works, as well as standard fiction in several languages. There was also a good assortment of maps, charts, mathematical and astronomical instruments, and an excellent pair of globes.'[11]

Why the Robinsons do not use these maps and instruments to determine just where they are, and on what island, is never explained. (Their island is, according to the Godwin version introduction, near New Guinea.[12]) Their incuriosity is no doubt because it is a fundamental feature of the story that they not know where they are, or even the full size and contours of their island. Robinson Crusoe, on the contrary takes full measure of his smaller island, as does Coetzee's Cruso. *Robinson Crusoe* is mentioned explicitly twice in *The Swiss Family Robinson*, as well as named as a model in that original preface, present in the Godwin version but not in the later ones in print today. Though it takes some enterprise to rescue so many things from what remains of the wreck, nevertheless their availability tips the balance in the Swiss family's favour, as also happens for Robinson Crusoe. In both cases, the basic materials of European civilization are brought ashore, flamboyantly so in *The Swiss Family Robinson*.

Since Wyss's goal was to teach his children natural history, he notoriously jumbled together animals, fish, and plants from all over the world on this one tropical island, in absurd co-presence: penguins, jackals, hyenas, elephants, kangaroos, bears, buffalo, lions, tigers, a boa constrictor, salmon, seals, walruses, whales, sturgeon, herring, ducks and pigeons of every sort, quails, partridges, antelopes, rabbits, honey bees, potatoes, rice, Indian corn (maize), cassava, vanilla, coconuts, calabashes, rubber trees, cotton bushes, figs, and so on, a virtually endless list.

Besides killing and eating, or taming, the creatures they encounter, the Swiss family does one more very eighteenth-century thing with them. Museums, as well as encyclopedias, were an important feature of the Enlightenment. The Robinson family gradually collects, in a museum at their 'Rockburg' dwelling, specimens they have preserved and stuffed. Taxidermy is another of the arts the father teaches his children. These specimens include a stuffed condor, the giant boa constrictor, and many other victims.

Wyss's 'New Switzerland' is an Edenic world of profusion, of plenitude. It is a world swarming with things to be shot, tamed, or eaten, or farmed and then eaten, if you are clever enough to know how to do so, as in this description of the results of the family's vegetable garden labor: 'Fortunately, in this beautiful climate little or no attention was necessary to our kitchen garden, the seeds sprang up and flourished without apparently the slightest regard for the time or season of the year. Peas, beans, wheat, barley, rye, and Indian corn seemed constantly ripe, while cucumbers, melons, and all sorts of other vegetables grew luxuriantly.'[13] Poor Cruso, in Coetzee's *Foe*, by contrast, has no seeds. I found all the abundance in *The Swiss Family Robinson* and all the descriptions of eating (even eating odd things like kangaroo meat) wonderfully reassuring when I was a child. This book, plus early camping experiences and some actual knowledge about the woods, has left me still with the belief, no doubt only partly true, that I would be able to survive all right, thank you, in the woods, at least for a while. I would survive especially if I had some company, though perhaps not quite so splendidly as does the Swiss Family Robinson.

Robinson Crusoe, on the contrary, stresses the difficulty and precariousness of going it alone in a wilderness. With a few exceptions, Crusoe is not sure of the names of any of the animals, birds, and plants on his island, nor does he know which are useful, nor how to use them. He has great difficulty getting his few grains of wheat and rice to germinate. Whatever Crusoe does, he does with great effort, with much trial and error, and with many failures. His life is, in Hobbes's words, 'nasty', 'solitary' and 'brutish', if not 'short'. Crusoe stresses

> the exceeding laboriousness of my work; the many hours which, for want of tools, want of help, and want of skill, every thing I did took up out of my time. For example, I was full two and forty days making me a board for a long shelf, which I wanted in my cave. ... My next concern was to get me a stone mortar, to stamp or beat some corn in; for as to the mill, there was no thought of arriving to that perfection of art with one pair of hands. To supply this want I was at a great loss; for, of all trades in the world I was as perfectly unqualify'd for a stone-cutter as for any whatever; neither had I any tools to go about it with.[14]

Coetzee's *Foe* makes this helplessness hyperbolic, whereas building bridges, houses, and boats seems relatively quick and easy for the Swiss Family Robinson.

Robinson Crusoe responded to another American myth I had been taught. This was the belief that if you were lost and alone in the wilderness you would have a hard time of it, but might possibly survive if you were brave, resourceful, and lucky. In the United States today versions of that myth are still active in survival tales dramatized in books, films, and on television.

In contrast to *Robinson Crusoe*, the Swiss family Robinson know the names of everything they find on their island, what each thing is good for, and how to do everything needful. It is as though Wyss were deliberately responding to *Robinson Crusoe* by saying, in effect: 'A good Swiss family with rural experience and knowledge of natural history would fare immeasurably better in the wilderness than this maladroit urban Englishman. I'll show you how.'

The Swiss Family Robinson, finally, is a relatively early example of colonial or imperialist literature. This is so in a way different from *Robinson Crusoe*. The latter blandly endorses slavery, for example, and sees South American natives as all cannibal savages in need of conversion to Protestantism. Crusoe, however, condemns Spanish conquistadores for being Catholic and for their indiscriminate slaughter of indigenous South Americans. The Swiss Robinsons, however, recreate on their desert island, without any interference from 'savages', a nearly exact replica of Swiss rural culture. Their plantation is spoken of several times toward the end of the book as a 'dominion' or 'colony'. They name this colony 'New Switzerland' (like 'New England' in the United States). They decide, even after they are rescued, to stay there, to remain in charge of their colony, to enlarge it, to add more people to it, and to make it more and more an outpost of Swiss culture. Later German and English versions I have seen, however, all specify that it will perhaps be an English colony, part of the then-growing British Empire. All this is missing from the first versions, for example the first English translation of 1814. The Robinson family in even the first versions, however, has already sprinkled the settlement with European place-names, given in straightforward vernacular in the English translations: 'Walrus Island', 'Cape Farewell', 'Cape Pug Nose', 'Flamingo Marsh', 'Monkey Grove', 'Safety Bay', and so on. The houses and settlements the family build are given names too: 'Falconhurst', 'Woodlands', 'Tentholm', and 'Rockburg'. These are translated more or less accurately, from the German original.

The land of New Switzerland is not taken from 'natives.' It is rather taken from the animals already there. Nor does the motif of slavery enter in, as it most certainly does in *Robinson Crusoe*. Nor is any hint given of homosociality, such as queer theorists might find in the relation of Crusoe to Friday. Nor is anything present like the slight edge of prurience involved when a young girl enters 'the awkward age', such as hovers over the 'Alice' books, as over Henry James's *The Awkward Age*. Until that penultimate episode when Fritz rescues a castaway English girl (she is destined to be a future wife for him), sexuality is wholly absent from *The Swiss Family Robinson*, except as it is implicit in the multiplying of farm animals. Even of the animals, however, nothing whatever is said about their reproduction. The reader is not told, for example, how the sow they save from the wreck comes to produce a swarm of piglets.

The Swiss Family Robinson, in short, when read slowly, *lento*, with a critical eye, reveals itself to be the expression of a definite ideology. This is the ideology of the author, the writer that I as a child wanted to deny even existed, along with the superadded ideologies of all those who augmented the text. The reader must remember here my earlier definition of ideology as 'a taken-for-granted local set of socially shared convictions that is incorrectly assumed to be natural and universal'. The ideology of *The Swiss Family Robinson* is most strongly reinforced, of course, by the implications of the stories themselves, as opposed to direct preaching. Occasionally, however, it is affirmed overtly, especially in later augmented versions:

> And my great wish is that young people who read this record of our lives and adventures should learn from it how admirably suited is the peaceful, industrious, and pious life of a cheerful, united family to the formation of strong, pure, and manly [!] character.
> None takes a better place in the great national family, none is happier or more beloved than he [!] who goes forth from such a home to fulfill new duties, and to gather fresh interests around him.[15]

This is from the opening of chapter 38, 'After Ten Years', in the Yearling Book edition. The Puffin Classics edition, source text for the version available on the World Wide Web (http://www.ccel.org/w/wyss/swiss/swiss.html), has 'those' for 'he' and 'them' for 'him'. I wonder who substituted the neutral plural for the sexist 'he' and 'him', and when. The later English versions end with a valedictory address somewhat similar to the interpolated passage just cited. The father speaks this passage to Fritz, who is carrying the father's journal to civilization:

> ... it is very possible that it [the journal] may be useful to other young people, more especially to boys.
> Children are, on the whole, very much alike everywhere, and you four lads fairly represent multitudes, who are growing up in all directions. It will make me happy to think that my simple narrative may lead some of these to observe how blessed are the results of patient continuance in well-doing, what benefits arise from the thoughtful application of knowledge and science, and how good and pleasant a thing it is when brethren dwell together in unity, under the eye of parental love.[16]

The last page in the twentieth-century German version I have obtained has a quite different concluding address to the reader. This page is completely absent from the English versions I have seen. This passage has, to my ear, a somewhat sinister Teutonic ring. Though the sentiments are innocent enough, the way they are expressed makes them sound disquietingly like twentieth-century German propaganda slogans. The passage is a direct apostrophe to Wyss's young readers. I give it first in German, to pay homage to the original language of *Die Schweizerische Robinson*, and for the untranslatable ring of that 'Wissen ist Macht, Wissen ist Freiheit, Können ist Glück':

> Euch Kindern aber, die ihr mein Buch lesen werdet, möchte ich noch
> ein paar herzliche Worte sagen:
> 'Lernt! Lernt, ihr junges Volk! Wissen ist Macht, Wissen ist Freiheit,
> Können ist Glück. Macht die Augen auf und seht euch um in der schö-
> nen Welt. Ihr glaubt gar nicht, was alles durch so ein paar offne, helle
> Augen in so einen jungen Kopf hineingeht.'
> (But to you children, who would read my book, may I still say a cou-
> ple of heartfelt words:
> 'Learn! Learn, you young people! Knowledge is power, knowledge is
> freedom, understanding is happiness. Open your eyes and look around
> in the beautiful world. You can scarcely believe all the things that enter
> a young head through a pair of open, clear eyes.' [my trans.])[17]

The Godwin version, closer to the German original of 1812, has a quite
different ending, one that has a different ideological exhortation. The final
paragraph rejoices in the family's success in creating a model community in
the wilderness. Father Robinson thanks Providence 'who had so miracu-
lously rescued and preserved us, and conducted us to the true destination of
man – to provide for the wants of his offspring by the labor of his hands'.
The whole text is presented, in the Godwin version, as a journal kept by the
castaway Swiss pastor. It ends with the following notation:

> Nearly two years have elapsed without our perceiving the smallest traces
> of civilised or savage man; without the appearance of a single vessel or
> canoe upon the vast sea, by which we are surrounded. Ought we then to
> indulge a hope that we shall once again behold the face of a fellow-
> creature? – We encourage serenity and thankfulness in each other, and
> wait with resignation the event![18]

This is followed by a fictitious 'Postscript by the Editor' which tells how an
English ship was driven to the island by a storm, made anchor in 'Safety
Bay', and sent men ashore who were met by Father Robinson alone. He gave
his journal to the Lieutenant to give to the Captain. Though plans are made
to meet with the whole family the next day, perhaps to rescue them, another
violent storm comes up. The English ship has to raise anchor and is driven
so far away it cannot return. Only the journal is taken back to civilization.

In this early version, the reader is to imagine the Swiss Family Robinson
left indefinitely on their island, like a virtual reality that can be visited only
indirectly, in this case through that journal. Endings are decisive for narratives. This original ending gives the whole book a quite different meaning
from the modern endings, including the ending in the modern German one
I have obtained. These endings all differ from one another, as well as from

the endings of *Robinson Crusoe* and *Foe*. The original Godwin ending fits better my childhood conviction that this enchanted island still exists somewhere, though it can be visited only through reading the book. In that somewhere the Robinsons remain forever, always having new adventures and always encountering new animals, plants, birds and fish.

Further reading

Coetzee, J.M, *Foe* (New York: Penguin, 1987).

Defoe, Daniel, *Robinson Crusoe* (Harmondsworth: Penguin, 1982).

Miller, J. Hillis, *On Literature* (London: Routledge, 2002).

Weber, Marie-Hélène, *Robinson et robinsonnades: étude comparée de Robinson Crusoë de Defoe, Le Robinson suisse de J.R. Wyss, L'île mystérieuse de J. Verne, Sa Majesté des mouches de W. Golding, Vendredi, ou, les limbes du Pacifique de M. Tournier* (Toulouse: Editions universitaires du Sud, 1993).

Wohlstadter, Jason, *Models of Education: Rousseau, Godwin, and the Subject of Childhood Reading* (Ph.D. Dissertation University of California at Irvine, 2001), Available from University Microfilms.

Wyss, Johann David, *Die Schweizerische Robinson* (Zürich: Orell Füssli, 1962).

Wyss, Johann David, *The Swiss Family Robinson* (New York: Yearling Books; Bantam Doubleday Dell Books for Young Readers, 1999). Also available online at http://www.ccel.org/w/wyss/swiss/swiss.html.

Notes

1. This essay is drawn, in somewhat revised and augmented form, from pp. 126–31; 139–55 of: J. Hillis Miller, *On Literature* (London and New York: Routledge, 2002). © 2002 J. Hillis Miller. I am grateful for permission to reuse this material.
2. The most rigorous affirmation of this view of autobiography that I know is Paul de Man's 'Autobiography as De-Facement', in *The Rhetoric of Romanticism* (New York: Columbia University Press, 1984), pp. 67–81.
3. Johann David Wyss, *The Swiss Family Robinson* (New York: Tor [A Tom Dohery Associates Book], 1996), p. iv.
4. Wyss, *The Swiss Family Robinson*, Tor edn, p. 298.
5. See Jason Wohlstadter, *Models of Education: Rousseau, Godwin, and the Subject of Childhood Reading* (Ph.D. Dissertation University of California at Irvine, 2001).
6. *The Family Robinson Crusoe: or, Journal of a Father Shipwrecked, with his Wife and Children, on an Uninhabited Island*, translated from the German of M. Wiss, 2 vols. (London: M.J. Godwin and Co., 1814), vol. I, p. xvi.
7. Daniel Defoe, *Robinson Crusoe* (Harmondsworth: Penguin, 1982), p. 182.
8. Johann Wyss, *The Swiss Family Robinson* (New York: Yearling Books; Bantam Doubleday Dell Books for Young Readers, 1999), p. 197.
9. As I have put this elsewhere: 'By "ideological" I mean masking an arbitrary arrangement of power and roles, an arrangement that could be otherwise, as a natural, universal way of living' (J. Hillis Miller, *Black Holes*/Manuel Asensi, *J. Hillis Miller; or, Boustrophedonic Reading* (Stanford: Stanford University Press, 1999), p. 257). See also Louis Althusser 'Ideology and Ideological State Apparatuses (Notes Towards an Investigation)', in *Lenin and Philosophy and Other Essays*, trans. Ben Brewster (New York: Monthly Review Press, 1972), p. 162: 'Idealogy is a

"representation" of the imaginary relationships of individuals to their real conditions of existence'; and Paul de Man, 'The Resistance to Theory', in *The Resistance to Theory* (Minneapolis: University of Minnesota Press, 1986), pp. 3–21, p. 11: 'What we call ideology is precisely the confusion of linguistic with natural reality, of reference with phenomenalism.'

10. *The Family Robinson Crusoe* (M.J. Godwin and Co.), vol. I, pp. xx–xxi.
11. Wyss, *The Swiss Family Robinson* (Yearling edn), p. 186.
12. *The Family Robinson Crusoe* (M.J. Godwin and Co.), vol. I, p. xxi.
13. Wyss, *The Swiss Family Robinson* (Yearling edn), p. 153.
14. Defoe, *Robinson Crusoe*, pp. 127, 133.
15. Wyss, *The Swiss Family Robinson* (Yearling edn), pp. 274–5.
16. Wyss, *The Swiss Family Robinson* (Yearling edn), p. 324.
17. Johann David Wyss, *Die Schweizerische Robinson* (Zürich: Orell Füssli, 1962), p. 378.
18. *The Family Robinson Crusoe* (M.J. Godwin and Co.), vol. II, p. 366.

5
The Implied Reader. Response and Responsibility: Theories of the Implied Reader in Children's Literature Criticism

Neil Cocks

As long ago as 1990 'The Reader in the Book' by Aidan Chambers was included in Peter Hunt's anthology of Children's Literature Criticism with the warning that it 'was written [...] in the very early days of response/reception criticism – at least in terms of its availability to a general audience. In this sense, the article has certain limitations, and Chambers has taken his arguments further since then.'[1] Michael Benton, in his 1996 survey-article of developments in 'reader-response criticism' within children's literature, however, still also sees Aidan Chambers's work as groundbreaking in particular respects, writing that Chambers's article is 'regarded as a landmark', but also that 'this lead has been followed so infrequently'.[2] Benton's explanation for this is that 'criticism has moved on'.[3] This chapter will argue instead that 'The Reader in the Book' is still relevant to the study of Children's Literature because contemporary criticism is still laboring under the same assumptions such texts make about the child and its reading, and employ many of the problematic moves made by that text. This 'Childist'[4] criticism may be read as an attempt to move away from what it regarded as the reductive simplicity of contemporary Children's Literature Criticism, seeking to 'break the power attributed to the text itself by the intrinsic criticism which dominated literary studies throughout the twentieth century, and empower the reader instead'.[5] However, despite focusing on readers and authors, this criticism also wanted to avoid falling into the trap of producing the kind of unproblematic autobiographical criticism that had also gained widespread acceptance among Children's Literature Critics.[6] Because it did not want to rest its claims to knowledge upon appeals to 'real' authors or readers, being only too aware of the dangers of the 'intentional fallacy',[7] it introduced terms such as 'Implied Author' and 'Implied Reader'. As we shall see, these terms were read as offering the opportunity of writing about child response to literature while still focusing upon texts. Although these critical terms are read as giving a more complex notion of how meaning is constructed, they bring with them many additional problems and finally, I would argue, can collapse into the very notion of intention they attempt to overcome.

I   Response

In the introduction to this book, Karín Lesnik-Oberstein reads the way Children's Literature Criticism always declares itself a complete departure from what went before while maintaining a fixed idea of its purpose. 'The Reader in the Book' does not deviate from this model in either its claims of originality or its concern with 'childist criticism'.[8] It makes the claim that criticism of Children's Literature has for too long neglected the child reader and in doing so has failed to understand the meaning of that literature. It claims that through this willful avoidance criticism has irresponsibly blinded itself to the needs of the children to whom this literature is directed and has been unable to keep up with developments in contemporary critical practice. It is claimed that such practice has increasingly concentrated not just on how meaning is structured by texts, but how meaning is shaped and understood by readers.[9] 'The Reader in the Book' wishes to re-introduce the child reader and its needs into a criticism it reads as ignoring them through understanding meaning as an occurrence within a negotiation between various parties involved in the reading process rather than simply being the fixed end product of an author's intention or an intrinsic quality of text. This approach 'derives from the understanding that it "takes two to say a thing" '.[10] In effect it suggests that in his book an author creates a relationship with a reader 'in order to discover the meaning of a text'.[11] For 'The Reader in the Book' a thing is only meaningful if it is received. Thus a study of the reader should be an indispensable part of contemporary critical practice.

This notion has been a corner-stone of the 'Signal Approach' to Children's Literature Criticism since 1970; an approach that is expounded in the sustained arguments of texts such as *Tell Me: Children, Reading and Talk – How Adults Help Children Talk*, but, I argue here, still finds expression in more recent work such as that of Barbara Wall (1991), Michael Benton (1992), or Peter Hollindale (1997),[12] as well as in recent educational publications and policy.[13] With its focus on 'practical' applications of theory to teaching, critics using this approach have often focused on studies of how individual children respond to texts.[14] 'The Reader in the Book' does not follow this path of practical response too closely. There is a repeated insistence on the 'need [for] a critical method that will tell us about the reader in the book' rather than a reliance on theories that require an unambiguous knowledge of what individual 'real' readers have to say about texts and what 'real' authors 'intend' to write. Rather, 'The Reader in the Book' argues that when reading a text a reader is made aware of the kind of reader that is 'desired' by the text[15] and the kind of author that it claims to be the creation of. It is not suggested that an actual, real author has in mind an actual, real reader. Rather the actual author constructs a 'second self' in writing whose writing implies a certain kind of reader. The actual reader can choose to align themselves temporarily with this implied reader to discover the 'true meaning' of the text.[16]

Thus we have the notion of five parties involved in the reading process and a 'true meaning' that is the sole property of none. There is the 'real author' who writes a narrator or 'second self'. This 'second self' writes for an 'Implied Reader', which is to say the 'second self' implies a certain reader through the kind of language it uses. For example, 'The Reader in the Book' claims that the 'concrete', 'active', 'everyday' 'Anglo Saxon' language of 'splashing and blotching' rain and 'smacking lips'[17] in Lucy Boston's *The Children of Green Knowe* implies a child reader. It suggests that a child reader can also be implied by the 'focus' of the narrative.[18] That focus can be inferred if that narrative includes nothing that would be outside a child's range of perceptions. The 'actual reader' of a text, that is any given reader in the real world, can choose to read as 'The Implied Reader' on a 'temporary' basis, even though they might themselves have very different abilities and sensibilities. If 'actual readers' are willing to 'give (them)selves up to the book' in this way they can gain access to the 'true meaning' of the text.[19] This meaning is one that takes in more than an individual reader's limited understanding. The individual reader must weigh their own prejudices, beliefs and knowledge against those that are implied as being 'correct'. 'Correct understanding [...] often depends principally upon correct recognition of the implied reader'.[20]

'The Reader in the Book' attempts to avoid reading meaning as originating at a single source of 'real' 'author' or 'reader', or of being a quality of a given 'book' that exists independently of any act of interpretation. Meaning is 'a negotiation of insight' occurring in the 'second' world of the text. As such the theory of meaning in 'The Reader in the Book' seems, in the words of Jonathan Culler, 'eminently sensible', an attempt to 'do justice to the creative, participatory activity of readers, while preserving determinate texts which require and induce a certain response'.[21] However, as Culler also suggests, the 'dualistic theory' of such a reading 'cannot be sustained, the distinction between text and reader, fact and interpretation, or determined and undetermined breaks down and [the] theory becomes monistic'.[22] What happens in such theories is either that one element in the 'negotiation of meaning' is singled out as that which always determines all meaning. For example, the author will finally be shown to be in total control of the text and the response to it. A different element can be given total control over all meaning at different stages of a reading. This ends up as the same thing, as reader, text and author variously take up exactly the same position: that which determines, or 'authors', meaning. This chapter will read the breakdown of the 'sensible' 'dualism' in 'The Reader in the Book'. It will question how far reading is a free 'negotiation' of meaning if meaning exists in an inviolate state waiting to be 'discovered' while at the same time being dependent on a temporary taking on of another point of view. Or, to put it another way, we will read how negotiation is set up as a dialectic movement towards a correct truth that must always already exist despite being the result of a singular and temporary relationship.

II   Negotiation

'The Reader in the Book' sets up meaning as 'negotiation'.[23] Initially it could be argued that it is 'the book' that initiates this process. The book is said to contain 'potential meanings'[24] the reader is guided towards. Thus it has within it a limited amount of meanings waiting to be actualized. These meanings exist prior to any reading. The book appears fully formed before the reader. The reader 'receives'[25] it as a coherent identity. The book makes 'demands'[26] that the reader must submit to. It also is read as offering an 'invitation'.[27] The reader must 'give [himself] up to the book'.[28] The reader can be 'led through whatever experience'[29] the book has to offer, the idea being that the book already exists as a space that the reader can discover. 'The Reader in the Book' quotes F.H. Langham's assertion that:

> I do not say we need to know what readers had in mind [...] but the work itself implies the kind of reader to whom it is addressed and this may or may not coincide with the author's private view of his audience.[30]

So the work, rather than the author, is that which implies, and therefore allows, meaning. Yet the reader 'submits' to 'author guided desires'.[31] Although it is the 'second self' that makes meaning possible by 'drawing in' the reader, this 'second self is created by his [the author's] use of various techniques'.[32] Likewise, the 'reader's second self' is also created by the use of 'various techniques'.[33] This might suggest again that it is 'the book' that is creating 'potential meanings'. It is also used to argue that the 'implied reader' 'persona' is at least active in the 'discovery' of already established meanings. However, both 'persona' and 'book' are controlled by the author, the former being 'guided by the author towards the book's potential meanings'.[34] The notion is put forward that:

> The child implied reader and the critical method that follows from it helps us to establish the author's relationship with the [child] reader implied in the story, to see how he creates that relationship, and to discover the meaning[s] he seeks to negotiate.[35]

The whole negotiation is set up by the author. The meaning that the negotiation seeks to move towards is already established. Despite this, that meaning may still be 'negotiated'. What is not up for negotiation, however, is that the meaning being 'negotiated' is the 'correct' meaning.[36]

There is also a sense in which the reader is that which makes meaning possible. The author requires the child reader to accept the text. The only successful book for children is one that 'take[s] the child as he is then draws him into the text'. The child reader makes its own demands in its 'unyielding'[37] state that necessitates it must be written to, a book 'requires a reader to complete the work'.[38] If the 'complete' text is the true text, which 'The Reader in the Book' argues that it is, then the reader is that which guarantees that truth. Yet, as I will argue, as well as the guarantor of the truth, the reading child in 'The Reader in the Book' is that which must learn to change in order to access truth. Only through the abandonment of self can the child access truth and only through the access to truth can the self be 'fulfilled'.[39] 'The Reader in the Book' claims that 'we shall call fruitlessly for serious attention to be paid to books for children, and to children as readers by others than that small number of us who have come to recognize their importance'.[40] So the child reader is of importance, but the reason for its reading is to learn to divest itself of the thing that makes it so.

The five stable identities that 'The Reader in the Book' sets up as engaged in the negotiation of meaning are therefore not as stable as they might first appear. We begin with an idea of the author authoring meaning. However, the reader is also granted the privilege, as is the book. The apparent 'dualism' does not hold. We end up with the idea that the child must give himself up to the author and the book. Differences collapse. What is offered as 'negotiation' between stable parties is no such thing. The competing claims are either entirely contradictory or not competing claims at all. Furthermore, negotiation can only take place if the nature of 'meaning' has already been determined prior to reading. What a meaning means is up for debate, but that a certain meaning is a forum for debate is not. There is a tension between the idea that meaning is something to be completed, a process, and that which is already always there waiting to be discovered. Meaning is both a potential and its fulfillment.

III Fulfillment

'The Reader in the Book' commends the critic Wayne C. Booth for expressing in his work 'something mature literary readers have always understood: that a requirement of fulfilled readership is a willingness to give oneself up to the book'.[41] Booth quotes the 'mature literary reader' testifying that 'it is only as I read that I become the self whose beliefs must coincide with the author's. I must subordinate my mind and heart to the book if I am to enjoy it to the full'.[42] This, in the words of C.S. Lewis, will allow the mature reader to be 'a thousand people yet remaining my self'.[43]

A very distinct notion of reading is thus being put forward. This is a qualitative account where the goal of reading is a fulfillment that is achieved through enjoyment and a recognition of the 'correct' meaning of a text. 'Fulfilled' reading is 'always' the same, whether the reader is child or adult, regardless of either cultural context or the specificity of the demanding object. No evidence is given of how 'Booth' has established that this has always been the case. The 'maturity' of the reader can be read in the way it understands both its own desires and exactly what it must do to meet them. 'Fulfillment' is the sign of maturity. Fulfillment can only be gained by submission. Submission to the demands of another is the sign, or the condition, of mature pleasure and the guarantor of its satisfaction. It is very important that this intellectual and emotional subordination must be carried out of the reader's own volition, that the reader knows exactly what is going on. With the submission of 'head and heart' the self is surrendered, or ceases to be, so it may be fulfilled. To fulfill the self, to 'complete'[44] it, necessitates that one is not oneself. One must have an understanding of one's own fulfillment before one is fulfilled. The self that is in the process that leads to fulfillment is never anything less than the fulfilled self waiting for fulfillment. This is because the 'mature' reader has been fulfilled before and is aiming to be so again (and a thousand times again). Fulfillment here is oddly 'temporary'. The rounded notion of completion that 'fulfillment' appeals to sits uneasily with the unquenchable excess of being a thousand people. It seems that a succession of identities must be taken on to confirm the genuineness of the identity 'myself'. The process is further complicated by the idea of negotiation. If one is never quite oneself in the process that leads to one's fulfillment neither is one ever quite alone.

'Fulfillment' can only be gained by the 'mature' and, according to 'The Reader in the Book' 'children, of course, have not completely learned how to do this'.[45] Child readers are read as 'unyielding',[46] resistant to submitting to the 'demands' made upon them by texts, the demand of taking on another's viewpoint or ideas. 'Children' are constructed as already established identities that lack the ability to 'shift the gears of their personalities'[47] that will make them fulfilled as mature individuals. They are complete identities that somehow lack the completeness that can only be gained by taking on the identities of others.

'The Child Reader' needs to develop its ability to 'receive a text'[48] if it is to enjoy a 'fulfilled' understanding, and it is the task of Children's Literature to develop this ability (this development is also necessary for the Child to gain the 'true meaning' of the text that will allow it to gain the maturity that will allow it to access the 'true meaning'[49] of the text etc.). 'Maturity' is something learnt. The child can 'develop his ability to receive a text as a literary reader'. 'The Reader in the Book' offers an ideal of reading that is as true for the Child as it is for the Adult, and involves the willing subordination of the self to the demands of the book in order for the fulfillment of mature pleasurable demands and an avoidance of 'non-literary' purposes.[50]

IV   Adoption

Because it is argued that children must learn the art of submission that they are (naturally, according to these arguments) resistant to it is very important for a writer for children to:

> Draw a child reader into his book [...] this narrowing of focus by the adoption of a child point of view helps keep the author's second self – himself in the book – within the perceptual scope of his child reader.[51]

To write for children involves something subtler than the simple demands of the adult text. 'The Reader in the Book' claims that the author must take on a quality that is both 'child-like' and 'visual' to make his adult writing appeal to children.

The whole process of meaning is initiated by the author here. We have already read the 'second self' to be a creation of the author. This 'second self' is constructed by a 'visual' quality that is 'narrower' than the author's 'own' vision. The 'adoption' of the child reader, being the 'temporary' responsibility for that child while existing in the space of the book, is achieved through non-inclusion. The author may only include things that may be seen by the child. What constitutes a child's range of perceptions is left unclear. 'The Reader in the Book' claims that 'if literature for children is to have any meaning at all, it must primarily be concerned with the nature of childhood, not just the nature commonly shared by most children but the diversity of childhood nature too'.[52] The child reader may still be offered something that diverges from its own vision. Yet, somehow, this alien vision is still its own, as still the vision of childhood, as still within its own 'perceptual scope'.[53]

The child reader still requires access to something beyond its own vision even when it receives a vision that chimes exactly with its own. The 'narrowing of focus'[54] is not only something that happens in the author's writing of the 'second self'. It is also something that happens as the child is reading. 'Narrowing of focus' is linked to a notion of 'drawing in'[55] the resistant child. The child is read as resistant to adopting the alien. However, it is claimed that well-written books for children also 'draw' the child reader in because it gradually becomes aware that it is seeing its own vision. This necessitates that it must, in the beginning of the process of 'drawing in', be aware of another vision, a vision that is outside its own limited sight, a vision of the 'other' it is 'naturally' resistant to. It is an appeal to gentleness, to consent that necessitates this move. There can be no sudden moves, no 'didactic' force.[56] Yet this move requires a child who begins the reading process seeing an alien sight, a sight it cannot have access to.

In 'mature' reading 'fulfillment' is gained through the temporary acceptance of the alien, through subjection to the demands of reading as another. Yet where child readers are concerned the author and the book must take on the 'mature' reader's position of taking on the alien. The child takes on the position of the demanding author/text. Yet that does not mean that the child initiates the reading process. It is drawn into a book by an author whose desires initiate the process. The child reader differs from its 'mature' counterpart through lacking an awareness of its own submission. The child is drawn in to an already existing text, a text that has adopted the unyielding identity it is trying to appeal to. Only the identity of the child in the text is not the same as the identity of the child reader:

> The child, finding within the book an implied author whom he can befriend because he is of the tribe of childhood as well, is thus wooed into the book. He adopts the image of the implied child reader and is then willing, may even desire, to give himself up to the author and to the book and be led through whatever experience is offered.[57]

The narrow vision that draws the child in because it offers nothing in excess of his own vision is actually not his own. The vision is one the child reader must itself adopt. Thus the child reader adopts the vision of childhood as an alien sight. When the child has taken on this alien vision, which is his own, he is capable of giving himself up. Yet this giving up of the self requires two selves, one that is given up and one that gives, one alien identity that is entirely adopted (even though it is the child's own) and one compacted identity that may be led through and already existent text, experiencing something that is already complete. The vision that is the child's own, yet not its own, contains within it the author. The author has not had to give up his identity. Rather, he has surrounded himself with an adopted identity, an identity that is a disguise, an addition, a family, a tribe.

'Adoption' constructs the relationship between the child and its language as familial while situating the child as not in its 'own' family. Adoption simultaneously reads language as being the child's 'own' and that which is not its 'own'. The child's own self is only available to it as the demands of another. These demands appear to be the child, but are not it entirely. Yet the child is not itself yet either. It finds itself in reading. Adoption simultaneously confirms and threatens the family.

The problem of 'fulfillment' is repeated in the discourse of 'adoption'. Just as 'fulfillment' was read both as an end and a continuum, a mark of transformation that bore no change, a promise of understanding that could always be understood, so the child is both unyielding, temporary, itself, not itself, that which is adopted and that which adopts. Apparently existing outside of the troublesome, shifting identities of individual child readers and texts are certain 'hard, impacted'[58] identities: 'the implied child reader' and 'child language'. These exist independently of any individual linguistic act. Wandering concepts waiting to be adopted, available to us prior to any reading, they are knowable, unquestioned and inviolate.

V   Writing as real

It has been established in the arguments read so far that the child is 'drawn' into a book that he may experience as he journeys through it.[59] This requires a notion of a text as something that exists as a physical space prior to the intervention of the reader, thus collapsing a notion of response as dualism into one of monism. The child is 'guided by the author towards the book's potential meanings'.[60] The text has meanings already established and they already exist in a place that the child can access but only if it is helped. There is a repeated insistence that the act of reading occurs within a specific geo-graphic environment; the child 'enter [s] into the book' and the good book for children 'take[s] [the child] as he is but then draw[s] him into the text'.[61] The author also 'puts himself into the narrator'. So 'the narrator', a function of the book, contains the 'actual author'. The author exists absolutely as itself, just covered in something else that 'The Reader in the Book' has named 'the narrator'. Just as it is argued that the narrator absolutely contains the author, so the book is said to totally contain the child. The narrator and the book are excesses, coverings, external spaces that do not diminish in any sense the self they contain. The child, however, is not itself when reading because the self that is guided through the book is the 'sec-ond self', a self that is 'created' by a narrative 'technique'.[62] So, although the child has been taken 'as it is' by the 'author', the child that enters the book and is guided through it is not the child. Let us recap: The author is in the narrator who is in the book that takes the child as it is by constructing a new child that recognizes the 'implied reader' as itself, even though the self that 'implied reader' is leading through the book is not itself. To further compli-cate matters the book is trying to 'discover the reader it seeks'.[63] So, as the (implied) reader is entering the book, the book is traversing some undis-closed space wherein dwells the thing it wishes dwelt within it.

Because 'The Reader in the Book' wishes to establish that a certain book has been written for a certain reader who is a child, it claims that this book must focus on a child character, 'putting at the centre of the story a child through whose being everything is seen and felt'.[64] Again we have an idea of a book that has physical properties – it has a center.[65] It also means that this center is sensory. Further appeals to the physical reality of the text follow: 'this narrowing of focus by the adoption of a child point of view helps keep the author's second self – himself in the book – within the perceptual scope of his child reader'. Thus the child reader understands not through language, but through the 'perceptual scope' of sight.[66] The child has a limited vision and will only understand a text if the text replicates that vision. What the child is seeing is an image of the author. It would seem that 'adoption' here is about writing taking on an alien form, that is the visual, while still maintaining its status as written. This allows the written to take on terms such as 'immediacy' that are, of necessity, not available to it.

These struggles can be understood as pointing towards an attempt to overcome what I will write as one of the great difficulties of writing: it can make no claim to the idea of the certainty and authority of experience.[67] When I have written these words down they exist as language, language that produces meaning through certain rules that exist before the particular language act they enable. In a sense this chapter has always already been written in the language that enables it. My 'presence' as an individual who wrote these words and thinks he has a definite idea of the 'correct' meaning of them is not directly and immediately available to you (or me). I am not here. My 'presence' is not stamping its authority on the text in any immediate way. This chapter existed in language prior to my writing it and the structure that enabled that language to mean anything is one that linguistics has argued to be built upon difference, combination and substitution; which is to say that meaning is never immediate, never a thing in itself. The whole idea of why something means something is that it is different from another thing. Nothing in writing means anything on its own as an immediate, sensory experience.[68] Yet it is precisely such an experience that 'The Reader in the Book' is describing the act of reading to be. There is an insistence upon the 'real', 'physical' and 'sensuous'[69] qualities of the text, just as there is an insistence upon the idea that the mental activity involved is played out in some specific physical environment. There is an appeal to the auditory senses, a notion that one can 'hear the voice of speech'[70] when reading a certain text. There is also an insistence on the visual quality of writing. Child readers must 'see' the story, the author must make an 'image'[71] of himself and his reader, 'the text reveals its implied reader'[72] and a reader's 'evaluation' of the book 'often depends upon correct recognition of the implied reader'.[73] These notions of visual understanding enable an idea of a distance between viewer and book that allows for notions of objectivity and lack of investment while, conversely, offering the idea of sensual intimacy that grants the idea of total and unmediated knowledge. The idea of the 'book' enables an idea of the work of art as a thing in itself, with a knowable meaning that exists independently from any act of textual interpretation. With the insistence on the immediacy of the spatial phenomena there is also an idea of the distance between the writer and the addressed, a space in which the author can 'offer' books to the reader. This is a distance that must always be reduced into a notion of physical experience, leading to 'a critical approach which concerns itself less with the subjects portrayed in a book than with the means of communication by which the reader is brought into contact with the reality presented by an author'.[74] What does 'contact' mean here? It allows for a sensual certainty, a notion of a present reality that exists, in some knowable form, prior to its 'representation'. It also allows the distance between adult author and child reader to be safely established. The two are utterly separate. The only time they ever join up is in the specific act of reading. The child is brought, rather than forced, to make 'contact' with a reality (not an 'author' or a 'second self' or anything specific enough to be dubious) that is separate from either author or child. This reality is 'presented', it overwhelms neither party. Rather it is some enclosed object that may be shown. Yet soon the child will be within this reality, engulfed by it rather than handling it.

'The Reader in the Book' wishes to establish a case for the certainty of meaning.[75] It wants to claim that books have an inviolate meaning, a definite audience and a clear purpose. It can only do this by constructing books out of the stuff of certainty. So books are sensed and felt and walked through rather than read, and the children to whom they are addressed are characterized by their ability to sense and feel and walk. Books are granted the absolute quality of 'reality' to give them the absolute quality of truth. The danger is that 'real' authors are having 'real' 'contact' with 'real' children. There is a paedophilic threat that must be countered by the reality-quashing notion of the 'implied' rather than the real status of those negotiating meaning.[76]

VI Writing the real

Lucy Boston's *The Children of Green Knowe* is an apt choice of text for a reading that wishes to put forward a notion of 'negotiation of insight'. In the text a young child, Tolly, goes to stay with his aunt, Mrs Oldknowe, who lives in a castle, cut off from the rest of the world. When Tolly first arrives he asks if 'things happen' in the castle like they do 'in books':

> 'Oh yes, things happen in it.'
> 'What sort of things?'
> 'Wait and see! I'm waiting too, to see what will happen now you are here. Something will, I'm sure.'[77]

The next morning things do indeed start to happen. It seems that the ghosts of children who lived in the house many years ago might be starting to appear. Yet they only do so when Mrs Oldknowe and Tolly are together. Even then these appearances are ambivalent, final proof is always withheld. 'The Reader in the Book' argues that there is a 'collusion' between Mrs Oldknowe and Tolly. The book is also said to be 'amicably halved' between author and reader, it has a 'referential gap' of meaning that must be filled in by the second party. Together, author and reader 'collude' to create the 'true meaning' of the text. That 'true meaning' is the uncertainty as to whether the ghosts are real or are fictions dependent on the presence of the two characters that have created them. Thus *The Children of Green Knowe* is read as not only the perfect example of a text for children that produces meaning through the process of 'negotiation' but is also fundamentally concerned with this nego-tiation. Tolly is the child reader, Mrs Oldknowe the author and the children are the book and its meaning. 'The Reader in the Book' goes on to assert that Mrs Oldknowe allows Tolly to take part in their creation in two ways. Like a 'wise play leader'[78] she offers opportunities for Tolly to:

> Enjoy himself through experiences that enliven the world around him [...] the book is laden with instances in which Tolly encounters objects and, by sensing them and playing with them, imaginatively per-ceives the life in them.[79]

Mrs Oldknowe also more directly influences Tolly to see 'the life' in the children by telling him four stories about them. According to 'The Reader in the Book' the children have an 'undeniable reality'[80] in these stories, unlike the deniable 'reality' they have when Tolly sensuously encounters them. It is claimed that Tolly and Mrs Oldknowe also have a:

> Reality in their own right only as characters in Mrs Boston's stories about them. Stories, Mrs Boston is telling us, are a means by which we give life to ourselves and the objects around us. Stories, in fact, create meaning.[81]

One problem is that if the reading strategy of 'The Reader in the Book' is replicated in *The Children of Green Knowe*, so are the issues regarding the 'negotiation of insight' read above. There is a referential 'gap' that must be filled in, but rather than this giving half of the authority of meaning to the reader, the reader is placed into a situation where he may only choose between two already existing 'correct' meanings that have already been established by the author/book. In the same way, Tolly encounters objects and grants 'life' to them yet Tolly's playful and 'sensuous'[82] understanding of these objects is legitimized because the life recognized is the 'correct' life that existed in the objects before, an already established meaning he recognizes rather than authors. The apparent dualism once more breaks down into the notion of singular authorship, of meaning existing before interpretation.

The idea that 'reality' is always dependent on reading appeals to the notion of 'construction' in criticism argued in the work of Karín Lesnik-Oberstein and Jacqueline Rose, their idea being that 'reality' is something that is always imbued with the very idea of unstable (because linguistic) meaning it attempts to extricate itself from. Yet in Children's Literature Criticism these attempts at 'construction' always collapse into their oppo-site.[83] 'The Reader in the Book' claims that the ghostly children exist in Mrs Oldknowe's stories 'independently' of Tolly's interpretation of them. Only in these stories is their 'reality' not open to the 'tell tale gap'.[84] The reader can be certain that Tolly has not conjured these children. So 'reality' here is that which is absolutely certain. Yet it has been established that there is a notion that the act of reading as amicable division between writer and reader is the mark of deniable 'reality'. This is also the mark of 'reality', because stories are a negotiation of meaning, gaps are that which enable negotiation and stories are responsible for creating 'reality'. 'Reality' is, at different stages of the reading, ambivalence and certainty, a 'gap' to be filled and an already established and independent entity. 'Reality' is also linked to the idea of the 'purely sensational'.[85] It is 'sensuous discovery'[86] that enables Tolly to 'perceive' life in objects. There is also the idea that it is the presence of Mrs Oldknowe or the child reader that grants 'reality'. Yet the presence of Mrs Oldknowe is precisely what the text can never grant as Mrs Oldknowe is constructed by language. Each character in *The Children of Green Knowe* 'adopts' many parts. Tolly is that which allows child readers to touch 'sensuous' reality, that which listens to 'undeniably real' stories and cannot affect them, a part of an 'undeniably real' story, the locus of a 'tell tale gap' that must be filled in by a child reader.

These shifting positions cannot be easily resolved. 'The Reader in the Book' claims that reading, interpretation and language grant meaning and without these there can be nothing 'real'. Yet it also sets up this 'reality' as that which contains no language, or at least the language it uses transcends the bounds of language, being 'direct' and 'sensual'. 'The Reader in the Book' quotes Lucy Boston stating:

> I [...] would like to encourage children to use and trust their senses for themselves at first hand – their ears, eyes and noses, their fingers and the soles of their feet, their skins and their breathing, their muscular joy and rhythms and heartbeats, their instinctive loves and pity and their awe of the unknown. This, not the telly, is the primary material of thought. It is from direct stimulus that imagination is born.[87]

The world of action and physicality is being praised over the world of the separate viewer: a primary interaction with the 'real', rather a secondary reaction to representation. 'The Reader in the Book' then states that:

> Nowhere has an author so exactly stated her aims, and in few books has an author achieved her highest aims so certainly [...] Through Tolly, guided by Mrs Boston's second self, her implied reader is brought to grips with the direct sense stimulus that gives birth to life expanding imagination.[88]

The move that 'The Reader in the Book' makes is to state that primary physical reality is necessary for the child to develop thought and that the language of *The Children of Green Knowe* allows such direct, unmediated access to such 'reality'. The language allows the child to get to 'grips' with the world of the 'direct'. In short, 'The Reader in the Book' must constantly praise the primary (physical) life over the secondary (representational) while, in the specific case of Children's Literature, simultaneously granting the 'representational' the same qualities as the 'real'.

VII Close reading

Towards the end of 'The Reader in the Book' the opening four paragraphs of *The Children of Green Knowe* are quoted, and a claim is made to engage in a close reading of them to show that they are written in a language that is specifically directed at children (this extended quotation, and a further discussion of it, are included below). 'The Reader in the Book' also quotes a shorter passage from *Yew Hall*, a text that it claims is aimed at an adult audience. The language of *Yew Hall* is said to include 'experiential demands' outside the range of children: one has to know what St Paul's Cathedral is, for example.[89] To define childhood thus, however, can be read as very problematic as, according to that logic, a seven-year-old would cease to be a child if they lived in the vicinity of that building. The language is said to be more 'confidently natural', 'closer' to its author's 'thinking voice', 'witty', 'slightly superior' and tending 'towards the Latinate'.[90] Compared to this *The Children of Green Knowe* is 'much more firmly Anglo-Saxon'.[91] Although as 'richly textured' as *Yew Hall*, it is more 'active', 'direct, clear, polite, firm, uncluttered' and 'more concrete' in an 'everyday child appealing sense'.[92]

Here we have an attempt to still or stop meaning by appealing to ideas of the physical (active and concrete) and to a lack of interpretation (clear, firm and uncluttered). The child is constructed as that which finds this language 'appealing'. This is a construction that is granted an unquestioned truth that is then set up as the guarantor of the text's 'true' meaning. Literary 'appeal' to children is not something refined, separate or intellectual. It is 'everyday', simple, unchanging and 'real'. 'Adoption' is introduced through the notion of an adult literature being a 'natural' representation of adult thoughts. This constructs Children's Literature as an 'unnatural', 'public' event. It also constructs childhood as something that is not about thinking. The text is read as certain in order to enable claims about the child that have certainty.

Yet 'The Reader in the Book' can only make such claims by ignoring the language it purports to read. A close reading of the first four paragraphs allow for other possibilities of meaning and, I would argue, troubles any notion of a reader finally 'completing' the text in a 'correct' way.[93] Here is that extended quotation from *The Children of Green Knowe* that I will go on to discuss further:

> A little boy was sitting in the corner of a railway carriage looking out at the rain, which was splashing against the windows and blotching downward in an ugly, dirty way. He was not the only person in the carriage, but the others were strangers to him. He was alone as usual. There were

two women opposite him, a fat one and a thin one, and they talked without stopping, smacking their lips in between sentences and seeming to enjoy what they said as much as if it were something to eat. They were knitting all the time, and whenever the train stopped the click-clack of their needles was loud and clear as two clocks. It was a stopping train – more stop than go – and it had been crawling along the flat-footed country for a long time. Everywhere there was water – not sea or rivers or lakes, but just senseless floodwater with the rain splashing into it. Sometimes the railway lines were covered by it, and then the train noise was quite different, softer than a boat.

'I wish it was the Flood', thought the boy, 'and that I was going to the Ark. That would be fun! Like the circus. Perhaps Noah had a whip and made all the animals go round and round for exercise. What a noise there would be, with the lions roaring, elephants trumpeting, pigs squealing, donkeys braying, horses whinnying, bulls bellowing, and cocks and hens always thinking they were going to be trodden on but unable to fly up on to the roof where all the other birds were singing, screaming, twittering, squawking and cooing. What must it have sounded like, coming along on the tide? And did Mrs Noah just knit, knit and take no notice?'

The two women opposite him were getting ready for the next station. They packed up their knitting and collected their parcels and then sat staring at the little boy. He had a thin face and large eyes, he looked patient and rather sad. They seemed to notice him for the first time. (Lucy Boston, *The Children of Green Knowe*)[94]

A good point of departure, in terms of the passage, is that the women who ignore the child utilize the kind of language that 'The Reader in the Book' claims to appeal to the child reader: 'they talked without stopping, smacking their lips in between sentences and seeming to enjoy what they said as much as if it were something to eat'.[95] This language is public utterance rather than 'natural' interior thought. It is constructed as so 'purely sensational'[96] that it wholly lacks content, interchangeable with the physical pleasure of eating. Thus, in this instance, the language that is read as 'childlike' alienates the child. It could be argued that this is because the adult language is more to do with self-pleasure than 'sensuous discovery'. The ladies are using language for 'non-literary' pursuits,[97] pleasuring themselves with their own words whose content is constructed as irrelevant.

Throughout these opening paragraphs I read a concern with things that stop and do not stop. Not stopping is read as 'senseless'. The water does not stop. It has no definition. Or, rather, its identity is purely negative. It is not like a variety of things. In this it shares a quality with the women's language. The public sensual language of the adults is not granted specific clauses. Exactly what it is, or what it is about, is constructed by the text as something that escapes it. However, there is also a sense in which the adults' language does stop. In between sentences there is a 'smacking' of the lips that is the same as talking. These gaps in dialogue (which are not gaps in the text) mark both continuum and break. If the content of the women's language is constructed as a gap in the text, an unavailable public utterance, then Tolly's language, which is private, is constructed as available speech. Although not stopping is read as something that alienates the child, is 'senseless' and a feature of adult language, Tolly's own interior monologue is read as ongoing. In Tolly's language there is a list of animals that are differentiated. Although the list is specific because all the animals are different and are granted different actions, they are also about sameness, as they are still all animals being linked to a single action. The build-up of these animals is, in a sense, senseless because the addition of animals explains nothing but confusion, a train of thought without destination. A noise is created by the actions of the animals. No such noise is created by the senseless flood. The flood is an exterior scene, the animals are in the interior world of the Ark. But all of this is 'interior' because there is a notion of the story and what is outside of it: the content of the ladies' speech that cannot be included. The private world of Tolly is constructed as the availability of his language, the public world of the ladies is constructed by the unavailability of theirs. The animals are noisy and should be noticed but are not. Tolly, also, is noisy yet unrecognized. Although Tolly's thoughts are noisy, there is no 'noise' in the text. His language, which is private, is available (and therefore the proper focus of attention) precisely because it is internal. The idea is that internal places create something differentiated, confusing and accessible. The external is that which escapes access, that which is never available as itself in the text. Yet the adult language, which cannot be contained in the text, is the 'internal' language of the text that constructs Tolly's 'point of view'.[98] However, if the Ark is the mind that contains it, it is also the train, outside of which is the flood. And thus the ladies are, at some stage, internal to the mind that they alone cannot sense, as they have been 'adopted' in the position of Mrs Noah. Although the train, unlike the flood, does stop, this is not read as beneficial to its passengers. The train 'crawls' and when it does stop it is replaced by the knitting that has the relentless constancy of a clock, a 'senseless' flood-like quality.

I read two notions of the 'gap' here. One is negotiated by ideas of constancy and change. Tolly's language, the flood and the women's conversation do not stop. There is in all of them the desire for a 'gap'. A lack of a 'gap' in something means that thing is 'senseless', an absence or 'gap' in meaning. There is also an idea of stopping: the train, the women's language, Tolly's thoughts (as they are suddenly unavailable at the end). The idea of stopping here is about one thing becoming another, a question of rest and motion. The train stops and goes but all the time in a 'crawling' way which negates any notion of a final end to the journey: Tolly's destination is never mentioned. The women's voices are replaced by a 'smacking' sound, the train becomes a boat, the needles replace the train. The idea of the 'gap' is also about things escaping the text. The notion of constancy should, therefore, be about what is included, exemplified by the endless floods, but these floods are also a 'gap' in the text as they can only be explained in language in terms of things that they are not. The public language of the ladies is also a 'gap' in this sense, as it is constructed as that which escapes the text. Yet it is also the language of 'Children's Literature' that allows this escape to occur. Private language, on the other hand, may be accessed. Yet it is also a 'gap' because access is granted then taken away. There is a noisy sound of interiority that is always there but never available as noise even when attention is drawn to it, and at most other times it is a 'gap' in our knowledge.

'The Reader in the Book', then, has claimed *The Children of Green Knowe* to be a novel about complex, dualistic states. The children are both ghosts and fictions and many other things can be two different states at once: a train is a ship, the private is the public. The idea of sensuous language is another such state as it signifies the alienation of the child while also being constructed as the language of child appeal. The 'gaps' in the text are also claimed by 'The Reader in the Book' to be dualistic states. They allow the whole notion of collaboration and negotiation because they were created by the author and filled by the reader. When this happens a 'complete' book is read as made. The difficulty is that this apparent dualism always collapses into a monism of authorial creation. I have instead read *The Children of Green Knowe* as offering a more complex notion of what a 'gap' and a 'presence' might be in literature. Rather than a hole waiting to be filled in an utterly predetermined fashion, there is, in my reading, a complex set of shifting meanings in which a presence is always also an absence, and absence always a presence, and both always differentiated from each other. To me it allows the questions: How can anything be totally present in writing? How can we say something exists outside a text (such as a 'gap') without saying what it is? How can one thing 'adopt' the identity of another?

Instead of asking such questions I read 'The Reader in the Book' as offering a call for 'responsibility'. There are dangers it wishes to still. One can be read in the lack of complexity in its close reading of what it means to have a 'gap' in a text, a complexity that I do read in the text it attempts to read. For 'The Reader in the Book' to engage in close reading might allow the reader to impose a meaning on the text that is not 'correct'. There is no justification for why a particular reading is 'correct'. There is, however, a resistance to engage in a close reading that might suggest other possibilities. That is because the argument of 'The Reader in the Book' collapses into a call for the restoration of authorial intention. Another concern is that adults might neither be writing for children or 'adopting' an additional voice to do so. Hence the self-pleasuring ladies who consume phrases rendered meaningless because of their lack of another destination. The purpose of the 'literary' for children is the ignorant 'pursuit' of one who is not oneself.

Conclusion: Why this is still important

I wish to conclude this chapter by briefly introducing the critical response to 'The Reader in the Book'. I do this not only to suggest further avenues of research, but also to argue that no previous readings offer anything like a 'new approach' to either the text or the question of the child reading. I will then offer some connections between the ideas put forward by 'The Reader in the Book' and the work of recent critics that claim to have 'moved the debate on'.

All the critics who have responded to 'The Reader in the Book' admire the text but have issues with certain aspects of it and, like Peter Hunt and Michael Benton, read a certain lack of sophistication in its interpretative strategies. Ruth B. Bottigheimer in her 1998 essay 'An Important System of Its Own' offers such a reading.[99] According to Bottigheimer 'The Reader in the Book' offers a reading that 'works well' at determining authorial intent. However, it is a reading that is only relevant to 'contemporary'[100] Children's Literature. Bottigheimer agrees with the notion in 'The Reader in the Book' that one can tell that an author intends to write for children because of his use of Anglo Saxon rather than Latin vocabulary, his use of the Child's Point of View, and his acknowledgment of 'immediate childhood experience'. However, these indicators are read as less valuable when reading earlier Children's Literature:

> For whose intended readers authors often provided sexually sophisticated plots (like Potiphar's wife attempting to seduce Joseph), explicit vocabulary (blood and gore in eighteenth century histories of 'Tom Thumb') and mature thematic concerns (early death and torments of Hell) that are fundamentally alien to contemporary views of child orientated reading material.[101]

All such texts are read as containing 'ambiguity'. Thus 'contemporary' (twentieth century) texts such as *The Children of Green Knowe* are read as utterly free from ambiguity. The Child that 'contemporary' authors write for is constructed as one that requires singular meanings and a lack of sexuality and 'explicitness'. Although Bottigheimer's criticism of 'The Reader in the Book' points to certain limitations, it does so to validate a construction of The Child that is knowable, non-textual and 'real'. Bottigheimer has no issue with the notion that an author introduces 'referential gaps that imply immediate Childhood experience'. The real is made available as an absence in the text that the Child completes. This completion is read as based on non-textual experience because it is 'implied' by the text rather than a part of it and because this is a child's un-read 'experience' rather than readable thought or language.

As Michael Benton also argues,[102] John Stephens offers a more sustained criticism of 'The Reader in the Book'. He criticizes the text for suggesting that there is text that can only be accessed by a reader's 'internalization of the text's implicit ideologies',[103] as a move that Stephens regards as privileging a dubiously passive construction of the reader. Moreover, he reads 'The Reader in The Book' as offering a very specific ideology that it refuses to recognize. 'The Reader in the Book' offers a reading of texts concerned with 'the individual [striving] for autonomous selfhood'. Stephens continues:

> The message which the literature overwhelmingly communicates is that people ultimately wield their own subjectivity as the grounds to their beliefs and actions. And this is the central tenet in the doctrine of the implied reader within reader response theories of reading.[104]

In addition to understanding the ideological import of reader response, Stephens also wishes to offer a more 'complex' reading. He argues that texts can be read in a number of different ways, not just in one 'correct' way. He also wishes to problematize the simple 'dualisms' that reader response appeals to. For example, he questions the simple dualism between text and reader, pointing out that the reader is not completely separable from the text, being a fundamentally linguistic construction:

> Since the subject is constituted within a structure of linguistic differentiations, it also follows that the subject is inscribed within language and can communicate only by conforming his or her speech to subject positions constituted within various discourse types.[105]

Stephens's account of reader response is complex and deserves to be read in full. However, even from just the quotation above, this is an account that may be read as replicating many of the problems it seeks to overcome. The subject, according to Stephens, is 'constituted' by language and as such cannot easily be separated from the text it engages with. Yet this is still a subject that is forced to 'conform' to the discourses that are read as constituting it. So, despite its apparent linguistic construction, the self still is available as a state prior to the 'conformity' of the discourse that constitutes it. Hence the 'reader' and 'text' here are not so different from those offered by 'The Reader in the Book': apparently distinct identities. Likewise, Stephens's attempt at rescuing reader response from the idea of a 'correct' reading of the text does not go as far as it claims. Stephens merely moves from the notion of a singular 'correct' meaning to a multitude of possible, yet stable, meanings. Thus Stephens claims that 'William Mayne's *Salt River Times* constructs at least ten possible subject positions, and, it should be stressed, as many ideological positions.'[106] In reading 'The Reader in the Book' Stephens states:

> Chambers argues from assumptions of determinate meanings and uses such formulations as 'the book's true meaning'. Wolfgang Iser, who was

Chambers' primary inspiration, did not. Iser argued that inferences were a matter of choices, and in excluding some possibilities a reader constructs a meaning which includes only parts of the text's potential, so there can be no determinate meanings.[107]

The text still has 'potential', the reader a limited set of 'choices'. This argument has not extricated itself from the problems of determinate reading introduced above.

It is not only those critics who seek to criticize 'The Reader in the Book' that cannot extricate themselves from the ideas about childhood and reading that I have read as problematic in it. Children's Literature Criticism is constantly appealing to notions of the immediacy of language, the physicality of the book, and the 'real' child that accompanies the child of construction. For example, the introduction to this book contains a detailed reading of David Rudd's theories of Children's Literature. I read the notion of 'adoption' argued for by 'The Reader in the Book' in the arguments concerning 'hybrid forms' 'mimicking' adult language in Rudd's work. There is also the idea of an increased sophistication in criticism that moves away from simplistic notions of authorial intention and response. Like such ideas in 'The Reader in the Book' these are read as collapsing into exactly what they attempt to avoid. The constructed child in Rudd's reading is merely a shifting notion that exists on top of the indisputable and immutable 'real'. This is exactly the way that the 'implied' child reader in 'The Reader in the Book' can be read as a dispensable covering under which the 'real' child exists, demanding texts that fulfill its desire for 'public', 'concrete', 'Anglo-Saxon language'.

Any recent critic of Children's Literature can be read through the reading of 'The Reader in the Book' offered here to establish how far their 'arguments' have 'moved on'.[108] Unfortunately, I have little faith that such an enterprise would yield readings of progression. To indicate how deeply the ideas I have read in 'The Reader in the Book' are entrenched in Children's Literature Criticism we might turn to a statement by Peter Hunt. Hunt has been mentioned before in this chapter, and is viewed (with good reason) as an innovative, theoretical critic by both 'Signal' critics and 'new' critics alike. However, in writing about 'response' and Children's Literature, Hunt claims that 'we are talking about how real readers read – not students or critics or others who deliberately read in a deviant way'.[109] The child is 'real' here. It is also knowable, as is its reading. This reading is the 'true' meaning of the text. All other readings are 'deviant': sexual, transgressive, dangerous, supplementary. They are so because they are 'deliberate'. The child has no 'intention' or thought. Its reading is natural, pure, 'correct'. And that reading is also Hunt's reading. Hunt has no difficulty in reading the child's reading. 'We' all agree what the child takes the meaning to be and 'we' all agree it is correct. 'We' are not critics. I do not read Hunt as defending 'the child' here. I do not see Hunt acting in a more 'responsible' way than the 'students' he berates. I do not read him as defending the child's experience from thoughtful deviants. Rather, I see 'the child' helping Hunt to secure meaning. Hunt has access to the 'true' interpretation of a text because he claims to have total access to the unmediated response of the audience for whom this text was written. Put succinctly, Children's Literature Criticism uses an idea of 'the child' to defend its interpretation of texts against the claims of others.

Suggested further reading

The problems associated with 'The Reader in the Book' can all also be read in: Wolfgang Iser, *The Implied Reader, Patterns of Communication in Prose Fiction from Beckett to Bunyan* (Baltimore and London: Johns Hopkins Press, 1976).

To deal with the issues of text and reader at a more rigorous level, I would recommend reading the critical debate around 'The Purloined Letter' by Edgar Allen Poe. Here notions of what might be termed 'authority', 'intrinsic quality' and 'interpretation' are read in a way that may 'provoke' or 'inspire' more detailed thinking. The debate comprises Jacques Lacan's reading of 'The Purloined Letter', Jacques Derrida's reply to this, and Barbara Johnson's complex overview of the 'traps' of reading both theorists find themselves caught up in. The following collection contains all of the above as well as additional, helpful essays:

John P. Muller and William J. Richardson (eds), *The Purloined Poe: Lacan, Derrida, and Psychoanalytic Reading* (Baltimore: Johns Hopkins University Press, 1990).

As far as issues of Theory and Children's Literature's Literature are concerned two books are essential:

Lesnik-Oberstein, Karín, *Children's Literature: Criticism and the Fictional Child* (Oxford: Clarendon, 1994).
Rose, Jacqueline, *The Case of Peter Pan, or, The Impossibility of Children's Fiction* (London: Macmillan, 1984).

Notes

1. Aidan Chambers, 'The Reader in the Book', in: Peter Hunt (ed.), *Children's Literature: The Development of Criticism* (London: Routledge, 1990), pp. 91–114.
2. Michael Benton, 'Reader-Response Criticism' in: Peter Hunt (ed.), *The Routledge International Companion Encyclopedia of Children's Literature* (London: Routledge, 1996), pp. 71–88, p. 83 (This article is also reprinted as 'Readers, Texts, Contexts: Reader-Response Criticism' in: Peter Hunt (ed.), *Understanding Children's Literature* (London: Routledge, 1999), pp. 81–99).
3. Benton, p. 84.
4. A classic example of 'Childist' criticism is Aidan Chambers, *Tell Me: Children, Reading and Talk – How Adults Help Children Talk* (Stroud: Thimble Press, 1993). For a selection of this criticism, dealing with a diverse range of subjects, see Perry Nodelman's web page: this is currently running and is advertised as a guide to Children's Literary Theory, expanded to include work published in 2002, at http://www.uwinnipeg.ca/~nodelman/resources/allbib.htm (2003).

    The ideas of 'Childist' criticism, and problems with it, are dealt with throughout this chapter. The first kind, which is explicitly 'Childist', may be read in the work contained in the journal *Signal*. Despite the recent closure of this groundbreaking journal, 'childist' criticism is still widely argued for: On the Cardiff University website Sebastien Chapleau states that:

> As it has been noted quite repeatedly [...] the fact that children's books are written by adults for children often leaves the child (whom the book is supposed to belong to) out of the equation – this being due to the ideological pressures that are encapsulated within the adult – child relationship. Developing [...] 'childist criticism' I believe that writing and criticising children's literature are possible endeavours [...] Including the child in the writing of children's books, I also wish to link childist criticism to current debates on critical pedagogy, and thus introduce the notion of 'childism'. (2004, at: http://www.cf.ac.uk/encap/staff/chapleau.html)

5. John Stephens, *Language and Ideology in Children's Fiction* (London: Longman, 1992). Stephens is not simply a supporter of 'Childist' criticism, see below.
6. For more on this debate see Peter Hollindale, 'Ideology and the Children's Book', *Signal* 55, 1988, 3–22.
7. See William Wimsatt and Monroe Beardsley, *The Verbal Icon* (New York: Noonday Press, 1958).
8. A defining moment in 'Childist Criticism' is Peter Hunt's seminal 'Childist Criticism: The Subculture of the Child, the Book and the Critic', *Signal* 43, 1984, 42–59. For readings of difficulties with such ideas see Karín Lesnik-Oberstein, *Children's Literature: Criticism and the Fictional Child* (Oxford: Clarendon, 1994).
9. Chambers, 'The Reader in the Book', p. 91.
10. Chambers, 'The Reader in the Book', p. 92.
11. Chambers, 'The Reader in the Book', p. 92.
12. Barbara Wall, *The Narrator's Voice: The Dilemma of Children's Fiction* (Basingstoke: Macmillan – now Palgrave Macmillan, 1991); Michael Benton, 'Possible Worlds and Narrative Voices', in: J. Many and C. Cox (eds) *Reader Stance and Literary Understanding: Exploring the Theories, Research and Practice* (Norwood, NJ: Ablex, 1992); Peter Hollindale, *Signs of Childness in Children's Books* (Stroud: Thimble Press, 1997). For an extensive analysis of the problems in Barbara Wall's argument, parallel to what I am arguing here, see: Karín Lesnik-Oberstein, *Children's Literature: Criticism and the Fictional Child*, pp. 143–8.
13. See above. For the pedagogical use of this see, for example, Martin Coles and Colin Harrison, *The Reading for Real Handbook* (London: Routledge, 1992).
14. See, for example, Hugh Crago, 'The Roots of Response', in *Children's Literature Association Quarterly*, vol. 10, no. 3, 1985, 100–4. Again, texts on the same subject published up until 2002 are included on Nodelman's web page.
15. Chambers, 'The Reader in the Book', p. 94.
16. Chambers, 'The Reader in the Book', p. 112.
17. Chambers, 'The Reader in the Book', pp. 107–8.
18. Chambers, 'The Reader in the Book', p. 98.
19. Chambers, 'The Reader in the Book', p. 111.
20. Chambers, 'The Reader in the Book', p. 92.
21. Jonathan Culler, *On Deconstruction: Theory and Criticism After Structuralism* (London: Routledge, 1989).
22. Culler, p. 75.
23. Chambers, 'The Reader in the Book', p. 92.
24. Chambers, 'The Reader in the Book', p. 92.
25. Chambers, 'The Reader in the Book', p. 93.
26. Chambers, 'The Reader in the Book', p. 94.

27. Chambers, 'The Reader in the Book', p. 93.
28. Chambers, 'The Reader in the Book', p. 93.
29. Chambers, 'The Reader in the Book', p. 98.
30. Chambers, 'The Reader in the Book', pp. 91–2.
31. Chambers, 'The Reader in the Book', p. 102.
32. Chambers, 'The Reader in the Book', p. 92.
33. Chambers, 'The Reader in the Book', p. 102.
34. Chambers, 'The Reader in the Book', p. 95.
35. Chambers, 'The Reader in the Book', p. 93.
36. Chambers, 'The Reader in the Book', p. 92.
37. Chambers, 'The Reader in the Book', p. 93.
38. Chambers, 'The Reader in the Book', p. 91.
39. Chambers, 'The Reader in the Book', p. 93.
40. Chambers, 'The Reader in the Book', p. 92.
41. Chambers, 'The Reader in the Book', p. 93.
42. Chambers, 'The Reader in the Book', p. 93.
43. Chambers, 'The Reader in the Book', p. 93.
44. Chambers, 'The Reader in the Book', p. 91.
45. Chambers, 'The Reader in the Book', p. 93.
46. Chambers, 'The Reader in the Book', p. 93.
47. Chambers, 'The Reader in the Book', p. 93.
48. Chambers, 'The Reader in the Book', p. 93.
49. Chambers, 'The Reader in the Book', p. 111.
50. Chambers, 'The Reader in the Book', p. 93.
51. Chambers, 'The Reader in the Book', p. 98.
52. Chambers, 'The Reader in the Book', p. 98.
53. Chambers, 'The Reader in the Book', p. 98.
54. Chambers, 'The Reader in the Book', p. 98.
55. Chambers, 'The Reader in the Book', p. 93.
56. 'Didactic' here is used as a pejorative term. The move to differentiate between 'didactic' teaching and 'child-centered' teaching is common to both Children's Literature Criticism and recent trends in educational theory and practice. See Karín Lesnik-Oberstein, *Children's Literature*, pp. 69–99 and p. 116, for a reading of how Children's Literature Critics use the term. A linked move to 'liberate' the child from all adult power (while still educating it in an institution) was argued for by Carl Rogers and Jerome Freiberg in *Freedom to Learn* (New Jersey: Prentice Hall, 1994). This move is still sanctioned by the educational policy of the current British government, implemented in flagship colleges, and remains a key notion in PGCE provision. My issue here is with the disavowal of authority required on the part of the institution, rather with some notion that the child should be subject to a more or less 'didactic' education.
57. Chambers, 'The Reader in the Book', p. 98.
58. See Stephen Greenblatt, *Renaissance Self-Fashioning: From More to Shakespeare* (Chicago: University of Chicago Press, 1980), p. 235.
59. This is a prevalent notion in writing about Child response, one questioned by John Stephens in *Language and Ideology in Children's Fiction*.
60. Chambers, 'The Reader in the Book', p. 102.
61. Chambers, 'The Reader in the Book', p. 93.
62. Chambers, 'The Reader in the Book', p. 92.
63. Chambers, 'The Reader in the Book', p. 91.
64. Chambers, 'The Reader in the Book', p. 98.

65. John Stephens offers a critique of 'The Reader in the Book' in his *Language and Ideology in Children's Fiction*. However, he finally agrees with that text on many matters, including the importance of a text having a center.

66. This notion is recurrent in Children Literature Criticism. See Perry Nodelman, *Words About Pictures: The Narrative Art of Children's Picture Books* (Athens & London: University of Georgia Press, 1988). Nodelman claims that Louise Rosenblatt's *The Reader's Eye: Visual Imaging as Reader Response* (Baltimore and London: Johns Hopkins, 1994) is 'persuasive' (http://www.uwinnipeg.ca/~nodelman/resources/allbib.htm (2003)). See also Jane Doonan, *Looking at Pictures in Picture Books* (Stroud: Thimble Press, 1993).

67. Experience has no certainty or authority either, or rather, experience is only available to us as something that is certain and immediate if we have an idea about what 'experience', 'certainty' and immediacy' are. See, for example, Jacques Derrida, *Of Grammatology*, trans. Gayatri Chakravorty Spivak (Baltimore: Johns Hopkins, 1976).

68. See, for example, Ferdinand de Saussure, *Course in General Linguistics* (New York: McGraw-Hill, 1959).

69. Chambers, 'The Reader in the Book', p. 113.

70. Chambers, 'The Reader in the Book', p. 96.

71. Chambers, 'The Reader in the Book', p. 92.

72. Chambers, 'The Reader in the Book', p. 94.

73. Chambers, 'The Reader in the Book', p. 92. But is this only true for the reader that 'The Reader in the Book' is appealing to, or 'the child reader'? The point is unclear.

74. Chambers, 'The Reader in the Book', p. 104.

75. See Jacqueline Rose, *The Case of Peter Pan, or The Impossibility of Children's Fiction* (London: Macmillan, 1984).

76. See James Kincaid, *Child Loving* (London: Routledge, 1994).

77. Chambers, 'The Reader in the Book', p. 110.

78. Chambers, 'The Reader in the Book', p. 111.

79. Chambers, 'The Reader in the Book', p. 111.

80. Chambers, 'The Reader in the Book', p. 112.

81. Chambers, 'The Reader in the Book', p. 112.

82. Chambers, 'The Reader in the Book', p. 112.

83. There are many examples. See Perry Nodelman's 'Hidden Meaning and the Inner Tale: Deconstruction and the Interpretation of Fairy Tales' *Children's Literature Association Quarterly*, 14(3), Fall 1989, 143–8. Nodelman argues for the notion of 'construction' before finally acknowledging the 'real child' and his unquestioned knowledge of it. A slightly different attempt can be read in the work of Kimberley Reynolds and Judith Plotz. These critics attempt 'theoretical' histories of Children's Literature and write about shifting 'representations' of childhood. The notion that a 'representation' is a construct is fine for such critics. The notion that there is a consensus as to the nature of the a-historical identity 'child' it represents cannot, however, be questioned. See Neil Cocks, 'Death and Absence in *Tim* by H.O. Sturgis' in *Nineteenth Century Contexts* (forthcoming).

84. Chambers, 'The Reader in the Book', p. 111.

85. Chambers, 'The Reader in the Book', p. 113.

86. Chambers, 'The Reader in the Book', p. 113.

87. Chambers, 'The Reader in the Book', p. 36.

88. Chambers, 'The Reader in the Book', p. 112.

89. Chambers, 'The Reader in the Book', p. 108.

90. Chambers, 'The Reader in the Book', p. 106.
91. I do not read the notion that the 'diversity of children' find 'Anglo-Saxon' appealing as particularly 'responsible'. The link between the child, nature and 'original' national identity has been rigorously read by Stephen Thomson in: 'Substitute Communities, Authentic Voices: the Organic Writing of the Child' in Karín Lesnik-Oberstein (ed.), *Children in Culture: Approaches to Childhood* (Basingstoke: Macmillan – now Palgrave Macmillan, 1998), pp. 248–73 and Jacqueline Rose's reading of Rousseau in *The Case of Peter Pan*.
92. Chambers, 'The Reader in the Book', pp. 107–8.
93. This lack of 'closure' need not be read as a 'Postmodern' demand to be 'lost in the funhouse' of meaning, the kind of a-political, reactionary notion Christopher Norris reads in *What's Wrong With Postmodernism: Critical Theory and the Ends of Philosophy* (Hemel Hempstead: Harvester Wheatsheaf, 1990), pp. 164–93. One might, instead, turn to the closing chapter of Karín Lesnik-Oberstein's *Children's Literature*. Here, in a reading of issues in Child Psychotherapy, there is an argument for a construction of meaning that eschews the short term, reductive demand in favour of an ongoing negotiation of meaning. Unlike the work of Carl Rogers and the Critics of Children's Literature, this negotiation is one that does not wish to deny issues of authority that are internal to, and constitutive of, it. For more on this see the introduction to this book.
94. Quoted in: Aidan Chambers, 'The Reader in the Book' in Peter Hunt, *Children's Literature: The Development of Criticism*, p. 107.
95. Chambers, 'The Reader in the Book', p. 107.
96. Chambers, 'The Reader in the Book', p. 111.
97. Chambers, 'The Reader in the Book', p. 93.
98. Chambers, 'The Reader in the Book', p. 98.
99. See Ruth Bottigheimer. 'An Important System of Its Own: Defining Children's Literature', *Princeton University Library Chronicle*, Winter 1998, 190–210. Other readings include Barbara Wall's *The Narrator's Voice: The Dilemma of Children's Fiction*. Wall reads 'The Reader in the Book' as too simplistic yet still confirms the idea of reading as immediate and physical.
100. Bottigheimer, 'An Important System of Its Own', p. 9.
101. Bottigheimer, 'An Important System of Its Own', p. 9.
102. Benton, p. 84.
103. Stephens, *Language and Ideology*, p. 66. For more on this see Stephen Thomson's chapter on ideology in this book.
104. Stephens, *Language and Ideology*, p. 57.
105. Stephens, *Language and Ideology*, p. 55.
106. Stephens, *Language and Ideology*, p. 56.
107. Stephens, *Language and Ideology*, p. 66.
108. To do this, simply go to: http://www.uwinnipeg.ca/~nodelman/resources/ allbib.htm. Again, this is Perry Nodelman's present Children's Literature theory web page. No author collected in this book is represented on this page. Every work of Children's Literature Criticism listed here could productively be read through any chapter of this book.
109. Peter Hunt, *Criticism, Theory, and Children's Literature* (Oxford: Blackwell, 1991), p. 4.

6
Children's Literature, Science and Faith: *The Water-Babies*

Lila Marz Harper

The once vastly popular children's book, *The Water-Babies or a Fairy Tale for a Land Baby* (1862–63) by Charles Kingsley does not appear to be translatable to modern times; it is considered a particularly Victorian work, one marked by the era's spiritual crisis, a crisis that was brought to a head by the 1859 publication of Charles Darwin's *Origin of Species*.[1] Yet, after its 1863 publication, *Water-Babies* was apparently popular up through the 1920s. The story provided inspiration for beautiful illustrations by Linley Sambourne, W. Heath Robinson and Rosalie K. Fry, all of whom were engaged by the detailed natural history illustrations prized by Victorians. The best known are those by American artist Jessie Willcox Smith (1863–1935), who was born the year of *Water-Babies'* publication. Her illustrations for the 1916 Dodd, Mead and Company edition with its scenes of babies encountering gloriously detailed sea and pond life underwater are the most memorable and mark the height of the book's popularity. Conversely, the book's reduction in popular appeal might be seen as signaled by the failure of a 1940 attempt by Walt Disney to use the title in a picture book that only dealt with water fairies (and bears and Snow White) and did not touch on the natural history theme.[2]

Thirty-five years after *Water-Babies'* publication, the *Pall Mall Gazette* listed it 'as the sixth most popular children's book in England'.[3] In Britain, a film was made of the book in 1907 and there was even a musical in 1973, indicating familiarity lasted longer in Britain, but today few Americans appear to have ever heard of *Water Babies*.[4] Yet in its time, its social impact was quite noticeable. Within a year of its publication, the popular outrage over the story of Tom, the chimney sweep, and his mistreatment had created the Chimney Sweepers Regulation Act that 'forbade the use of children for sweeping chimneys' (an act that was not repealed until 1971).[5] Certainly, by the 1950s, *Water-Babies* appears to have lost its popular audience. Most children's editions available today are reprints of the 1928 abridged version, lacking the social criticism and references to fights among major scientific figures, and this edition or excerpts are what most adults today remember.[6] The book nearly went out of print in the United States. In 1982, F.J. Harvey

Darton in his history of children's literature comments that, 'Like other well-loved children's books, [*Water-Babies*] is a story which is very likely more talked about by grown-up people today than re-read by them'.[7] Deborah Stevenson in her examination of the process that creates children's classics particularly focuses on *Water-Babies* as an example of an 'unretrievable' text, by which she means that adults no longer see a reason to direct their children to the work.[8]

Although it is not possible ever to completely recapture the thought processes of the readers of a particular historical period (after all, we only have access to the responses of a few readers), approaching a work historically, speculating on how a Victorian reader might respond to a particular work, is still worthwhile since the effort to think according to other ideologies allows us to better understand current ideologies and see them as subject to flux. I argue that those criteria that might move parents and teachers to identify a work as 'good' for children in the nineteenth century are not going to be quite the same as in the twenty-first century and it is important to trace how those valuations change and why. Therefore, this chapter will examine differing ideas about childhood, childhood and adult reading, what was considered as 'suitable' reading for these readerships, and why. Changes and shifts in the views on 'suitable books' may lead to editing, censorship, abridgement, or the forgetting of (children's) books. The history of the reception of *The Water-Babies* may serve as an illuminating example of these processes at work.

The scientifically-minded book-purchasing parents of 1860s England, one might assume, faced a problem finding material to read to children since much of the earlier material provided for children's consumption served the purpose of teaching a faith that no longer seemed to provide the answers in a post-Darwinian world. If we assume that the crisis in religious faith that impacted many Victorian writers carried over to parents' selection of children's literature, we can gain a sense of why *Water-Babies* might have been adopted as part of the children's reading lists and why it later lost its appeal or no longer seemed as relevant to the adults' sense of what children needed emotionally and spiritually.

There is some question as to why *Water-Babies* was ever considered children's literature in the first place. It was first published in an adult periodical and it can be seen as adult fantasy.[9] It may have been moved into the children's literature genre because the narration is addressed to a child. There are also biographical reasons. According to his wife, Kingsley wrote the book for his son, Grenville Arthur Kingsley. She claims he dashed off the first chapter in an half-hour:

[O]ne spring morning, while sitting at breakfast, his wife reminded him of an old promise, 'Rose, Maurice, and Mary [Kingsley's other children] have got their book, and Baby must have his.' He made no answer, but got up at once and went into his study, locking the door. In half an hour he returned with the story of little Tom. This was the first chapter of *The Water Babies*, written off without a check.[10]

Two of Kingsley's previous novels were read by adolescents and he had been appointed tutor to the Prince of Wales, so there was a general perception that he did write for children and this reputation also made it more likely that the book would be marketed for children.

What is observable is that *Water-Babies* sold well and continued to sell well as adults chose to place the work in their children's hands. It is one of the earliest books marketed for children about nine years of age. In a chapter titled 'Literature of the Little Ones' from his 1888 study of children's reading preferences, Edward Salmon observed that

> The last quarter of a century has been rich in marvels for the nursery. Whilst a literature has sprung up for the older boys and girls, that for babes – or rather the smaller boys and girls – has undergone developments which carry it altogether beyond anything previously written. In 1863 Kingsley published *Water-Babies*; and a year later Tom Hood was delighting the world with such works as *The Fairy Realm, The Loves of Tom Tucker* and *Bo-Peep, Funny Fables for Little Folks*, and *From Nowhere to the North Pole*.[11]

After noting that *Water-Babies* marked the beginning of a collection of works marketed to younger children, Salmon continues to focus on Hood's books and never returns to discuss *Water-Babies*.[12] Salmon's need to acknowledge *Water-Babies* and yet not discuss the work's contribution to 'the mental and moral welfare of the rising generation' may be perhaps linked to some Victorian critics' uncertainty as to whether *Water Babies* was really for children or if it spoke to adults' ideas of children's thinking. Generally, concerns made shortly after 1863 focused on the use of satire. *The Westminster Review*, noting some general concerns about the adult material in *Water-Babies* observed, 'It [*Water-Babies*] is complained of as unsuited to the capacity of the good little boys to whom it is dedicated'.[13] Salmon appears to agree indirectly about the inappropriate nature of satire in children's books. He continues with his discussion of Hood's stories by stating that despite being humorous, Hood's satire 'hardly fitted him to be regarded … as a successful writer for children'.[14] Although *Water-Babies* is not discussed, the placement of these two authors side-by-side suggests an unmentioned concern that *Water-Babies*, although well established, was also more satirical than considered appropriate for a child's reading. These concerns were, however, dismissed by the earlier *Westminster Review* assessment, which, after acknowledging that children would not understand everything in the book, continued stating: 'but we believe the children will find quite as much that they can understand as they ever find in any book that is worth putting into their hands, and quite as much probably as will be revealed to the understanding of most grown-up folks'.[15] Thus, it was recognized that *Water-Babies* had an adult readership, yet it was still seen as a worthwhile book for children.

While attempting to gain a better sense of what the 1860s audience valued in *Water-Babies*, my approach is to bring together those works considered 'scientific' and juxtapositioning them with 'non-scientific' works. By doing this, I am examining how literary works may have contributed to the history of science. This approach challenges the generally assumed division between the literary world and the scientific: a dominant belief of modern culture with its understanding of science as a professional field of study.[16] The Victorian period offers a rich area of study in science and literature as scientific disputes were often carried into the popular press and the general public was eager to learn about the latest discoveries and to speculate how they might affect the future.

The Water-Babies' removal from the canon of modern children's literature is indicative of the particular role that *Water-Babies* appears to have played in its time. Victorian parents may have chosen *Water-Babies* to address a major conflict between church and religion and explain the conflict to their children. The pedagogical role of the novel may, then, have been defined in relation to Darwin's publication, and may have been seen less strongly as the impact of Darwin's work was absorbed into wider debates and other publications. Generally speaking, Victorian culture was intensely aware of the growth of knowledge and was concerned about the impact of new knowledge on cultural development; this, as Alan Rauch observes, led to a 'general uneasiness about how to interpret the world', which in turn 'prompted elaborate efforts to reconcile the secular and the spiritual'.[17] This concern is expressed in *The Spectator's* review of *Water-Babies*, which identifies the book's purpose as pedagogical – to 'adapt Mr Darwin's theory of the natural selection of species to the understanding of children by giving it an individual, moral and religious as well as a mere specific and scientific application', a purpose that *the Times* praised as a 'fine' goal.[18] Thus, it was quickly recognized that *Water-Babies* helped clarify a moral and religious position that accommodated natural selection.

Children's literature has a long history of scientific education. Rauch points to John Newbery's *The Newtonian System of Philosophy* (1761) as an important early work for children.[19] Most of such works followed John Locke's call for investigation into nature as the appropriate material for children's reading. At this time, a natural linkage between religion and nature study was assumed. By the mid-1800s, however, clergyman naturalists were avoiding direct mention of the word 'God', particularly in works intended for children, and there were concerns that when combining science and religious messages in a single text, the emphasis on 'reason' might contribute to the teaching of materialism if children were put into a position of choosing faith or scientific reasoning.[20] Elizabeth Eastlake commented in 1842 that it may not be 'conducive to the soundness of this future faith to accustom a child to believe only what he can understand'.[21] While it was felt children should be taught about scientific ideas, the conflict between science and religion that centered on Darwin made writers and purchasers of children's literature concerned about how to present scientific material and not risk promoting ideas that could undermine future religious belief.

Although the connection between discussion of natural selection and *Water-Babies* has been noted,[22] the religious crises that affected Victorian society have not really been considered in modern critical assessments of *Water-Babies*. For the most part *Water-Babies* has not received the attention from children's literature scholars given to later Victorian and Edwardian children's literature. Humphrey Carpenter's chapter on *Water-Babies*, entitled 'Parson Lot Takes a Cold Bath', reads the narrative in narrowly biographical terms. Kingsley's writing of the novel is perceived as psychologically 'lightening him of a burden'.[23] It is apparent that Carpenter's reading of *Water-Babies* is inspired by Susan Chitty's biography of Kingsley, a biography that declares that '[w]hen Kingsley wrote it [*Water-Babies*] he dived deep into his own unconscious, although he was probably quite unaware of the fact'.[24] There is no evidence though that Kingsley's contemporaries were aware of it either or that his readers saw such post-Freudian symbolism. Chitty outlines several critical treatments of the late-1960s and early-1970s, which, like similar treatments of Lewis Carroll during these years, tended to focus on sexual symbols whenever possible.[25] Carpenter views all of Kingsley's previous work as showing he 'had been a destroyer rather than a creator, a critic of society who had no idea how to set it right and perhaps scarcely cared, a sexual sadist (in imagination if not fact) who delighted in the destruction of women's bodies'.[26] *Water-Babies*, he concludes, serves as a 'perfect vehicle for an adult's most personal and private concerns', particularly guilt about sex.[27] Such assessments, unfortunately, say more about the modern erroneous perception of the culture of the Victorian period as being unusually prudish and sexually warped, than that it really informs us about the role *Water-Babies* played in the major intellectual exchanges of the period.

Understanding *Water-Babies*' great appeal in its time requires an understanding of the cultural/scientific context of the Victorian period and how this book, although marketed for the use of children, had a great influence on the popular understanding of evolution. It gave parents a way to present a new form of scientifically-supported moral teachings to children in a world quickly losing its connection to past spiritual guidelines, and also to reassure themselves of the possibility of a reconciliation between faith and science. Although historians of Victorian culture tend to overlook *Water-Babies*, they acknowledge the importance of Kingsley as a spokesperson for the concerns of the mid-nineteenth century. While Kingsley was the most active and energetic of the many Victorian advocates for the advancement of knowledge, he was also one whose ideas were more conventional, more reflective of the middle-class Victorian readership, than other intellectuals and, thus, Alan Rauch sees him as crucial to 'understanding the currents of knowledge in Victorian England'.[28] Rauch admits that '[t]here is a helter-skelter quality to Kingsley's works that makes them somewhat difficult to analyze and, I dare-say, somewhat difficult for contemporary audiences to read. Kingsley is … less interested in the conventions of plot than in the need to make statements in his work'.[29] By contemporary standards, *Water-Babies'* plot is not well-organized, but Victorian middle-class readers tended to focus on moral positions and a lack of narrative consistency was seen as less of a problem. So major a figure of mid-nineteenth century culture was Kingsley that G.M. Young called him 'very nearly the central man of that period of swift change'.[30] Understanding Kingsley's stature is key to understanding the impact that *Water-Babies* had during a time of major intellectual upheaval.

Certainly something seemed to have been fueling an interest in children and fairies in the 1860s. An 1863 review of *Water-Babies* in *The Saturday Review* particularly grumbles over an apparent fascination with imagined children's responses to such fantasies and shows a surprisingly sophisticated theoretical understanding of the problems inherent in defining the child reader. The review opens with a discussion of how 'grown-up persons amuse themselves with thinking how nearly like children they can feel, and it is supposed that there is something morally and artistically good in the process'. This 'latest fancy of sentimentalists', which the reviewer calls 'the child-heart', 'is an attempt to write a child's story really for grown-up people, but nominally for children … the sort of performance which is dearest to those who are made sentimental by a fantastic liking for an artificial child-hood'.[31] Similar narratives of childhood might be read today. Recently, in a hospital's mammography X-ray room, I found, as elements of the interior decorating, a teddy bear in a flowered lace-decked dress, a plaque with religious sentiment on the wall and a vase of flowers. These items may be read as symbols of a childhood, faith, and nature which are seen as appropriate to warding off, for the adult, fears of the unknown, or of an invasive and threatening 'science' or 'technology'.

As Stevenson, and many other children's literature critics, explains, canonical status in children's literature differs strikingly from other forms of literature since, for the most part, books are not selected by children (and are never produced by them), but are selected for them by adults: 'generally someone other than the buyer is the intended reader'.[32] At the same time, these books must be seen as having an awareness of children, at least as the adult understands children.

It may be assumed that adults would purchase books that they remembered and this would keep certain titles on children's reading lists.[33] Yet, basing an argument about the success of a work on adult attempts to recapture their own childhood is problematic. It is impossible to really come to grips with what a particular child might find in a particular text, even one that is remembered fondly. *The Water-Babies*, along with the *Dr Dolittle* books, was my father's childhood favorite. During his childhood, I suspect these books evoked pleasant summertime memories of exploring the woods outside his grandparents' farm at a time when he was sick, confined inside with scarlet fever, and his window showed only the drab dirty world of an industrialized city, which, on consideration, might well evoke an experience not much different from the experiences of many Victorian-era children. And while I can imaginatively evoke his childhood, I do not really know why this work became a favorite for him or for anyone else. Any generalizations would be merely guesses. The problem with adult attempts to recapture their own childhood is apparent in the confessions of adult re-readers that their memories of the book do not agree with what they thought they would find in *Water-Babies*. For example, Gillian Beer, upon re-reading the book, suddenly realizes that the main character drowned. She muses that 'it was not until I read the book as an adult that I recognised that'.[34] For Julian Huxley, grandson of T.H. Huxley, *Water-Babies* was important because there was a picture of his grandfather in it. He writes, 'when I was nearly five, I read Kingsley's *The Water Babies* and was much intrigued by the picture in the book representing my grandfather and Professor Owen examining a bottled water-baby with magnifying glasses'. Julian Huxley saved the letter he wrote to his grandfather, asking, 'Have you seen a water-baby? Did you put it in a bottle? Did it wonder if it could get out? Can I see it some day?'[35] How much was actually read at age five is difficult to ascertain; however, Julian Huxley did later refer to *Water-Babies*, apparently having read it again later on.

Apparently, the scientific Huxley family chose *Water-Babies* as an appropriate text to present to their son. Certainly, T.H. Huxley's answer (dated 24 March 1892) suggests that the work was valued at least partly because of the author:

> I never could make sure about that Water Baby. I have seen babies in water and babies in bottles, but the baby in the water was in a bottle and the baby in the bottle was not in water. My friend who wrote the story of the Water Baby was a very kind man and very clever. Perhaps he thought I could see as much in the water as he did – There are some people who see a great deal and some who see very little in the same things.[36]

Kingsley was remembered fondly by T.H. Huxley because he went out of his way to send his sympathies when Huxley's four-year-old son died in 1860 and this led to a correspondence between the minister and scientist over religious concerns.[37]

In order to try to recapture the interest *Water-Babies* evoked in its original audience, it is helpful to consider its role in the cultural understanding and social integration of evolutionary concepts during the late nineteenth century. In the history of ideas, three authors are often noted as initiating the modern era: Marx, Freud, and Darwin. In the case of Charles Darwin, however, there is a curious disconnection between the ideas advanced in *Origin of Species* and how those ideas were perceived and used in the general public. As Robert M. Young notes, 'It is very difficult indeed to assess what it was about the Darwinian theory which was so influential and how its influence was felt'.[38] I argue here that the difference between how natural selection is defined in *Origin* and how it was quickly perceived by the Victorian public is the result of two books that were both published in 1863, four years after *Origin*: T.H. Huxley's *Man's Place in Nature* (Jan. 1863) and Charles Kingsley's *Water-Babies* (Aug. 1862–March 1863). While Arthur Johnston concludes his fine article on Kingsley's debt to Darwin with the statement, 'The metamorphosis of Tom [the hero of the novel] into a water-baby is not more wonderful than the metamorphosis of the *Origin of Species* into *The Water Babies*',[39] I am not too sure about the direction of the transformation. *Water-Babies* appears to have had a transforming effect on the reception of *Origin of Species*. Bearing in mind that assumptions of clear distinctions between the 'scientific' and the 'non scientific' were simply not there in 1863,[40] the moral and religious implications of new knowledge were debated by the entire reading public. The very word 'scientist' itself was not coined until the 1830s. The universities did not grant degrees in the subject and there were few professional societies. In fact, we can see in Huxley's *Man's Place in Nature*, a need to establish that very distinction, now, thanks to C.P. Snow, commonly referred to as 'the two cultures'.[41]

Therefore, as I have already argued above, the distinction between scientific and popular was not so clearly marked in the 1860s. While Kingsley was a minister and a novelist, he was also a naturalist and a member of the Geological Society.[42] He did not just observe the evolutionary debates from afar: he was an active participant in these debates and helped shape what would be the perception of evolution in the 1890s–1920s.

Modern scholars emphasize the religious life of Kingsley (1819–75) and some assume simply because he was an outspoken religious figure that he was a powerful force for conformity. Although Kingsley was Canon of Westminster (appointed 1873), a professor of modern history at Cambridge, and an individual who held high public and royal approval,[43] he was a controversial and complex character, a member of one of the most eccentric families of England. Kingsley early on took a militant response to those he disagreed with, arguing with Cardinal John Henry Newman,[44] and supporting social reform, while at the same time condemning the Chartist labor movement. Influenced by the writings of Frederick Maurice, he belonged to a group known as Christian Socialists, who believed in a socialist alternative to laissez-faire economics and a rejection of competition and individualism. It was not religion, but natural history and writing that was the unifying interest among the Kingsley family.

Kingsley's close attention to natural history was not unusual in the latter half of the nineteenth century. The study of natural history was closely associated with the Broad Church movement within the Church of England. Many ministers followed the call of William Paley's *Natural Theology* (1802) to find proof of the existence of God in the natural world, working under the assumption that observing the patterns and complexity of organic structure would lead to an understanding of God's mind.[45] This loosely affiliated group believed in a liberal, metaphorical understanding of scripture and, thus, was opposed by Evangelicals and Tractarians. So it was not surprising that Charles Kingsley was a member of several natural history societies and was particularly known for his studies of seashore and ocean life. His *Glaucus: or the Wonders of the Shore* was very popular at a time when it seemed the entire population of England was in love with tidepools. The association of religion with natural history study ironically made the discussion of evolution a major part of the general intellectual discussion of Victorian England: it was never isolated to a group of scientific societies. As John Burrow put it, 'Bughunting was the Trojan horse of Victorian agnosticism'.[46] It was only because ministers were heavily vested in the study of natural history that Britain in particular faced a spiritual crisis when confronted with natural selection. And because the Church of England was so engaged in the use of natural history as evidence for the existence of God, the intellectual community could not ignore the subject and they were challenged to find some way of communicating a sense of ethical and moral stability to the next generation.

At the time Kingsley was working on *Water-Babies*, there were well-publicized and closely followed conflicts between traditional anatomists such as Richard Owen, who insisted on the existence of clear delineatable physical distinctions between humans and primates, and T.H. Huxley (who nicknamed himself 'Darwin's Bulldog' as a declaration for his support of Darwin's work), who argued that humans were clearly primates.

The year 1863 produced several scientific additions and interpretations of Darwin's 1859 ideas. Janet Browne groups together three scientific works for that year which developed from, yet also diverged from, Darwin's original thesis, and changed the popular perception of evolution. Charles Lyell's *The Geological Evidences of the Antiquity of Man* provided the expression 'missing links' as Lyell pushed back human origin before the glacial period. Henry Walter Bates's travel narrative, *The Naturalist on the River Amazons* [sic], introduced evidence of natural selection at work in the form of insect mimicry and evolutionary diversification among butterflies. And then there was Huxley's *Man's Place in Nature*.[47] And to this list, we must add *Water-Babies*.

Gillian Beer points out that Kingsley and Huxley's works parallel each other. Both are concerned with human–primate connections and Huxley's discussion of the theme of 'man-apes' in legends closely fit in with Kingsley's 'Doasyoulikes'.[48] Huxley's book, *Man's Place in Nature*, made explicit the connection between primates and humans, a connection that Darwin only very discreetly implied in *Origin*. Huxley also showed the relationship between species as hierarchical, in direct opposition to Darwin's explanation. Darwin carefully avoided the teleology that marked such earlier evolutionary discussion, such as that of Lamarck and his own grandfather, Erasmus Darwin, producing a scheme that was completely based on contingency rather than a future goal.[49] His metaphorical discussion used a tree structure, and he focused on divergence as illustrated by the branches of the tree growing out from a trunk: ancestral forms formed the trunk for branching new species. Huxley, however, was seemingly wedded to a teleological understanding of the world. His 'question of questions for mankind' asks 'whence our race has come; what are the limits of our power over nature, and of nature's power over us; to what goal we are tending...'[50] His discussion arranged species along a ladder structure, not unlike the Renaissance Great Chain of Being, and he even spoke of 'lower races of mankind', giving the impression of evolutionary movement and progress toward some goal[51] – and this metaphorical discussion left the door open to a possible backward movement and degradation of a species.

Just how degraded humans could become is hinted at in Huxley's shocking incorporation of a 1598 imaginative engraving of a cannibal's butcher shop,[52] a scene that Huxley links to the African explorer Paul Du Chaillu's description of the Fan people of West Africa, whom Du Chaillu accused of cannibalism.[53] (We will soon see how the questions over Du Chaillu's honesty played a role in the evolutionary debates.) This engraving and discussion Huxley confesses 'is not strictly relevant to the matter in hand', but he could not refrain from mentioning it,[54] even though just the page before he dismissed Du Chaillu's authority with the enigmatic statement: 'It may be truth, but it is not evidence'.[55]

In some ways, Huxley was more attracted to the opportunity to oppose religious involvement in science than he was committed to Darwinian natural selection. While Darwin sought to explain his ideas to the greater reading community, Huxley felt that the scientific community was more likely to progress if it were separated from the general public discussion, and particularly if the religious community was no longer involved. Huxley delineated a difference between 'scientific' understanding and that of the general readership: in effect, Huxley segregated scientific writings to a professional sphere, setting up a division that broke the hereto understood fabric of common intellectual debates that can be seen as the hallmark of Victorian culture. Yet, paradoxically, his inability to move away from a teleological understanding of natural processes led to a version of natural selection that was more closely linked to Victorian ideas of progress, religion, and race, than to a scientific methodology.

While Huxley's work was distinctly aimed at an adult audience, Kingsley's novel is, as his subtitle indicates, 'A Fairy Tale for a Land-Baby', and, as discussed earlier, it was aimed toward a dual audience of adults and children, or of adults reading to children. There is a tendency to assume since Kingsley was a minister that Darwin triggered a religious crisis. Carpenter concludes his generally appreciative evaluation by describing *Water-Babies* as 'predominantly a work of destruction rather than construction, written at a time when its author's religious faith had nearly crumbled. One has a sense that in the book he was trying to remedy that loss of faith, was fumbling towards the creation of some kind of alternative religion, which was made up of things that really mattered to him'.[56] While such descriptions might apply to such authors as Philip Grosse,[57] a good friend with whom Kingsley argued, it does not match how Kingsley was viewed by his contemporaries. It is difficult to see, however, just how Kingsley's faith would have been undermined by evolutionary ideas. He was confident that eventually science would support religion. In an 1846 lecture, Kingsley expressed this view:

> I have watched scientific discoveries which were supposed in my boyhood to be contrary to revelation found out one by one to confirm and explain revelation, as crude and hasty theories were corrected by more abundant facts, and men saw more clearly what the Bible and Nature really did say; and I can trust that the same process will go on forever, and God's earth and God's word will never contradict each other.[58]

While rejecting scientific materialism, Kingsley presented in *Water-Babies* a welcoming response to evolution.[59] He did not see Darwin as being a threat to his faith. Darton similarly finds Kingsley difficult because, 'He simply could not write without a moral purpose' and the incorporation of his missions 'spoils much of his fiction'.[60] Such views reflect modern tastes and forget that adult Victorian readers considered the presence of a moral message a necessity.

Like many Victorian novels, Kingsley's work first appeared as a magazine series beginning in the August 1862 edition of *Macmillan's Magazine* and continued in each issue until the March 1863 issue. Two months later in May 1863, the work was published as a book.[61] The appearance of the Irishwoman (a disguised fairy) in the beginning, the section 'The Isle of Tomtoddies', and other alterations in the last chapter, were added in the book edition.[62]

Water-Babies begins with Tom's experiences as an apprentice to a chimney sweep, Grimes, and his limited urban world-view becomes apparent when he is taken into the country for a job at an estate. The rich detail of the natural world is immediately apparent, and Tom, the soon-to-be transformed chimney sweep, stares in wonderment when he is first introduced to the woods after knowing only the urban landscape. His lack of knowledge of nature, his inability even to identify bees,[63] is telling. His lack of religious education and his lack of cleanness are tied to his lack of exposure to nature: they are part and parcel of what Kingsley saw as the same moral absence. Tom is not the delicate misplaced higher-born child seen in *Oliver Twist*: he is sturdy and active. While capable of empathy, he is also equally capable of cruelty and misbehavior. He is mistreated, but he also enjoys life. He delights in mischief, throwing bricks and rocks as a game, but, on occasion, he does pause and consider the consequences of his actions. He is on the verge of transformation though and the question is in what direction he will evolve. When going to an estate to clean the chimneys, Tom wants to pick flowers and bathe,[64] suggesting that Tom has the potential for goodness; but his master scorns such behavior. The poor adult role model presented by Grimes, rather than Tom's physical mistreatment, attracts the most attention from Kingsley. A mysterious prophetic fairy (added by Kingsley to the beginning for the book edition) follows Tom and observes. She emphasizes a controlling nature, one which will correct such unnatural behavior as that of Tom's master, as she warns: 'Those that wish to be clean, clean they will be; and those that wish to be foul, foul they will be. Remember'.[65] Kingsley's fantasy evokes an overseeing intelligence in nature, one that responds to individual drives.

After falsely being accused of theft, Tom flees and then drowns in a river, and his soul is separated from his body, leaving him transformed into a tiny 'water-baby', a sort of a newt, who has adventures in the water, learning moral lessons in the process. The major lesson that he learns is a new morality, one inspired by *Origin of Species* – that his behavior as an individual can affect the direction of human evolution. Kingsley was quite familiar with Darwin's argument: as a public intellectual, he was sent a presentation copy of *Origin* by Darwin, which he responded to favorably and Kingsley became a major supporter of Darwin.[66] Darwin, in turn, looked to Kingsley with a certain amount of relief since Kingsley's approval indicated there was hope for religious acceptance. Kingsley was the first clergyman to see in Darwin's ideas 'an internal beauty that could be shared by science and spiritual revelation alike'.[67] At the time of publication, Kingsley was Canon of Westminster and he is the 'celebrated author and divine' cited by Darwin in his second edition of *Origin*, a mention that was retained in all later editions.[68] Having faced increasingly hostile responses to his ideas from the Church, Darwin was particularly concerned that opportunities for accommodation between religion and science be explored. He stated in *Origin* that 'I see no good reason why the views given in this volume should shock the religious feelings of any one'.[69] Then, as support for his claim that natural selection and religion were not at odds, Darwin quotes from a letter from Kingsley where Kingsley writes that he has 'gradually learnt to see that it is just as noble a conception of the Deity to believe that He created a few original forms capable of self-development into other and needful forms, as to believe that He required a fresh act of creation to supply the voids caused by the action of His laws'.[70]

While Darwin had not wanted to include the idea of a creator in his argument, he modified his later editions as a compromise in the face of heated religious oppositions. Following the line of argument that Kingsley offered,

Darwin added a couple of changes to the second edition. In the first edition, he wrote of life being breathed into some original primordial forms; this was altered so there was mention of 'the breath of the Creator'.[71] Additionally, he included one more epigraph to the front of the book, an extract from Joseph Butler's *Analogy of Revealed Religion*, that associated the word 'natural' with the presence of a creator.[72] While he later regretted his changes, they stayed as Darwin hoped that other theologians, like Kingsley, would find in them the opportunity to accept evolutionary ideas. Yet, Darwin strongly resisted the idea of a directed process as being responsible for human intellectual development. In a letter of 1859 Charles Lyell asked Darwin, 'Must you not assume a primeval creative power which does not act with uniformity, or how could man supervene?' Darwin repeated the question in his answer and then replied:

> We must, under present knowledge, assume the creation of one or a few forms in the same manner as philosophers assume the existence of a power of attraction without any explanation. But I entirely reject, as in my judgment quite unnecessary any subsequent addition 'of new powers and attributes and forces'; or of any 'principle of improvement,' except in so far as every character which is naturally selected or preserved is in some way an advantage or improvement, other wise it would not have been selected. If I were convinced that I required such additions to the theory of natural selection, I would reject it as rubbish, but I have firm faith in it, as I cannot believe, that if false it would explain so many whole classes of facts, which, if I am in my senses, it seems to explain.[73]

Darwin, however, was fighting against a very strong social desire to see future movement toward improvement as the driving force of evolution, and Kingsley was both a supporter and a re-interpreter of Darwin's ideas.

Shortly after responding to Darwin and accepting evolutionary ideas (or at least his interpretation of them), Kingsley became closely associated with the famous 'hippocampus minor' debate as scientists argued whether there was an anatomical difference in the brain that clearly separated humans from other primates. The question of the relationship between humans and primates quickly became a major topic in the press as various types of apes came to symbolize everything that made people uneasy about evolution, producing a complex nexus of theology, questions over human connection with the divine, morality, class distinction, racism, basic species ethnocentrism, and straightforward sensationalism.[74] In *Water-Babies*, Kingsley took the opportunity to satirize several prominent scientists, particularly Richard Owen and Huxley, using the debate to poke fun at scientific positivism, but also to drive home his point that degradation was both possible and a moral danger.

To add fuel to the debate between Owen and Huxley, the African explorer Du Chaillu brought to the lecture circuit gorilla specimens and his well-embellished, colorful and largely fictionalized tales of horrific gorilla attacks; these he placed at the service of Owen, who arranged for a presentation at the Royal Geographical Society meeting on 25 February 1861. This well attended show was followed by Du Chaillu's *Explorations and Adventures* published later that spring. *Punch* had a field day, publishing a satiric verse (by Sir Phillip Egerton, a Tory MP) in their May 1861 issue that featured a gorilla asking 'Am I a Man and a Brother?'[75] *Blackwood's Magazine* followed, to the tune of 'He's a Jolly Good Fellow', with 'Pouters, tumblers, and fantails are from the same source;/The racer and hack may be traced to one horse:/ So Men were developed from Monkeys, of course,/ Which nobody can deny./ Which nobody can deny...'[76] So great was public attention that *Punch* dedicated its 1861 Christmas Annual to the gorilla theme.[77]

Owen described Du Chaillu's specimens in lecture and print claiming that part of the brain, the 'hippocampus minor', was only found in humans and marked a distinct difference between humans and apes, responsible for major differences in behavior and anatomy. Huxley and Owen then carried out an increasingly personal debate in the letter columns of the *Athenaeum* and the *Annals and Magazine of Natural History*.[78] Public opinion quickly shifted to Huxley's side after Du Chaillu's book was published, when John Edward Gray of the British Museum accused Du Chaillu of lying and revealed, through analysis of the donated gorilla skin from the animal Du Chaillu had shot, that the animal was shot in the back and had not been the aggressive creature that was suggested by Du Chaillu in his illustrations.

Kingsley followed every movement of the furor with much interest. At the 1862 British Association for the Advancement of Science meeting Owen presented two anti-Darwinian papers that were effectively dealt with by Huxley's friends. Kingsley gleefully produced a privately printed skit poking fun at the anti-Darwinians and then incorporated this scientific brouhaha into *Water-Babies*, having, as Browne puts it, 'the last word'.[79] Making reference to 'hippopotamus majors,' Kingsley's narrator declares, via a *reductio ad absurdum* argument, that 'You may think that there are other more important differences between you and ape, such as being able to speak, and make machines, and know right from wrong, and say your prayers, and other little matters of that kind: but that is a child's fancy, my dear'.[80] Rather, speaking mock-seriously, the narrator continues to his assumed child audience:

> Nothing is to be depended on but the great hippopotamus test. If you have a hippopotamus major in your brain, you are no ape, though you had four hands, no feet, and were more apish than the apes of all aperies. But, if a hippopotamus major is ever discovered in one single ape's brain, nothing will save your great-great-great-great-great-great-great-great-great-great-great-greater-greatest-grandmother from having been an ape too. No, my dear little man; always remember that the one true, certain, final, and all-important difference between you and an ape is, that you

have a hippopotamus major in your brain, and it has none; and that, therefore, to discover one in its brain will be a very wrong and dangerous thing, at which every one will be very much shocked, as we may suppose they were at the professor. – Though really, after all it don't much matter ... nobody but men have hippopotamuses in their brains; so, if a hippopotamus was discovered in an ape's brain, why it would not be one, you know, but something else.[81]

This delight with Owen's grasping at straws in order to attack Darwinian views followed a similar discussion over the question of materialistic evidence as Kingsley raises the question of the existence of a water-baby, or a soul: the dialogue follows on the limits of scientific inquiry as Kingsley's narrator declares: '... no one has a right to say that no water-babies exist, till they have seen no water-babies existing; which is quite a different thing, mind, from not seeing water-babies; and a thing which nobody ever did, or perhaps ever will do.'[82]

In reply to the question of 'How do you know that somebody has not?' the narrator continues to argue that if someone had, 'they [naturalists] would have put it into spirits, or into the *Illustrated News*, or perhaps cut it into two halves, poor dear little thing, and sent one to Professor Owen, and one to Professor Huxley, to see what they would each say about it'.[83] Anticipating a challenge that water-babies were against nature, the narrator continues with a tongue-in-cheek lesson that mentions several of the major scientists of the time:

You must not say that this cannot be, or that that is contrary to nature. You do not know what nature is, or what she can do; and nobody knows; not even Sir Roderick Murchison, or Professor Owen, or Professor Sedgwick, or Professor Huxley, or Mr Darwin, or Professor Faraday, or Mr Grove, or any other of the great men whom good boys are taught to respect. They are very wise men; and you must listen respectfully to all they say: but even if they should say, which I am sure they never would, 'That cannot exist. That is contrary to nature,' you must wait a little, and see; for perhaps even they may be wrong.[84]

And throughout the story, there are peppered references to Du Chaillu,[85] pterodactyls and other topical scientific news. A giant naturalist who 'had a heart, though it was considerably overgrown with brains', seemingly an agglomerate of naturalists, debates with Tom as he collects specimens obsessively.[86] The basic message seems to be not that scientists are foolish, but that there is both wisdom and foolishness in science and that the reader should not see science as the source for all information. In a time when the scientific community and the religious establishment were both profiling themselves as sources of authoritative pronouncements, this message may have provided parents with a much needed way of explaining religious and scientific conflicts.

Although there are several references to Victorian Darwinian debates, the more important connection with science lies in the teleology that Kingsley advances, first in the natural observations that he presents, and then in the form of an allegorical fable with the moral fairy Mrs Bedonebyasyoudid who tells the history of Doasyoulikes.[87] This story is based on a form that Diane Purkiss finds first used by Catherine Sinclair in her *Holiday House* (1839).[88] *Holiday House* is unusual, according to Purkiss, in that the text presents children's disobedience as entertaining: the substitute parent, a doting uncle, delights in the children's pranks. The book was still being distributed to children in the 1860s. Carpenter observes that '*Holiday House* was presented by Lewis Carroll to the Liddell children in 1861, before he entertained them with *Alice's Adventures*, suggesting some possible subtle inspiration there.'[89]

In the case of *Water-Babies*, the influence is more direct. In *Holiday House* a rather tongue-in-cheek moral story entitled 'Uncle David's Nonsensical Story About Giants and Fairies' is told to the children by their uncle. The story concerns an idle glutton child named Master No-book, 'a very idle greedy, naughty boy', who is visited by two fairies, Do-nothing and Teach-all. The child is asked to choose between a life of ease in Castle Needless or a life of purpose in the Palace of Knowledge. The child chooses a life of amusement and gluttony with the fairy Do-Nothing, only to find he has been moved lower down the food chain and is being fattened up for consumption by a local giant, Snap-'em-up, who bears some resemblance to the traditional British giant in 'Jack and the Beanstalk'. The fairy Do-nothing allowed him to help himself to children and was, in turn, invited to dine with him. Master No-book is then hung high on a hook facing a horrific image of butchered children (suggestive of Huxley's butcher shop). From this position, Master No-book observes the life of children at Teach-all's and their ability to fight off the giant. Teach-all kills the giant and rescues the boy and gives him a good lecture on 'activity, moderation, and good conduct'.[90] Sloth and cannibalism, as a symbol of degradation, are thus linked.

In Kingsley's tale, the punishment for self-gratification and laziness is not to be eaten but to face de-evolution. Kingsley's narrator anticipates that there would be questions raised about the possibility of degradation and he responds rhetorically to 'Cousin Cramchild' (possibly a reference to Dickens's Gradgrind of *Hard Times*), who represents the new trend in positivist educational reform, and considers the claim 'that things cannot degrade'.[91] In response the narrator points to the change in the free-swimming larval and stationary adult form of goose-barnacles and 'the still stranger degradation of some cousins of theirs, of which one hardly likes to talk, so shocking and ugly it is'.[92]

Brian Alderson footnotes this last comment in his edition and identifies it as a reference to Darwin's eight years of extensive work on barnacles. He thinks Kingsley is referring to a crustacean larva that became parasitic, losing all functioning parts except the reproductive organs,[93] but while I agree that this is a reference to Darwin's barnacle studies done before he wrote *Origin*, I suspect the 'shocking and ugly' response refers to Darwin's discovery that in the genera *Ibla* and *Scalpellum*, the male is parasitic on the female and lives under the female's carapace. As Darwin reported to his friend Henslow in a letter, the 'odd fact' is that 'the male, or sometimes two males, at the instant they cease being locomotive larvae become parasitic in the sack of the female, & thus fixed & half embedded in the flesh of their wives they pass their whole lives & can never move again'.[94] Thus, Kingsley is making a knowing comment on the unmentionable sexual reduction of the male barnacle. Degradation can be worse than becoming parasitic: it could lead to becoming but an appendage of one's mate.

The issue of degradation, of de-evolution, is quickly foreshadowed in *Water-Babies* when Tom sees himself for the first time in a mirror after working in the chimneys and sees 'a little black ape'.[95] When he flees the false accusation of theft, he heads for the forest barefooted, 'like a small black gorilla'. This indicates his intermediate position before he dies and becomes a water-baby. The theme of species degradation arises again when Tom moves from his stream, where he played with caddises and trout, into the ocean where he encounters a pair of salmon. The salmon regard the trout with disgust as degraded relations who were too lazy to move beyond their streams. The male aristocratic salmon explains,

> ...I am sorry to say they [the trout] are relations of ours who do us no credit. A great many years ago they were just like us: but they were so lazy, and cowardly, and greedy, that instead of going down to the sea every year to see the world and grow strong and fat, they chose to stay and poke about in the little streams and eat worms and grubs: and they are very properly punished for it; for they have grown ugly and brown and spotted and small; and are actually so degraded in their tastes, that they will eat our children.[96]

The message of the salmon is that staying too close to home cannot only change the physical appearance of a species, but create cannibals. The barnacles indicate that one should keep moving or be trapped forever in a single spot, reduced to sperm production. Tom, as part of his moral education, must then venture out into the world and struggle so as to insure the progress of the species to higher spiritual levels.

This lesson is further developed, as Tom, along with other water-babies, is instructed by Mrs Bedonebyasyoudid, who shows them a book that begins with the description of a land where no work was required, called 'Readymade'. Each page she turns moves the story ahead 500 years, showing natural selection in process. The next page shows the explosion of a volcano that eliminates two-thirds of the population. As the food becomes limited, and the population is preyed on, the people move to the trees and 'only the strongest and most active ones who could climb the trees, and so escape'.[97] The population grows in strength through sexual selection since 'the ladies will not marry any but the very strongest and fiercest gentlemen, who can help them up the trees' out of harm's way.[98] Another page and 500 years pass as the population grows strong but smaller; the feet change to allow the grasping of tree limbs. When the children ask if the fairy is responsible for the change, she replies: 'Yes, and no. ... It was only those who could use their feet as well as their hands who could get a good living: or, indeed, get married; so that they got the best of everything, and starved out all the rest; and those who are left keep up a regular breed of toe-thumb-men, as a breed of shorthorns, or skye-terriers, or fancy pigeons is kept up'.[99] The reference to domestic breeds is a restatement of Darwin's analogy between natural and artificial selection, the basis of his argument that selection can make major modifications in a species.

A 'hairy one' is then noticed in the historical progression whom the fairy predicts will be 'a great man in his time, and chief of all the tribe' as he had more hairy children, who had 'hairier children still'.[100] As the climate grew colder, all the other children died of consumption (tuberculosis). The next 500 years show altered curved backs and Tom declares, 'they are all apes'. The fairy explains that

> They are grown so stupid now, that they can hardly think: for none of them have used their wits for many hundred years. They have almost forgotten, too, how to talk. For each stupid child forgot some of the words it heard from its stupid parents, and had not wits enough to make fresh words for itself. Besides, they are grown so fierce and suspicious and brutal that they keep out of each other's way, and mope and sulk in the dark forests, never hearing each other's voice, till they have forgotten almost what speech is like. I am afraid they will all be apes very soon, and all by doing only what they liked.[101]

The phrase 'by doing only what they liked' signals the moral that each individual's effort can overtime move evolutionary change in a particular direction, and it is possible to go backwards: two concepts that are in opposition to Darwinian natural selection but which became incorporated into popular notions of evolution.

The final page shows only one survivor who is shot by Du Chaillu while trying to say, 'Am I not a man and a brother?' – much like the previously mentioned *Punch* cartoon. The description of the survivor 'roaring and thumping his breast' fits Du Chaillu's description of the gorilla he shot. The phrase 'Am I not a man and a brother?' is from a well-known Wedgewood anti-slavery medallion; the phrase was adopted by the London Anti-slavery

Society.[102] After the story, the child audience is as quiet as Sinclair's, but in addition to absorbing the message that work is good, they also make the connection between primates and humans as Kingsley sarcastically notes: they 'really fancied that the men were apes, and never thought, in their simplicity, of asking whether the creatures had hippopotamus majors in their brains or not....'[103] The fairy concludes:

> Folks say now that I can make beasts into men, by circumstance, and selection, and competition, and so forth. Well, perhaps they are right; and perhaps, again, they are wrong....But let them recollect this, that there are two sides to every question, and a down hill as well as an uphill road; and, if I can turn beasts into men, I can, by the same laws of circumstance, and selection, and competition, turn men into beasts.[104]

The potential for transformation thus gripped the Victorian imagination. While Darwin pointed to changes in domestic breeds of animals as the result of farmyard and breeders' selection, Huxley and Kingsley leaped to insect metamorphosis as a major metaphor for evolution as a process. In *Man's Place in Nature*, Huxley writes:

> In a well-worn metaphor, a parallel is drawn between the life of man and the metamorphosis of the caterpillar into the butterfly; but the comparison may be more[,] just as well as more novel, if for its former term we take the mental progress of the race. History shows that the human mind, fed by constant accessions of knowledge, periodically grows too large for its theoretical coverings, and bursts them asunder to appear in new habiliments, as the feeding and growing grub, at intervals, casts its too narrow skin and assumes another, itself but temporary. Truly the imago state of Man seems to be terribly distant, but every moult is a step gained, and of such there have been many.[105]

This optimism about human progress is continually built upon as Huxley declares, 'thoughtful men, once escaped from the blinding influences of traditional prejudice, will find in the lowly stock whence man has sprung, the best evidence of the splendour of his capacities; and will discern in his long progress though the Past, a reasonable ground of faith in his attainment of nobler Future'.[106] It is in a new science though, not religion or 'traditional prejudice', that Huxley finds his faith; but it is still a kind of faith.

Kingsley, more imaginatively, chose his aquatic locale because it gave the author of books on tidepool life the opportunity to have Tom watch the change of a caddis and a dragon fly who wants to break out of its exoskeleton: 'I am sure I shall split. I will split!'[107] This insect then was transformed from 'a very ugly dirty creature' with 'six legs, and a big stomach, and a most ridiculous head with two great eyes and a face just like a donkey's'[108] to a creature with 'the most lovely colours…blue and yellow and black, spots and bars and rings [and] out of its back rose four great wings of bright brown gauze; and its eyes grew so large that they filled all its head, and shone like ten thousand diamonds'.[109] While not everyone is as likely to see dragon flies as pretty as butterflies, under Kingsley's treatment we view the creature again and Tom's viewpoint allows Kingsley to transmit his sense of wonder.

I have argued, then, that the Victorian response indicates that the book was taken more seriously than one would expect today where the divisions between popular and research scientific works are more pronounced. *Water-Babies* was the only novel to have been reviewed in the *Anthropological Review*, the official journal of the Anthropological Society, and its reviewer, while acknowledging its 'flashes of wit and humour' also noted that the novel marked 'the period of an epoch in our biological literature' and that it required a 'competent knowledge of biological controversy'.[110] *The Times* also noted the connection with *Origin*: 'Tom's education would have been impossible had not Mr Darwin published his book on the *Origin of Species*.' And, as noted earlier, *the Spectator* gave a clear indication of the value of *Water-Babies*:

> The purpose of this tale, – and it was a fine one – seems to have been to adapt Mr Darwin's theory of the natural selection of species to the understanding of children, by giving it an individual, moral and religious as well as a mere specific and scientific application. He took the watery world, principally because he knows it so well, and because the number of transformations which go on in it are so large and so easily capable of a semi-moral significance, that it served best to illustrate his purpose. For example the specific difference between salmon and trout, Mr Kingsley interprets as a difference between enterprise and industry on the one hand, and stupid greediness on the other; wherever moral qualities, or the germs of moral qualities, begin, there, at least, is a turning point of natural development or degradation in the individual, and thence also in the species.[111]

The idea of a directed evolution was far from Darwin's purpose and his theory of natural selection did not allow for a reversal of evolution, yet many of Darwin's contemporaries tried to 'compromise by swallowing evolution but rejecting natural selection'.[112]

By 1869, early anthropology texts were focusing on the possibility of human degradation. In particular, the Duke of Argyll, in his book, *Primeval Man* (1869), insisted that humans had degenerated from an earlier more perfect non-primate form; he preferred that rather than accepting a kinship with animals.[113] His major argument was that humans could not compete with apes, therefore they could not have evolved from primates: 'Place a naked high-ranking elder of the British Association in the presence of one of M. du Chaillu's gorillas, and behold how short and sharp will be the struggle'.[114] For Kingsley and Huxley though, the primate connection was not problematic. Both saw it as a promise of future greatness, a reason for optimism and also a reason for worry if human sloth was not sufficiently contained. Their major area of division was the role traditional religious practices played in the transformation of post-Darwin culture. But as Huxley led an atheistic material movement, Kingsley allowed his reading public to have it both ways and maintain a sense of divinely led morality while still accepting evolution.

While both Huxley and Kingsley, then, saw potential greatness for the future and were optimistic about the possibility of the human somehow becoming better, the future history of these ideas is linked with disastrous attempts at social engineering. Eventually, fears of species degradation would, with the popularity of eugenics, become a fear of racial degradation, and there was a cultural panic at the turn of the century as a range of social changes, including mixed racial marriages and women's education, were seen as signs of future degradation, a degradation that would undermine British manhood and produce effeminate men and Amazonian women. This has often been seen as the dark side of Darwinian evolution, but it is really the dark side of Huxley and Kingsley's interpretation. It is far too easy to see the racial symbolism in Tom's soot and see a justification for British imperialism in the association of manhood with leaving home. The repeated focus on skin color can be read as presenting distasteful racial overtones, facilitating as association of colonized people with apes.

Huxley was successful in separating scientific study from natural theology and such minister naturalists as Kingsley, and establishing a group of professional specialists. But in doing so, he also established the dangerous belief that the practice of science is not affected by its social context, but a practice that leads to a higher truth. The result of such a view may be that too often social assumptions are not examined so long as the label 'scientific' is used and texts outside the professional sphere are not viewed as having a bearing on scientific thought. We may be said to be coming to terms with how these assumptions affect the field of science. By the end of the century, science was seen as approving of colonialism because non-English peoples were perceived as less evolved and needing to be governed. Similar non-Darwinian interpretations of evolution led to restrictive immigration practices in the United States that blocked entrance to any group seen as a threat to the dominance of the northern European population base. To understand how such ideas became formulated, we need to go back and investigate works outside the standard histories of science and see how they shaped the popular understanding of scientific research and human potential.

Recommended further reading

Allen, David, *The Naturalist in Britain*, 2nd edn (Princeton: Princeton University Press, 1995).

Altick, Richard, *The English Common Reader: A Social History of the Mass Reading Public,*
   1800–1900 (Chicago: University of Chicago Press, 1957).
Barber, Lynn, *The Heyday of Natural History: 1820–1870* (Garden City, NY: Doubleday,
   1980).
Beer, Gillian, *Open Fields: Science in Cultural Encounter* (Oxford: Clarendon Press, 1996).
Chapple, J.A.V. *Science and Literature in the Nineteenth Century* (Basingstoke: Macmillan –
   now Palgrave Macmillan, 1986).
Darwin, Charles, *Darwin: A Norton Critical Edition,* ed. Philip Appleman, 2nd edn (New
   York: Norton, 1979; orig. pub. 1859).
Gillespie, Neal C. *Charles Darwin and the Problem of Creation* (Chicago: University of
   Chicago Press, 1979).
Gould, Stephen Jay, *Ever Since Darwin* (New York: Norton, 1977).
Keynes, Randal, *Darwin, His Daughter, and Human Evolution* (New York: Riverhead,
   2002).
Morton, Peter, *The Vital Science: Biology and the Literary Imagination, 1860–1900*
   (London: George Allen and Unwin, 1984).
Uffelman, Larry K. *Charles Kingsley* (Boston: Twayne, 1979).

Notes

1. Yet, at the same time, it did survive longer than other similarly popular and topical Victorian novels; certainly it continued to sell for some time after Kingsley's other works.
2. Walt Disney and Georgiana Browne, *The Water Babies* (Boston: Heath, 1940).
3. Susan Chitty, *The Beast and the Monk: A Life of Charles Kingsley,* p. 216.
4. Chitty, p. 216.
5. Chitty, p. 222.
6. Lynn L. Merrill, *The Romance of Victorian Natural History* (New York: Oxford University Press, 1989), p. 221. The Puffin edition, for example, is abridged.
7. F.J. Harvey Darton, *Children's Books in England: Five Centuries of Social Life,* 3rd edn (Cambridge: Cambridge University Press, 1982), p. 252.
8. Deborah Stevenson, 'Sentiment and Significance: The Impossibility of Recovery in the Children's Literature Canon or, The Drowning of *The Water-Babies*', *The Lion and the Unicorn,* 21(1) (1997): 112–30.
9. Colin Manlove treats the tale as a significant Christian fantasy, making no mention of a child audience. Similarly, George MacDonald and C.S. Lewis's works are not labeled as children's literature but are seen as a continuum of the Christian fantasy in Dante, Spenser and Milton. (See Colin Manlove, *Christian Fantasy: From 1200 to the Present* (Basingstoke: Macmillan – now Palgrave Macmillan, 1992), pp. 183–208.)
10. Frances E. Kingsley, ed., *Charles Kingsley: His Letters and Memories of His Life* (London: Macmillan, 1890), p. 245.
11. Edward Salmon, *Juvenile Literature As It Is* (London: Henry J. Drane, 1888), pp. 169–70. Salmon attempted to determine 'What do children read?' and 'What is written for them' (p. 12) based on a survey that was sent out to school children aged 11–19. In this survey of adolescent reading, Kingsley was ranked 11th by 28 boys out of 790, coming under Lytton, but the favorite book title was *Westward Ho!* (ranking 12th). About a thousand girls responded and listed Kingsley as their third favorite (p. 103) with Dickens and Sir Walter Scott coming in as first and second. *Westward Ho!* was the top favorite (p. 34) and *Hypatia* (p. 5) was ranked at 38th (pp. 21–2).

12. *Water-Babies* continually has been noted as marking a change in the development of books for children, but after that observation critics usually pass onto later works.
13. 'Belles Lettres', *The Westminster Review*, 24 (July and October 1863), 307.
14. Salmon, p. 170.
15. 'Belles Lettres', 307.
16. In the past 20 years, there has been a call to reassess the reputations of many writers of nineteenth-century popular science and increased recognition has been given to several writers, many of them women, who contributed to the larger body of scientific activities. See Barbara T. Gates, *Kindred Nature: Victorian and Edwardian Women Embrace the Living World* (Chicago: University of Chicago Press, 1997); Barbara T. Gates and Ann B. Shteir, eds, *Natural Eloquence: Women Reinscribe Science* (Madison: University of Wisconsin Press, 1997); Lynn L. Merrill, *The Romance of Victorian Natural History* (New York: Oxford University Press, 1989); Bernard Lightman, ed., *Victorian Science in Context* (Chicago: University of Chicago Press, 1997).
17. Alan Rauch, *Useful Knowledge: The Victorians, Morality, and the March of Intellect* (Durham: Duke University Press, 2001), p. 11.
18. Quoted in Arthur Johnston, '*The Water Babies*: Kingsley's Debt to Darwin', *English*, 12 (1959): 215–19, 217.
19. Alan Rauch, 'A World of Faith on a Foundation of Science: Science and Religion in British Children's Literature: 1761–1878', *Children's Literature Association Quarterly*, 14(1) (1989): 13–19, 14.
20. Rauch, 'A World', 17.
21. Elizabeth Eastlake, 'Review of Gallaudet's *Child's Book on the Soul* and Other Books', *Quarterly Review*, 71 (1842–43): 54–83, 71; quoted in Rauch, 'A World', 17.
22. See Gillian Beer, *Darwin's Plots: Evolutionary Narrative in Darwin, George Eliot and Nineteenth-Century Fiction* (London: Routledge, 1983), pp. 129–39; Arthur Johnston, '*The Water Babies*: Kingsley's Debt to Darwin', *English*, 12 (1959), 215–19; Robert M. Young, *Darwin's Metaphor: Nature's Place in Victorian Culture* (Cambridge: Cambridge University Press, 1985), p. 106; James G. Paradis, 'Satire and Science in Victorian Culture', in *Victorian Science in Context* (Chicago: University of Chicago Press, 1997), pp. 162–3.
23. Humphrey Carpenter, *Secret Gardens: A Study of the Golden Age of Children's Literature* (Boston: Houghton, 1985), p. 36.
24. Chitty, p. 220.
25. Chitty refers to Maureen Duffy's *The Erotic World of Faery* (London: Hodder and Stoughton, 1972), which reads Tom entrance into the water as a transformation into 'the questing penis' and argues the story warns about masturbation (see Chitty, p. 220).
26. Carpenter, p. 37.
27. Carpenter, p. 37. Chitty's biography reproduces a drawing by Kingsley showing him with his wife entwined together on a cross. This was found with his papers. Frances Kingsley saved many of Kingsley's papers and did not destroy material as much as was typical among Victorians. Many felt it was best to destroy potentially embarrassing material after someone's death.
28. Alan Rauch, *Useful Knowledge: The Victorians, Morality, and the March of Intellect*, p. 165.
29. Rauch, *Useful*, p. 176.
30. Quoted in Rauch, *Useful*, p. 168.
31. Review of *Water-Babies*, *The Saturday Review*, 23 May 1863, 665–6.

32. Stevenson, p. 117.
33. This is essentially Carpenter's argument.
34. Beer, p. 135.
35. Julian Huxley, *Memories* (New York: Harper, 1970), pp. 22–6. Julian Huxley's letter and T.H. Huxley's reply are reproduced in this autobiography.
36. Julian Huxley, pp. 24–5.
37. One of the great attractions of studying Victorian culture is the close relationships formed between many writers as families often intermarried and socialized together. There is a discussion of this exchange in William Irvine's 'Carlyle and T.H. Huxley', in *Victorian Literature: Modern Essays in Criticism*, ed. by Austin Wright (London: Oxford University Press, 1968), pp. 193–207.
38. Robert M. Young, *Darwin's Metaphor: Nature's Place in Victorian Culture*, p. 79.
39. Arthur Johnston, '*The Water Babies*: Kingsley's Debt to Darwin', 215–19, 219.
40. Alan Rauch, in *Useful Knowledge: the Victorians, Morality and the March of Intellect*, investigates the accumulation of knowledge and how Victorian culture saw it as a 'morally responsible activity' (p. 2), an assumption that was challenged when there was a general realization that knowledge was not neutral and that it was related to the questioning of religious, social and political structures. In response, efforts were made to 'reinforce the status of knowledge and to sustain its moral force' (p. 3).
41. From Snow's 1959 Rede Lecture, 'The Two Cultures and the Scientific Revolution'.
42. He was elected to Fellowship in 1863, the same year as the publication of *Water-Babies*. He was proposed by Charles Bunbury and was seconded by Charles Lyell. See Frances Kingsley, p. 249.
43. He was appointed Chaplain-in-Ordinary to Queen Victoria in 1859, the year *Origin of Species* was published.
44. Newman's 1864 *Apologia pro Vita Sua* was written in answer to Kingsley when he questioned 'whether the Roman Catholic priesthood are encouraged or discouraged to pursue "Truth for its own sake" ' in *Macmillan's Magazine*. See Frances Kingsley, *Charles Kingsley*, p. 258.
45. For a discussion of Paley and natural theology, see Stephen Jay Gould's 'Darwin and Paley Meet the Invisible Hand' in *Eight Little Piggies: Reflections in Natural History* (New York: Norton, 1993), pp. 138–52.
46. John Burrow, Introduction, *The Origin of Species* by Charles Darwin (London: Penguin, 1985), pp. 11–48, p. 19.
47. Browne, *Power*, pp. 217–26.
48. Beer, pp. 138–9.
49. Browne, *Power*, p. 61.
50. T.H. Huxley, *Man's Place in Nature* (Ann Arbor: University of Michigan Press, 1961, orig. pub. 1863), p. 71.
51. The argument that the linkages required in evolutionary theory makes the development of humans improbable is commonly used to argue for the existence of divine intent. Stephen Jay Gould addresses the history of this reasoning in his article, 'In a Jumbled Drawer', in *Bully for Brontosaurus* (New York: Norton, 1991), pp. 309–24.
52. T.H. Huxley, p. 69.
53. Interestingly, this appears to be the tribal group Kingsley's niece, Mary Kingsley, traveled with in her *Travels in West Africa* (1859). There is a rich body of criticism on the theme of cannibalism in literature. See the collection *Eating Their Words: Cannibalism and the Boundaries of Cultural Identity*, edited by Kristen Guest (Albany, NY: State University of New York Press, 2001).
54. T.H. Huxley, p. 69.

55. T.H. Huxley, p. 68.
56. Carpenter, p. 41.
57. Philip Grosse's crisis of faith is famously described in a 1907 memoir, *Father and Son*, written by his son, Edmund Grosse (Harmondsworth: Penguin, 1982).
58. Charles Kingsley, 'How to Study Natural History (1846)', in *Scientific Lectures and Essays* (London: Macmillan, 1893), 289–310, 304; quoted. in Alan Rauch, 'A World', 7.
59. Although James G. Paradis acknowledges that Kingsley was 'clearly supportive of scientific progress associated with the work of Lyell, Darwin, Huxley and others', he focuses on Kingsley's satiric comments on scientific behavior that he regarded as rigid and doctrinaire (p. 162). See James G. Paradis, 'Satire and Science in Victorian Culture', in *Victorian Science in Context*, edited by Bernard Lightman (Chicago: University of Chicago Press, 1997), pp. 143–75. This might leave the impression that Kingsley was a critical outsider of the scientific debates, rather than an involved participant who supported Darwin and his allies.
60. Darton, p. 254.
61. Carpenter, p. 23.
62. See Alderson, p. xxi–xxv; Johnston, p. 216.
63. Kingsley, p. 13.
64. Kingsley, p. 10.
65. Kingsley, p. 12.
66. Browne, *Power*, p. 95.
67. Browne, *Power*, p. 95.
68. Browne, *Power*, p. 95.
69. Darwin, p. 124.
70. Quoted in Darwin, pp. 124–5.
71. Browne, *Power*, p. 95.
72. Browne, *Power*, p. 96.
73. Quoted in Young, p. 102.
74. Browne, *Power*, p. 156. Some illustrations of ape cartoons from this period are reproduced in Paradis's article, 'Satire and Science in Victorian Culture', pp. 143–78.
75. Browne, *Power*, pp. 157–8.
76. Quoted in Browne, *Power*, p. 158.
77. Browne, *Power*, p. 158.
78. Browne, *Power*, p. 159.
79. Browne, *Power*, p. 160.
80. Kingsley, p. 83.
81. Kingsley, p. 83.
82. Kingsley, p. 39.
83. Kingsley, p. 39. This part was illustrated with a picture of Huxley and Owen and this is the picture that Julian Huxley alluded to.
84. Kingsley, p. 40.
85. Kingsley, p. 41.
86. Kingsley, pp. 161–4. Brian Alderson's notes suggest this is a self-portrait of Kingsley, but Randal Keynes sees this reference as a portrait of Charles Darwin (p. 262); the beetle-catching mania reference (p. 163) certainly does evoke a mention of such obsessions in Darwin's autobiography.
87. Kingsley's history of Doasyoulikes was, in turn, as Paradis notes, a clear inspiration for the title of Matthew Arnold's second chapter of *Culture and Anarchy*: 'Doing as One Likes'. (See Paradis, p. 162.)

88. Diane Purkiss, *At the Bottom of the Garden: A Dark History of Fairies, Hobgoblins, and Other Troublesome Things* (New York: New York University Press, 2000), p. 223. Catherine Sinclair, *Holiday House* (New York: Garland, 1976, orig. pub. 1839).
89. Carpenter, p. 9.
90. Kingsley, p. 194.
91. Kingsley, p. 43.
92. Kingsley, p. 43. What is disturbing about the threat of de-evolution is that it means the sequence that leads to adulthood is altered. When children have the potential to undermine species evolution, they, thus, become disturbing to the adults.
93. Alderson, p. 210, note 43.
94. Quoted in Browne, *Voyaging*, p. 477.
95. Kingsley, p. 17.
96. Kingsley, pp. 68–9.
97. Kingsley, p. 128.
98. Kingsley, p. 128.
99. Kingsley, p. 129.
100. Kingsley, p. 129.
101. Kingsley, pp. 129–30.
102. Kingsley, note 219.
103. Kingsley, p. 130.
104. Kingsley, p. 131. Gillian Beer also quotes this passage in relationship to Darwinian ideas; see p. 130.
105. Huxley, p. 72.
106. Huxley, p. 131.
107. Kingsley, p. 53.
108. Kingsley, p. 52.
109. Kingsley, p. 53.
110. Quoted in Johnston, p. 217.
111. Quoted in Johnston, pp. 217–18.
112. Browne, *Power*, p. 308.
113. Browne, *Power*, p. 308.
114. Quoted in Browne, *Power*, p. 308.

7
The Child, The Family, The Relationship. Familiar Stories: Family, Storytelling, and Ideology in Philip Pullman's *His Dark Materials*

Stephen Thomson

Introduction: family and ideology

I want to examine the role of ideas of family and the familiar in structuring the ideology, or ideologies, of Philip Pullman's *His Dark Materials*. First, however, a brief survey of recent criticism of ideology, and the problems it encounters, will be helpful in framing my own enquiry. Over the past decade, children's literature criticism has started to respond to areas of literary theory that inquire into the ideologies of texts. Indeed, of all the 'theories' criticism has touched upon, it could be argued that this is one of the most fundamentally pertinent to the field of writing for children. In teaching children to read stories, according to one commonly-held view, it is of the highest importance to be ideologically aware, and to pass that ideological awareness on to the children. Broadly speaking, this is a position that has been taken by, among others, John Stephens, Peter Hollindale, and Roderick McGillis. Stephens, who offers the most thorough account of ideology within children's literature criticism, advocates inculcating 'reading strategies' that will help child readers to avoid being trapped into a single subject position. All narratives have ideology, so any text will require an awareness of it on the part of the reader.[1] Furthermore, Stephens agrees with Hollindale that children's literature criticism has conceived of ideology too much in terms of more or less conscious agendas, and that this limits its purchase on unexamined assumptions.[2] Aidan Chambers's notion of texts leading children to question ideas in the guise of a friendly teacher is, says Stephens, as likely to lead to subjection as to liberation.[3] Thus far, Stephens offers a thorough critique of ways in which ideology has generally been conceived in children's literature criticism.

144

And yet, it is sometimes hard to see how his own proposals fundamentally differ from those he criticizes. Stephens's own version of ideological criticism arguably shares more with critics such as Chambers than he seems to suggest. When, for instance, he invokes the notion that poems create emotional spaces for the reader,[4] or appeals to gaps in the text that open up possibilities of interpretation,[5] Stephens is drawing on a body of critical ideas that are very widespread in children's literature criticism, and which can be seen at work in the article by Chambers which he criticizes.[6] The broad aim of such ideas is to devolve power from author to reader. But there is, in Chambers and Stephens alike, a constant pull back to evaluating the text in terms of its ability to foster active participation on the part of the reader. Thus the power and autonomy that was supposed to be granted the reader slips back to the text, and ultimately even to the author. I believe, in fact, that Stephens would agree with me in seeing this as a problem. I argue, however, that some of Stephens's own terminology undermines his stated position, and, perhaps more importantly, that his text does not raise or grapple with this difficulty within its own fabric.

Crucially, I would also suggest that this happens to the extent that the terminology in question forms a sort of second nature in children's literature discourse. The basic idea that it is the task of criticism to work out grounds for evaluating and recommending books in terms of their suitability for children, however that may be defined, is so fundamental to how the field functions that its status *as* a critical idea tends not to be put into question. Thus, while I would thoroughly agree with many of Stephens's comments – regarding, for instance, the importance of the construction of point of view – I would also question the idea that one can confidently judge some texts 'restrictive', and others, by implication, not restrictive.[7] Once again, an appeal to readerly freedom ends up producing a judgment about texts, dividing them into those that offer one, limited reading, and those that encourage diverse readings. The problem with this division is that it leaves even the putatively unrestrictive text firmly in control; it is credited with the ability to say how and when to interpret diversely. Stephens's more radical point, it seems to me, is that a liberal society has to hope for critical readers – readers who try to understand the process of their own reading, even as they are involved in it. But when texts are recommended because they are said to *teach* this critical disposition, there is a clash between the message and the way it is being taught: the reader's imagined relationship to the text that is said to coach her into freedom sounds dangerously passive.

There is a problem in any case with the assumption that a given text can and should fall, in its entirety, on one side or the other of such a criterion. Surely a critical reader will have to learn to tolerate, and indeed to articulate, more ambivalence and conflict in her readings than this neat division would imply? The quest for exemplary texts that stage the experience of ambivalence seems to be couched in, and to produce, a critical discourse that is rather anxious to avoid any ambivalence in its own judgments: it must be able to say finally, on behalf of the children, whether a text is essentially good or bad. At the same time, this critical tendency also demands that texts be divisible within themselves into discrete ideological and non-ideological components. Though this move may seem contradictory to the previous one, it nevertheless follows the same impulse: one has to be able to *locate* ideology so as to be able to deal with it, ultimately by distancing oneself from it. Stephens, for instance, locates ideology in what he sees as the *secondary* meanings of texts,[8] and describes it as a distinct figure inscribed within a primary, and implicitly neutral, structure.[9] Again, this cuts against the ambition of his critique to overhaul the existing concept's limitation to more or less conscious agendas. Stephens's notion of ideology does *not* infect the very fabric of thinking: it is an additional something that one can stand aside from, leaving a pure core at least notionally recoverable.

This idea of an innocent primary meaning is especially troubling here because it looks a lot like a prime piece of ideology. According to one highly influential strand of thinking about ideology, the claim to ideological neutrality is itself profoundly ideological. For the post-Althusser concept,[10] which Stephens seems in places to want to adopt, casts ideology as something like Baudelaire's devil: its best trick is to make us believe it does not exist.[11] If one pursues this notion, an analysis of ideology in children's literature will start from the very most basic, everyday, apparently 'natural' ideas and structures it finds therein; whatever one is tempted to call 'primary meanings' immediately come into question. The challenge for criticism will not be simply to identify flagrant instances of prejudice or authoritarianism, but rather to confront in itself the baggage of habits and structures, the very décor of the little world it carries about with itself, and which orders its own critical narratives. What I am proposing here is not, I should stress, some sort of psychological introspection. The scene of this little drama will have to be the critical text itself, and its struggle to make sense. The issue of ideology will never be more crucial or problematic than where the critical text finds it cannot quite dispense with, or excise from its own fabric, the idea it wants to put under the microscope; or where an idea seems so self-explanatory as almost to defy analysis.

The role of family and the familiar in children's literature would be a good example of both of these problems. And indeed some critics have proposed looking upon concepts of family as historically and socially 'constructed' and therefore variable. This is the line taken by Nikki Gamble in a recent collaboration with Nicholas Tucker on family fiction.

> It is now widely acknowledged that concepts of family are socially and culturally constructed, influenced by economic, religious and political trends. Change is also evident in the representations of fictional families from the early nineteenth century to the present day which generally reflect a trend towards more liberal attitudes and subversion of the traditional values.[12]

So Gamble heralds a new consensus around an attention to the cultural constructedness of concepts that previously passed beneath the critical radar. But there is a problem in the second half of this announcement: 'liberal attitudes' and 'subversion' surely once more entail a true, non-ideological core as a point of comparison. Are we to take it that the liberal attitudes themselves are *not* historically and socially constructed? Is there not an uneasy feeling here that finding the avowedly progressive values of one's own time more congenial than those of another may not strike such a blow against dominant or embedded ways of thinking as seems to be claimed by a term such as 'subversion'?

Indeed, I would argue strongly that Gamble is continuing one of the most fundamental narratives of children's literature criticism: the idea that children's literature is constantly progressing away from a state of subjection to ideology (sometimes associated with the 'didactic'), so as to eventually achieve a state of autonomy and liberation. This eventual liberation is supposed to occur when literature becomes properly fitted to those who read it; when it speaks as one child to another, without any imposition. This idea of children's literature criticism has been thoroughly criticized by Jacqueline Rose[13] and Karín Lesnik-Oberstein.[14] The implications of this critique have not, however, been anything like realized in the critical practice of even the most theoretically-inclined contemporary critics. Certainly the ideological status of the claim to overcome ideology has not been seriously shaken in any of the critics cited above. Ideology remains something over there, at a safe remove; something that critical writing can deal with, without being itself involved in it. The move, in the space of a paragraph, from bracketing off a concept such as 'family' as standing in need of analysis, to reinstating a given notion of family as simply right and fit, is symptomatic of the sort of theoretical limbo in which children's literature criticism resides as long as it grounds itself in its progressive historical narrative, and the need to recommend the good with which it is complicit.

In this context, family is not just any old concept. According to the progressive historical narrative, children's literature must free itself from the imposition of an external, unreasonable authority. The writing itself must cease to be imposed upon if it is to stop imposing itself ideologically on its readers. A great deal of creative and critical energy in the field of children's literature has thus gone into forging the imaginative and rhetorical effacement of authority. The holy grail of such a quest would be, not just a set of characters that act out in an allegorical fashion the putatively benign use of power, but a *form* of narrative – an address, or a 'voice' as critics often prefer to say – that would empower the reader.[15] This notion comes with a variety of inflections, from the downright utopian to the more cautious or even resigned. But the idea that 'story' can embody what is best in the world, and in our relation to it and to each other, is one of the most persistent refrains of children's literature criticism. Family finds itself curiously placed here. For it may be seen as the most natural site and model for educational relations in the broadest sense, and as the natural home of storytelling. But it may also appear dangerous for much the same reasons: its inevitability, its organic self-reproduction, may be read as *too* automatic, as an imposition on the individual who, after all, did not choose to be born into such and such a family. There is a long and complicated history of oscillation between these two positions. Arguably these oscillations are themselves symptomatic of an ambivalence inherent in the modern liberal idea of family as the relatively autonomous building block of civil society. At the heart of this ambivalence I think we can also find an anxiety of authority whose shadow falls over the very idea of adult-to-child cultural transmission. The drama I want to stage, then, has as its players the storyteller, the teacher, and the parent. Looking in depth at how these ideas are articulated in a particular case – in the present instance, in the work of Philip Pullman – will not, of course, say everything that needs to be said about the ins and outs of the history of educational theory. But it may suggest some reasons why the concepts of family and authority will never simply reconcile themselves, and why the longed-for *final* liberation is a chimera.

My critical materials: Pullman as case study

The terms of my discussion so far are, of course, guided to a certain extent by the case I have chosen to study. But if Philip Pullman's much-lauded *His Dark Materials* lends itself particularly well to a discussion of family, the familiar, ideology, authority, and storytelling, it is not because it is unique in the field of children's literature. Rather, Pullman's three novels[16] are of particular interest because they articulate a number of abiding concerns with particular vigor and have been widely praised for doing so. Pullman, more than anyone at present, has (and I will discuss this more fully later on) raised the banner of 'story' as the force that leads the way to a better world. In some of their more programmatic moments, the three novels that have made his reputation offer themselves as a critique of authority, in particular religious authority, and set up truth-telling story against lies and dogma. Moreover, it is possible to argue that the narrative premise of other worlds unsettles an unreflecting relation to the familiar and everyday. It is thus doubtless tempting for criticism to declare that the story *enacts* the critique of dogma that it announces. But I want to avoid this over-hasty conclusion as it seems to me to pre-empt analysis. Indeed, it risks falling back into a profoundly uncritical relationship to the familiar, to the extent that it implicitly accepts that some things *just are* familiar, as if in advance we were all agreed as to what constitutes 'our' world. On the contrary, I propose that what needs to be analysed in such a text is its *thesis* of familiarity; its way of thinking about what makes things expected or unexpected, normal or abnormal. And this thesis constitutes an important aspect of anything one could call a text's 'ideology'. In the case of Pullman, this will lead me on to the family, to see how its structure is related to notions of familiarity, and this will in turn lead me on to the questions of storytelling and authority.

The familiar

From the start, *Northern Lights* is much concerned with the familiar. Familiar objects occupy 'wrong' places or have names implying a different course in the history of knowledge: hence there is a reference to 'Pope John Calvin';[17] brandy is known by the etymologically related 'brantwijn',[18] a photograph is a 'photogram', and scientific instruments are 'philosophical instruments';[19] reference is made to the five planets,[20] and so forth. What is going on here, beyond a series of scholarly jokes? Is there a point beyond the local and incidental, and, if so, how are we to read it? A good place to start might be the opening sentences, where any novel has to insinuate a passage into a world that is somehow marked as other, but also as already existing.

> Lyra and her dæmon moved through the darkening Hall, taking care to keep to one side, out of sight of the kitchen. The three great tables that ran the length of the Hall were laid already, the silver and the glass catching what little light there was, and the long benches were pulled out ready for the guests. Portraits of former Masters hung high up in the gloom along the walls. Lyra reached the dais and looked back at the open kitchen door and, seeing no one, stepped up beside the high table. The places here were laid with gold, not silver, and the fourteen seats were not oak benches but mahogany chairs with velvet cushions.[21]

The narration adopts a sort of indirect discourse that asserts the familiarity of what it relates to the character in question in their own particular world, even as it marks differences. From the opening words – 'Lyra and her dæmon moved through the darkening Hall' – things such as dæmons present themselves without immediate explanation or qualification, as if they went without saying. The passage that follows, detailing the décor of the Dining Hall, is heavy on definite articles and capitalized titles that likewise intimate notions of routine and familiarity with each object. This does not make these things familiar *to us*, but it claims they are familiar to this world, most immediately to Lyra, but also by implication beyond her to a set of established relations and customs.

The abrupt introduction of the strange thus depends upon, and indeed simultaneously sets up, a background of familiarity. The ideas of 'fantasy' and 'other worlds' in *His Dark Materials* operate through slight displacements within what is presented as 'our' world. The unfamiliar or unexpected is thus narrated with the steady beat of routine: 'Rooks were cawing somewhere, and bells were ringing, and from the Oxpens the steady beat of a gas engine announced the ascent of the evening Royal Mail zeppelin for London.'[22] Against the stately progress of such a sentence, one could say that the attribution of familiarity to an implicit point of view wavers. One can ask at any given point – for *whom* is this familiar? But equally, one can ask – for whom is it supposed to be entirely *un*familiar? The two questions taken together, I would suggest, evade any neat or definitive attribution. Similarly, if one focuses on the *process* of narration – not what is told, but *how* it is told – it makes as much sense, if not more, to think of the other worlds and different points of view as products of the familiarity and unfamiliarity, and not the reverse.

Indeed, while Pullman's text is, as a story, necessarily committed to the idea that these worlds are out there waiting to be encountered, it is also interested in who is doing the encountering and, more importantly, how they conceive of difference. Passage from one world into another may thus be expressed as a dialectic of sameness and difference. Mary Malone's first view of the world of the *mulefa* takes in trees 'like juniper', flowers 'like cornflowers', and so forth.[23] Malone, a scientist, explains this *like*ness in terms of an evolutionary theory of other worlds: worlds that have split off from our own more recently are more like ours.[24] Mary's explanatory framework thus accommodates no idea of absolute difference, or at any rate of absolute unrelatedness. The encounter with the other is with the more or less 'like'. It is also worth noting that Mary's framework is, in many respects, very much *like* that which is most familiar in the narration throughout the three books. Whatever point of view it says it is articulating, and however different each is supposed to be, the very positing of difference entails an ultimate frame of likeness, and this frame is regularly explained in terms of relatedness.

Part of the interest of this sort of other-world fantasy is often supposed to lie, as suggested earlier, in defamiliarization; a coming-at the familiar from an oblique angle that foregrounds point of view, and so makes us question its construction. But I think it is possible to overplay the extent to which the imaginative effort to embrace otherness can be said to effect that embrace. By way of corollary, it is possible to miss the extent to which any such move reaffirms the familiar. In Pullman, and I think this is necessarily true of all other-world fantasy, some things remain constant throughout the text, forming an armature of regularity against which the differences are given relief. One might then say more judiciously that repetition *offers itself* to be read as an acting out, and thus as a corroboration, of the regularity that narration projects. The job of criticism, then, will be to ask how constants are established; not to accept them as constants.

The family as constant

In this context, it is especially interesting to ask what things are taken to be so like as to go without saying. That is to say, what sorts of things are *not* said to be 'like' because indeed they are *not* 'like' anything, but just are themselves. In Pullman, I would suggest, not the least of such invariable structures is that of family itself. It is not just that family retains the same shape regardless of point of view, it is that it is never marked as being a matter of point of view in the first place. Whereas many other objects and ideas are described in terms that mark out a given person or world, no other terminology or structure is ever articulated from which family might relativize, or be relativized, in this way.

Take, for example, Ama the Himalayan herdsman's daughter trying to make sense of Mrs Coulter and the drugged and sleeping Lyra: 'Sorcerers existed, beyond a doubt, and it was only too likely that they would cast sleeping-spells, and that a mother would care for her daughter in that fierce and tender way.'[25] The indirect discourse respects, one might say, Ama's point of view. But in so doing, and especially in the pathos and irony of 'beyond a doubt', it implies a master narrative subject *capable of* that respect; one that can survey many, if not all, such possible world-views and comprehend them all. *His Dark Materials* does not brashly assert the superiority of 'science' to other models of explanation; indeed, part of the point of Lyra's world is that it has arrived at knowledges apparently similar to our own using languages, social structures, and instruments that might appear superseded, pre-scientific. Similarly, Mary Malone is surprised that the *mulefa*, who figure to a certain extent as practically wise primitives, are able to understand complex mathematical ideas in their own terms.[26] This quasi-anthropological position is, nonetheless, arguably based on a notion of translatability of knowledge that posits an ultimate scientific positivity: different knowledges are able to converge on the same thing because there is a thing, and because it demands to be discovered in a way that is more or less compatible with 'science'. Viewed in these terms, even though the herdsman's daughter's notion of sorcery is far from adequate, it is nevertheless a distant cousin of science in its attempt, however far off course, to make sense in terms of cause and effect, regularity, and so forth.

But does the same sort of relativizing apply to the rest of Ama's view? For I have only discussed the first half of what I have quoted; and if the latter half is perhaps all too easily passed over, this is part of what I want to point out. My question is this: does the notion of a mother's fierce and tender love require one to juggle different world-views as I have suggested reference to sleeping spells does, and if not, why not? On the same page, at the start of the chapter, Ama is identified as 'the herdsman's daughter': in this world, family relations are conceived as they are in ours, and in Lyra's. Indeed, is there a world envisaged by *His Dark Materials* of which this would not be the case? The *mulefa* have a very different bodily structure, not to mention wheels, but nonetheless have two sexes who live 'monogamously in couples'.[27] In drawing attention to this I am not necessarily advocating that it ought to be otherwise; that the *mulefa*, for instance, should have baroque reproductive habits to match their unusual constitution. Still, I find it interesting that it is *family* that tends to remain constant in a text that explicitly touts an interest in variation and difference. Family here requires no anthropologizing or adjustment of world-view to be understood. Its job is precisely to provide a discreet backdrop of normality against which remarkable things such as science and magic stand out in relief. But this very function is, it seems to me, especially in the context of ideology, worth pointing out and bringing into question.

The fact that family plays this role is not, perhaps, in itself very surprising. Indeed, if anything, quite the contrary. Is it a simple accident that family turns out to be so familiar, and that discussion of likeness and relatedness of different worlds turns so readily to the structure of family? Can the family be discounted as just a convenient metaphor for a more fundamental concept of relatedness? Or are the two sets of ideas more intimately *related*? There are big and important questions at stake here, and I want to signal them precisely because I will not be able to deal with them adequately in this context. In particular, I want it to be as clear as possible that, whatever remarks I make about Pullman's particular take on family, I am not suggesting that he could have simply dispensed with all the problems in which he becomes entangled. Nevertheless, even if one decides this entanglement is, on some level or other, unavoidable, this is certainly not a reason to stop thinking about it. And, what is more, there is much that can be said about the particular ways in which Pullman's novels figure family relations, most especially as they relate to issues of power and right.

The right family: power and destiny

As I have been arguing, *His Dark Materials* posits family as a constant of all worlds, and moreover posits a family relation as the basis for the relative likeness of worlds. This already paves the way for naturalizing all relations by implying that they have a quasi-genetic explanation. And Pullman does go some way in this direction by maintaining certain hierarchies as family inheritances. One instance in which the relatedness of worlds and the everyday notion of family are in high tension with each other is perhaps Lyra's role as the new Eve. According to Church dogma she is 'in the position of Eve, the wife of Adam, the mother of us all, and the cause of all sin'.[28] As in the case of Ama, this view can be relativized from within the narration: the notion of 'sin' is part of what *His Dark Materials* is setting itself up to criticize and renegotiate; it is marked as belonging to the church. But can the narrative, for all that, quite do away with the notion of Eve, or of Lyra, as 'mother of us all'?

Lyra's final resolution to build the republic of heaven, with which the story ends, is exemplary. She is deciding to do what each of us must do each in our own world, and it is a work without end. To that extent, one might say the message is liberal and democratic; Lyra is not just doing something *on behalf of* everyone else. But Lyra's exemplary status is no accident, nor is it determined by a path laid down from within the work of her own life. Her instrumental role in setting the renewal of the universe in motion has been predicted from the first volume, and the prediction is shared by different peoples and discussed across worlds. Her actions mark an epoch for the whole universe of different worlds, and indeed different species. Her role is, in this respect, transcendental and retains from *Genesis* the idea of man's dominion. This is one sense in which Lyra's role is 'exemplary'. But in addition to this, I want to point to the simultaneous ordinariness and specialness that defines any child hero: she is at once only one individual child, and representative of all children. Following the odd logic of the exemplary, she represents 'the child' *better* than other children.

As in the 'Harry Potter' books, this tricky double shuffle is partly articulated, and naturalized, through the structure of family. At some points in the story, the narration is most insistent on *whose* children certain characters are. It is especially fond of patronymics. Lyra is, we are frequently reminded, Lord Asriel's daughter, just as Will is the son of Stanislaus Grumman, the shaman. In this way, with the frequent use of possessives, both Will and Lyra are defined as *belonging to* a lineage. And while they are supposed to be in some measure independent, there is also a notion of direct, genetic inheritance; that they are, constitutionally, their fathers' children. And this notion of belonging is strengthened, not weakened, by the fact that both come into their own belatedly. Lyra is, morally, set up as the appropriate daughter of Lord Asriel before she, or we, are told that is who she is. Similarly, Will only discovers just who and what his father was by venturing into other worlds, and after a tragic struggle with him, he consciously assumes his mantle. For he not only puts on 'his father's heavy cloak',[29] but also thinks his way into his father's way of thinking: 'His father, the soldier, the explorer, would have known exactly what to take. Will had to guess.'[30] Indeed, Will has been defined as taking his father's place from the very start of his story in *The Subtle Knife*, fending for his mother in his father's absence. And it is his mother who tells him he will take on his father's mantle, and the phrase sticks in his mind even though he does not understand it.[31]

The encounter with the unknown parent, then, serves to confirm, or to challenge one to realize, what one already potentially is. Initial concealment and belated inheritance thus make family a model of a sort of destiny in line with the witch Serafina Pekkala's notion of the necessary illusion of free will: we are all subject to fate but must act as if we are not.[32] It is worth also considering a less lofty notion of family destiny that underpins this one. Lower class societies, such as the gyptians and the college servants offer a security and continuity of identity that amounts to a sort of destiny by social reproduction. Mrs Lonsdale the Housekeeper emphatically reassures Lyra she is not the only one who cares what has happened to Roger: ' "None of that. I'm a Parslow, same as Roger's father. He's my second cousin." '[33] The Parslow family shares an organic structure with the college-world which it is their job to maintain.

> It had never been planned; it had grown piecemeal, with past and present overlapping at every spot, and the final effect was one of jumbled and squalid grandeur. Some part was always about to fall down, and for five generations the same family, the Parslows, had been employed full-time by the College as masons and scaffolders. The present Mr Parslow was teaching his son the craft [...].[34]

This passage seems to express strong approval of the idea of organic social reproduction: class belonging, in the context of a pre-capitalistic craft economy, is seen as a fit destiny. Lyra is a curious instance here. She frequents the lower classes and doesn't *speak proper*: her speech is marked with the colloquialisms of other Oxford street children. To this extent she might be said to be the product of her environment, but this is negotiable. The text is equally insistent that she is 'nobly born',[35] and the proof is that she soon imposes herself as leader over a gathering.[36] Her view of them as 'subjects' may well be ironized,[37] but the notion of nobility shining through is still there. Like the lost princes and princesses of romance, Lyra's belonging is no mere matter of contingent social relations.

Indeed, Lyra dreams her parentage before she knows of it, in a sort of family romance: 'Perhaps they would meet Lord Asriel. Perhaps he and Mrs Coulter would fall in love, and they would get married and adopt Lyra, and go and rescue Roger from the Gobblers.'[38] This projected union is itself the resolution of an orphan's dilemma: 'Oh, this *was* confusing. Mrs Coulter was so kind and wise, whereas Lyra had actually seen the Master trying to poison Uncle Asriel. Which of them did she owe most obedience to?'[39] Towards the end of *Northern Lights*, when she does know her parents' identities, she has a belated primal scene, seeing them in the gulf between worlds passionately embracing.[40] Even in the land of the dead, Lyra is spinning yarns of abducted nobility.[41] The narration dismisses this as nonsense; and yet it is part of its own story, and a structurally important part too.

Parentage and gender

Another important factor in Lyra's parentage is gender. Both parents have concealed their identity, and both play double hands, but it is the father who has the more gallant role. Despite her earlier fantasy, Lyra resents hints that she may be Mrs Coulter's daughter.[42] When, on the other hand, John Faa, king of the gyptians, has told her all – the adulterous affair between Asriel and the already-married Mrs Coulter, the concealment of her birth, the duel, and the death of Mr Coulter[43] – she dreams of 'her great imprisoned father'.[44] What accounts for this disparity? Broadly speaking, the family inheritance is riven along lines of gender: femininity is, one might say, charged with making the break. Or at least a certain model of femininity is viewed as duplicitous and dangerous. Mrs Coulter opens up a new world for Lyra: 'women so unlike female scholars or gyptian boat-mothers or college servants as almost to be a new sex altogether, one with dangerous powers and qualities such as elegance, charm and grace.'[45] A total contrast to the beauty of the college, 'grand and stony and masculine'.[46] Lyra regards 'female Scholars with a proper Jordan disdain'.[47] In each case, femininity is placed in relation to motherhood: the absence of motherly sentiment is either pathetic or downright poisonous.

There is a danger of oversimplifying here. What game each parent is playing at any given moment remains a slippery question throughout. When Asriel has captured Mrs Coulter, she is the one who defends her daughter's worth, while he says he has more important things to think about.[48] Here also the link between mother and daughter is asserted in a novel way: 'Mrs Coulter was more like her daughter than she knew. Her answer was to spit in Lord Asriel's face.' When Will takes Lyra from her, he cannot tell beyond her beauty whether or not her anguish conceals monstrous cleverness. And it is at this very point that she looks, to Will, 'uncannily like her daughter'.[49] But it is noticeable that these are references to trickster qualities, and that they liken mother to daughter, rather than daughter to mother. When it comes to the father, however, it is Lyra who is likened to Asriel, and it is a matter of noble, heroic qualities: so, for example, Lyra orders Iorek Byrnison 'in that imperious way, [...] very like her father'.[50]

On the basis of these plot twists, then, one might say that there is a degree of ambivalence in the moral balance of Lyra's parentage. And yet I would argue that certain distinctions prevail: even Mrs Coulter's motherly anguish is capable of something like calculation, and even Asriel's apparent coolness is consistently seen as having ultimately more genuine consideration for her well-being. The disapproval of a notion of feminine vanity can be seen in another figure who acts in an odd sort of motherly role towards Lyra: Mary Malone, the serpent or tempter of the piece. She, at one point, constructs a mirror: 'Not out of vanity, for she had little of that, but because she wanted to test an idea she had.'[51] The exemplary figure of science in *His Dark Materials* is thus a woman, but it is a woman expressly devoid of what is elsewhere identified as femininity: she is neither glamorous nor motherly. At this point, if one tries to continue this allegorical sort of reading, the message becomes hard to follow. Mary Malone is, like the Jordan scholars, not a mother-woman. Then again, the part she plays is not that of Eve but that of the serpent. Who, then, is Mrs Coulter? One could try to explain all this in terms of Eve's double role as tempted and tempter; the incomplete and overlapping allegories relaying this ambivalence. But whatever one makes of all these allegories of femininity, masculinity is never a problem in the same way in *His Dark Materials*.

The family as problem

Indeed, one could say that masculinity, or at least heroic masculinity, figures here most consistently as the freedom from relations. The figure who ventures alone into other worlds almost axiomatically steps aside from the family. So even though Will constantly acts for his mother, he does so by leaving her; and as it is the thought of her that breaks the subtle knife, he must try to act for her without thinking of her.[52] It should be noted that, if this stoic alienation constitutes 'masculinity' in *His Dark Materials*, then Lyra also follows the path of masculinity. One might read here the idea, which one also finds in other celebrated children's writers such as Alan Garner, that women have to be weaned off the silliness of femininity. But even then, it seems that Lyra's heroism reaches its end at the moment that she 'becomes a woman' in the sense of discovering sexual desire.[53] To make matters even more puzzling for an allegorical reading, she is then debarred from pursuing her love for Will and has to live on in renunciation. If these various threads point to anything, it is not so much a structure as the idea of a process that maintains the structure. At the close, everything is returned to its home because the separateness and wholeness of each world must be respected. The time of the story, then, the temporary arc outwards and then back again, can be likened to the family that sends its son out into the world so as to build another family in its likeness elsewhere. But while one can say that the figure of family works to naturalize this potentially contradictory structure, it is equally possible that the contradiction might threaten to make the family seem less homely than one might like to think.

My story about gender difference, I propose, works around an ambivalence within the idea of family that is resolved – in places, and by no means systematically, but nevertheless following a certain logic – along the lines of gender. The notion of femininity as a stability that the hero must reject is, for instance, readable in the ghost of an alternative family for Lyra with the gyptians. Mrs Coulter at first hid her with a gyptian nurse, and this is why the gyptians 'knew about [her] from a child'.[54] Lyra might have been raised among them, but, says the narrative, their low legal standing prevented this happening.[55] The gyptians stand as the epitome of tight and wholesome family relations, and this is associated with the notion of a domestic matriarchy that complements a political patriarchy. That is to say, Ma Costa is said to have a distinct sphere of power, but John Faa and Farder Coram are still in charge of the polity. Lyra is doubly alienated in the sense that the 'proper' family, the one where biological origin and family role match, is denied to her either way. Her 'real' (that is, biological) mother, on the one hand, is not a proper mother to her, and the proper mother she might have had is a nurse; a proxy or substitute. Proper femininity, low class, and pre-modern social structure are thus aligned with each other: 'in the tight-knit gyptian boat-world, all children were precious and extravagantly loved, and a mother knew if a child was out of *her* sight, it wouldn't be far from someone else's who would protect it instinctively.'[56] But one must not inherit this femininity if one wants to be a hero. Femininity is, in this respect, the enemy of story.

Story *in loco parentis*

There is, however, a striking moment where Lyra does, in a sense, come into her feminine inheritance, by apprehending her place in the chain of mothers. This is simultaneous with her realization of what it would be to be a child. Most tellingly, the whole episode is provoked by a female storytelling voice.

> In all the life she could remember Lyra had never been read to in bed; no one had told her stories or sung nursery rhymes with her before kissing her and putting out the light. But she suddenly thought now that if ever there was a voice that would lap you in safety and warm you with love, it would be a voice like the Lady Salmakia's, and she felt a wish in her heart to have a child of her own, to lull and soothe and sing to, one day, in a voice like that.[57]

So a non-human creature from another world (Lady Salmakia is a Gallivespian, a tiny winged creature) awakens a human child to a knowledge of true childhood, and it does so through the true voice of story, and this provokes in turn a desire to *have* as well as to *be* a child. The family bond speaks between strangers, across species, across worlds. Storytelling thus reconciles the most far-flung branches of the family tree and strikes an intimacy of which the proper biological agents may be incapable. Or, more simply, Pullman puts story *in loco parentis*.

The importance this gives to story will come as no surprise to anyone who has ever read an interview with the Author. And indeed Pullman articulates a notion of story that is very widespread in children's literature. It is worth noting, however, that this idea of story at once affirms and usurps the family proper. Or rather, literature of the right sort – one that speaks with the right voice – is seen as the proper substitute of the parent–child relation. Story is entitled to take the place of parent because it articulates what ought to have been there in the first place. Similarly, the story of childhood that springs to Lyra's mind is cast as a true one precisely to the extent that it comes from outside her experience: it tells itself spontaneously, immediately, with the force of a desire.

Again there is a tension between the idea that a child is destined to be what it is, and the idea that it must nevertheless learn to live this destiny, and may do so for better or for worse. If this can be read as corresponding to a tension between the claims of family and the claims of education, it is story that steps in to mediate. It is not just that the story of the books, the story one reads, presents itself as being, in part at least, the story of Lyra's life. Telling the story of her life is also an important part of what Lyra has to learn to do, so as to live better. One of Lyra's most important breakthroughs comes towards the end of *The Amber Spyglass* when she stops spinning romances and just says what has happened to her, and so, incidentally, talks her way out of the world of the dead.[58] Learning to live in *His Dark Materials* is learning to tell the right sort of story about oneself.

Stories about stories

The right story, on this account, eschews the romance of high parentage, on which *His Dark Materials* nevertheless arguably leans rather heavily. And indeed, for all his insistence on 'story', one should not assume that Pullman always tells the same story about it. These inconsistencies have, however, a certain consistency, in that they tend to follow the fault lines over issues of the authority of stories, and the family as their scene, which I have been tracing. I want now to turn to some of Pullman's statements, made in interviews, essays and lectures, on the subject of story. My point is not, I should stress, to privilege these as true stories just because they are told outwith the pages of fiction. Reading them in parallel with the fictional texts will, however, shed some interesting light on the ideas of authority with which all of these texts are grappling, and how these ideas relate to the different sorts of authority the various texts implicitly claim for themselves. On the whole, the refrain of Pullman the Author's pronouncements is that a story has authority to the extent that the author has surrendered his pretension to be the source, and has allowed his steps to be guided by the story itself. In his Patrick Hardy lecture, he tells the story of a girl overheard on a train writing a story with her sister who says, 'Are we allowed to write that she can do magic?. Pullman's point is not that this reflects a stultifying submission to the values of classroom discipline, but that the girl has realized something very important about stories; that they need rules.[59] Following from this, Pullman counsels a strict adherence to the story; one must not put one's writing in front of its dictates.

Another corollary of this is that one must not be afraid of the obvious. Pullman's concept of the 'obvious' not only seems to resemble what I have been calling the 'familiar'; it also expressly concerns the place of family in the story. Pullman tells how he considered at one point having Lyra discover that Lord Asriel and Mrs Coulter are not in fact her parents; apparently the discovery that they *are* her parents seemed, on its own, too obvious. But 'we shouldn't be afraid of the obvious, because stories are about life, and life is full of obvious things like food and sleep and love and courage which you don't stop needing just because you're a good reader'.[60] Family, then, is part of 'life', which is the basic raw material of story; the job of the writer when handling such material is to be as true to it as possible.[61]

The 'obviousness' of family as a part of 'life' needs a few comments here. Family is one of the fundamental struts of interviews and about-the-author blurbs, and this is nowhere more true than with children's authors. There is, indeed, a sense in which family is cast as a sort of scene of writing: children's literature criticism and biography abounds with anecdotes about first tellings of stories to the author's children, or their origins in the author's own childhood. But this location of storytelling is not perhaps made without equivocation or misgiving. In *Talking Books*, Pullman's profoundest wishes and gratitude go to his wife and sons (and pets, it is fair to add). At the same time, however, the tradition of storytelling is emphatically not traced on this occasion to his mother and father, but to a grandfather. Similarly, Pullman says he gained his own first audience and learned his craft as a teacher, not as a father. By the same token, in another interview, he says his imagination was shaped by moving around the globe following his father's service postings, and that he learned his craft telling the story of *The Odyssey* to his son Tom.[62] Do these different versions add up to an ambivalence over the place of family? The most consistently retold element of Pullman's story about his story-writing has him at work in a hut at the bottom of the garden. The relation made between family-as-milieu and story is thus at once intense and semi-detached. It is tempting, then, to trace a parallel between the hesitation over the place of family as an origin of being in the stories, and this hesitation over the family as an origin of stories that is told in these stories-about-stories.

The storyteller's responsibility

Putting the emphasis on the story, Pullman claims a form of authority based on the ostensive disavowal or abdication of authority. On the other hand, Pullman is not always shy about enjoying a certain mastery in the craft of storytelling. He prefers, he says in one interview, the third person 'omniscient' narrator because he likes 'swooping in and drawing back, and giving a panoramic view'; he likes 'directing the story'.[63] Whichever way one looks at it, the elevated status given to story places a high responsibility on the storyteller. *His Dark Materials* provides some pointers as to how seriously it wants to take this responsibility. That is to say, there are moments in the story that, by commenting on story, allow themselves to be enlisted as meta-commentary on the story in hand. One such passage will put a slightly different emphasis on the idea of story *in loco parentis*. The Master of Jordan College has just told the Librarian of Lyra's importance in coming events, and of the betrayal she will commit. The old men are unsure how best to fill their responsibilities and it makes the Master anxious: ' "That's the duty of the old", said the Librarian, "to be anxious on behalf of the young. And the duty of the young is to scorn the anxiety of the old." ' The chapter then concludes wryly: 'They sat for a while longer, and then parted, for it was late, and they were old and anxious.'[64] This discussion can be read as a parable of the role of parent, educator, or indeed children's writer. At this point, Lyra is an orphan and the Scholars are 'all she had for a family'.[65] Reciprocally, the Master has a tutelary responsibility towards Lyra, and this produces an anxiety over what to tell and how to tell it. She might even benefit from some scientific (or 'philosophical') instruction, 'if it were explained in a simple way', and this would make the Master less anxious.[66] At the same time, it has been predicted that she must carry out her role 'without realizing what she's doing'.[67] This point is later glossed by the Witch-Consul to Farder Coram: 'she must be free to make her own mistakes'.[68] These are also, however, classic questions often raised in criticism that asks how one should write for children. The Master's dilemma, like that of the children's writer, is that he cannot say where telling will become an imposition on the individual freedom of the child.

The idea that education, the passing on of ideas and values, might necessarily involve some sort of symbolic violence, or at least subjection, haunts thinking on education in general. The general problem is set out thus by Roderick McGillis:

> This situation in which children are shaped and organized by a larger and dominant group may be unavoidable if we accept adult responsibility for perpetuating a social order. On the other hand, to perpetuate a social order need not mean closing adult ears to childhood.[69]

McGillis wants to value an idea of understanding, implying a commitment and a process, over knowledge as a claim to mastery.[70] Like the Master, McGillis expresses anxiety not just on behalf of the child, but also on his own behalf; it is an educator's anxiety of power and control. Through the Master, the text is thus invoking concerns that haunt education and, by extension, children's literature.

Persons

But does it make a difference that the idea is here articulated in the form of fiction, rather than of criticism, or of educational theory? As I have already suggested, fiction opens up the possibility of reading an episode as a commentary on the whole. This is often thought of as being a particular facility of fiction, part of what distinguishes it from theoretical discourse. Because literary discourse is routinely thought of in terms of character, narration, plot, and point of view, one can readily say the narrative has the luxury of making a 'character' stand as a proxy for the 'I' of the text. But is it quite certain criticism's own 'I' does nothing of the sort, even on its own behalf, when one claim out of many is taken to stand above the others and guarantee them all? And in either case, what conclusion should one draw from such statement by proxy? Is one to read the Master's dilemma as a confession of the text's own failing? Or is one to say that, precisely by confessing through him, it exonerates itself? In other words, can a figure like the Master furnish a text with an alibi? Viewed in this way, one might even argue that critical and theoretical discourse are regularly allowed to outdo fiction at what is allegedly its own game, as positions are advanced, built upon, then ostentatiously rejected, without even leaving the trace of a distinct name or identity. Indeed, why treat fictional and critical discourse as freestanding entities that only happen to meet, when it would appear that they produce each other from the very start?

I am raising these problems here because the discussion of 'story' in Pullman tends, while affirming the primacy of the fictional form, also to draw heavily on Authorial statements, made *ex cathedra*. The pronouncement of a separation of functions thus tends to cut across the boundaries it says it is erecting. It is important to track this, not least because critical hymns to the power of story are able to draw on programmatic claims, with little or no regard to whether they are quoted from narrators, characters, or authors talking about their work, and without remarking any contradiction in this. The workings of authority here are more than a little slippery: God is replaced by family, is replaced by Author, is replaced finally by story. Or, I should rather say, the *claim* for story is that it has the last word. But I only have this on the say-so of critics, who are often quoting the author as an authority on the matter. And though he says, and his books say, they are questioning the authority of God and father, I am not sure that he, the Author, is not thereby casting himself in their image. In short, my inquiry into family, and story as its bond, leads me to question what has been vaunted as Pullman's moral victory over authoritarian religious dogma.[71] Most particularly, it leads me to question the equivocal role the idea of Pullman as author and authority plays in this.

The Authority?

Just as I find *His Dark Materials*'s apparent questioning of parents ambivalent, so I find its trumpeted rebuff to God the Father less than conclusive. If Milton fell unwittingly into Satan's party, I think one might say Pullman pulls the reverse stunt by falling, despite his avowals, in with God the Father. To make a very broad point indeed, the story of *His Dark Materials* is a case in point, with its angels and so forth, and with a cosmology somewhat less compatible with modern science – or even modern philosophy, or indeed modern theology for that matter – than the media figure of Pullman would have one believe. But I do not just wish to make the point that Pullman has not quite laid aside the paraphernalia of Christian myth. Pullman is perhaps happy to concede something of the sort himself when he describes himself as a 'Christian atheist', maintaining the structures of religion after the belief has gone.[72] And another person in this narrative, Lord Asriel, argues something similar by likening Adam and Eve, beyond the question of 'belief', to an imaginary number without which certain calculations are not possible.[73] The concern I am trying to pursue here is that in this way story has come to stand not just in the place of parental authority, but in the place of God too, not to mention the place of the Author.

Again, it is the family that provides the, I think less than accidental, framework for this series of substitutions. In the *Talking Books* interview, Pullman falls into romancing Lyra's parents yet again. But what interests me this time is the way the functions of author, God, character and so forth slide about.

> Lord Asriel and Mrs Coulter are Satan and the Ice Queen, if you like. They're very powerful, glamorous figures. [...] Mrs Coulter's young and beautiful. She wears expensive clothes and lives in luxury. Lord Asriel is powerful and Byronic. He sets everything in motion. We don't see very much of him: we see him at the beginning and the end of Book One; we don't see him at all in Book Two – but everything in that book happens because of him. He's a figure of enormous authority and power and we'll see more of both of them in the third book, of course.[74]

Mrs Coulter is *said* to be fascinating, but it is Lord Asriel who has seized this text's attention. As he is recounting Asriel's invisible power, Pullman himself seems to come under its influence, and Mrs Coulter is only hauled back into the story with a rather abrupt 'they' at the end, as if by way of a guilty after-thought. The position attributed here to Asriel, especially in Book Two, is analogous to the position of author: he is the unseen cause of everything *in the story*. What is more, this role is curiously closer to a metaphysical notion of God than the one who nominally fills that role in the books. The Authority, who masquerades as God, is debunked as a decrepit cosmic bureaucracy that has forgotten itself. But in the figure of Asriel as absent cause, at the Author's right hand, something like the grandeur of deity lives on.

One can also ask here what it means to attribute more power over the 'story' to a character than to the legally recognized author, Philip Pullman. This question relies on an equivocation over the word 'story': is it to be read as referring to the events recounted within the book, or to the entire book itself? But this is what Pullman's notion of story itself does. Pullman speaks here of his characters as entities over which he, as author, has limited control. He, like us, sees them appear and disappear: 'we' are watching together. In one sense, this move disclaims power and authority: Pullman casts himself as a mere conduit for stories. The story, as he has said on many occasions, is given; the telling is what the storyteller contributes. And, as we have seen, often the challenge for the teller is to do as little as possible to get in the way of the story. But the role imagined for and through Asriel is the converse of this: he makes things happen, but he keeps this fact well hidden. Is there a contradiction here in Pullman's idea of story?

Curiously enough, I don't think there is. The family resolves the tangle. I think one can read a parallelism here between the idea of the wise father who lets his child make her way in the world, and the wise author who gives the story its liberty. The daughter, like the story, is given, pre-ordained, but must be allowed to wend its own way. Following this reading, Pullman's admiration for Asriel's 'enormous authority and power' is most revealing. Suddenly the story, his own story, is no longer the story of Lyra's struggle. Another story opens up behind the one that is explicitly narrated in *His Dark Materials*; a back story. This power that works by its very invisibility, analogous to the power of the self-effacing author, cannot resist breaking out and proclaiming itself. Whether it calls itself Asriel, God or Philip Pullman is, to a certain extent, irrelevant: the figure of a single controlling entity has made a comeback just as it is being dismissed.

The point of all this is not, however, just to indict Philip Pullman for a sort of circuitous narcissism. And if there is an element of accusation in my analysis, then it is precisely there that I write myself into a quasi-theological power struggle and join God, Asriel, Philip, and all the rest, on the stage. Perhaps an element of this is inevitable, unless one wants to claim an even more transcendent posture entirely beyond the ideological struggle in question. Having said this, however, the pretension to be critical demands that I draw back from simply immersing myself in such a drama, and try instead to ask what it is all about: what is at stake in all this juggling of authority?

The question implicit in my discussion of Pullman's staging of Asriel is, I would suggest: where can power *decently* reside? Power, I am suggesting, is being anxiously shunted from one post to another, in search of a place where it is right and fit for it to exist. If I am right in this, what can one say, if anything, of that home position? One answer would seem to be that 'story' is the fitting owner of power, and this is the version most commonly touted by Pullman in his guise as the author talking about his creations. But, as I have been arguing, even in the very act of saying this, something opens up behind story. Or rather it opens up within story, both in the sense that that is where Pullman's recasting of his story places it, and in the sense that making 'story' the origin necessarily begs the question of origins. The humility of submitting to the story always harbors this pride.

Conclusion

Ultimately, both parents, Mrs Coulter and Asriel, redeem themselves by annihilating themselves.[75] Within the frame of *His Dark Materials*, it is the final instance where the ostentatious effacement of a figure charged with carrying a role of authority maintains, or even perfects, the function of that authority. The corollary of this is an author who is held in high regard as such at least in part for proclaiming his submission to the higher power of stories. In effect, if this is taken in good faith, children's writers and parents alike are held to ransom by story: they are only leased their authority on condition of keeping alive the true spirit of story. We must all learn to tell truly the things that make up 'life'. Pullman avoids the term 'fantasy' and prefers to stress the psychological truth of his stories, no matter how apparently fantastic their décor. If one looks for this life, and this psychological truth in *His Dark Materials*, as I have tried to do, I think one finds ideas of family and every-day life rather less radical or pluralistic than Pullman's profile would suggest. Indeed, the challenge for the storyteller, as Pullman conceives it, is that the message almost *has to* consist of a series of banalities we already know too well; the 'obvious' which we should not be afraid to tell. But if one took this line to be entirely representative of 'Pullman', this would have the curious consequence of reducing the story to rubble: it could, read according to some of the pronouncements on story contained within it, only be a fantastical confection that denies itself in the making; the only purpose of which would be to leave, in the space vacated by the ruin, a banality otherwise too banal to tell. For, as I hinted earlier, what can the supposed difference between the hackneyed romantic 'lies' that Lyra first tells to the harpies, and the true account of the story so far that wins approval as 'truth', possibly be? They seem, in substance, remarkably similar. Indeed, Lyra is remarkably fortunate as a teller of true stories in having armoured talking bears, cliff ghasts, and subtle knives to draw upon. And while it may be a lie in point of fact that her parents are the Duke and Duchess of Abingdon,[76] surely this is not so far from the true romance of her concealed nobility. Given all this, if one under-stands 'ideology' in terms of the décor and dramatis personæ of a story, one would be hard pressed to say what *His Dark Materials*'s ideology of story – or its ideology of family – is. Is the whole quasi-theological notion of family as destiny what the story is telling us, or what it is telling us to reject? Alarmingly, it seems to be both. But, to return to my introductory discussion, need we be looking for 'the ideology' in these terms at all? I think what I have found will not fit this pattern, for it is not a single, coherent, discrete, and detachable quantity. I have not found anything like the straightforward sub-version of traditional values; indeed, I have found some aspects that seem quite politically conservative. But I do not think these aspects can be simply isolated and held at bay: my reading has not been able to isolate and pin down discrete representations, mimetic pictures that can be held up to the world for comparison, and accepted or rejected accordingly. The ideas I have looked at – story, family, the familiar – have not had unique functions. Rather, they have slipped from being fictional ideas to critical ideas, from being events in the narrative to being structuring principles of narration. On a given occasion, something may be labeled as an event, a character type, an idea, and so forth: but none of them is limited to just one of these functions, and none of them operates on its own. I cannot thus tell you how to avoid the ideological bits of this, or any other, book, nor does it make sense to use 'ideology' as a benchmark for recommendation. This is the crucial point that hampers children's literature criticism's engagement with ideology: as long as it is committed to recommending 'good' books, it has to approve or disapprove of what it sees as their ideologies.

But what is one to do if one stops thinking of ideology as being like the parts of a story one wants to excise or quarantine? I propose one might think rather in terms of 'the ideological', a field of inquiry that concerns itself with how textual objects project, that is to say throw out before them, their preferred origins and the conditions of their reception. For the funny thing about familiarity, supposing something does function as such in a given reading of a given book, is that it has to give birth to its own family. Where material presents itself as at once itself, and as its own father, and as its own daughter, a certain amount of confusion is to be expected. Still, it is something like the confusion of persons literature has by tradition been allowed to have. One could say Pullman has produced an admirable fable of the difficulties of this situation. With a weird sort of fidelity and tenacity, by tying themselves in knots and belying their triumphant message, Pullman's three novels provide more food for thought than that pallid message ever could.

Suggested further reading

Carsten, Janet (ed.) *Cultures of Relatedness: New Approaches to the Study of Kinship* (Cambridge: Cambridge University Press, 2000).
Eagleton, Terry, *Ideology: An Introduction* (London: Verso, 1991).
Geertz, Clifford, *The Interpretation of Cultures* (London: Fontana, 1993).
Hunt, Peter and Millicent Lenz, *Alternative Worlds in Fantasy Fiction* (London: Continuum, 2001).
Lévi-Strauss, Claude, *Structural Anthropology*, trans. by Claire Jordan and Brooke Grundfest Schoepf (Harmondsworth: Penguin, 1972).
Zornado, Joseph L., *Inventing the Child: Culture, Ideology, and the Story of Childhood* (New York: Garland, 2001).

Notes

1. John Stephens, *Language and Ideology in Children's Fiction* (London: Longman, 1992), p. 8.
2. See Peter Hollindale, 'Ideology and the Children's Book', *Signal* 55 (January 1988), 3–22.
3. Stephens, p. 10.
4. Stephens, p. 14.
5. Stephens, p. 18.
6. Aidan Chambers, 'The Reader in the Book', in Peter Hunt (ed.) *Children's Literature: The Development of Criticism* (London: Routledge, 1990), pp. 91–114.
7. Stephens, p. 27.
8. Stephens, p. 3.
9. Stephens, p. 1.
10. Louis Althusser, *Essays on Ideology* (London: Verso, 1984).

11. Charles Baudelaire, 'Le Joueur généreux', in *Petits poëmes en prose* (Paris: Gallimard, 1973).
12. Nicholas Tucker and Nikki Gamble, *Family Fictions* (London: Continuum, 2001), p. 1.
13. Jacqueline Rose, *The Case of Peter Pan, or, The Impossibility of Children's Fiction* (Basingstoke: Macmillan, 1984).
14. Karín Lesnik-Oberstein, *Children's Literature: Criticism and the Fictional Child* (Oxford: Clarendon, 1994).
15. See Stephen Thomson, 'Substitute Communities, Authentic Voices: the Organic Writing of the Child' in Karín Lesnik-Oberstein, ed., *Children in Culture: Approaches to Childhood* (Basingstoke: Macmillan – now Palgrave Macmillan, 1998), pp. 248–73.
16. I will try, in line with Pullman's wishes, to avoid referring to them as a 'trilogy'.
17. Philip Pullman, *Northern Lights* (London: Scholastic, 1996), p. 31.
18. *Northern Lights*, p. 30.
19. *Northern Lights*, p. 21.
20. *Northern Lights*, p. 83.
21. *Northern Lights*, p. 3.
22. *Northern Lights*, pp. 62–3.
23. Philip Pullman, *The Amber Spyglass* (London: Scholastic, 2001), p. 87.
24. *The Amber Spyglass*, p. 90.
25. *The Amber Spyglass*, p. 48.
26. *The Amber Spyglass*, p. 234.
27. *The Amber Spyglass*, p. 132.
28. *The Amber Spyglass*, p. 71.
29. *The Amber Spyglass*, p. 12.
30. *The Amber Spyglass*, p. 17.
31. Philip Pullman, *The Subtle Knife* (London: Scholastic, 1998), p. 11.
32. *Northern Lights*, p. 310.
33. *Northern Lights*, p. 65.
34. *Northern Lights*, p. 34.
35. *Northern Lights*, p. 53.
36. *Northern Lights*, p. 58.
37. *Northern Lights*, p. 59.
38. *Northern Lights*, p. 86.
39. *Northern Lights*, p. 77.
40. *Northern Lights*, p. 394.
41. *The Amber Spyglass*, pp. 276–7.
42. *Northern Lights*, pp. 89, 92.
43. *Northern Lights*, pp. 122–5.
44. *Northern Lights*, p. 182.
45. *Northern Lights*, p. 82.
46. *Northern Lights*, p. 76.
47. *Northern Lights*, p. 67.
48. *The Amber Spyglass*, pp. 210–11.
49. *The Amber Spyglass*, p. 149.
50. *Northern Lights*, p. 380.
51. *The Amber Spyglass*, p. 233.
52. *The Amber Spyglass*, p. 253.
53. *The Amber Spyglass*, p. 492.

54. *Northern Lights*, p. 122.
55. *Northern Lights*, p. 124.
56. *Northern Lights*, p. 56.
57. *The Amber Spyglass*, p. 292.
58. *The Amber Spyglass*, pp. 329–31; see also pp. 455–6.
59. Philip Pullman, 'Let's Write it in Red: The Patrick Hardy Lecture', *Signal* 85 (January 1998), 44–62, 48.
60. 'Let's Write it in Red', 50.
61. In the same lecture, Pullman also says the best source of stories is myth and folk tale, but this, as is often the case in children's literature criticism, is itself seen as part of 'life' in opposition to literary writing.
62. Kate Kellaway, 'A wizard with worlds', *Observer*, 22 October 2000.
63. James Carter, *Talking Books: Children's Authors Talk about the Craft, Creativity and Process of Writing* (London: Routledge, 1999), p. 184.
64. *Northern Lights*, p. 33.
65. *Northern Lights*, p. 19.
66. *Northern Lights*, p. 33.
67. *Northern Lights*, p. 32.
68. *Northern Lights*, p. 176; see p. 310.
69. Roderick McGillis, '"And the Celt Knew the Indian": Knowingness, Postcolonialism, Children's Literature', in Roderick McGillis, ed., *Voices of the Other, Children's Literature and the Postcolonial Context*, (New York: Garland, 2000), pp. 223–35, p. 225.
70. McGillis, '"And the Celt Knew the Indian"', pp. 224–5.
71. See e.g. Anne-Marie Bird, ' "Without Contraries is no Progression": Dust as an All-Inclusive, Multifunctional Metaphor in Philip Pullman's "His Dark Materials"', *Children's Literature in Education* 32:2 (2001), 111–23. Pullman's newspaper and television interventions against the Christian myth of higher powers and after-lives are too numerous to list.
72. Kathleen Odean, 'The Story Master', *School Library Journal*, 1 October 2000 (online at www.slj.com).
73. *Northern Lights*, pp. 372–3.
74. *Talking Books*, pp. 190–1.
75. *The Amber Spyglass*, p. 430.
76. *The Amber Spyglass*, p. 307.

8
Reading Intertextuality. The Natural and the Legitimate: Intertextuality in 'Harry Potter'

Daniela Caselli

> No man can write a single passage to which a parallel one may not be found somewhere in the literature of the world.
>
> Alfred Tennyson[1]

Intertextuality is still a contentious notion, not only within children's literature criticism but also within criticism overall. If we look at a text which has recently been at the center of the children's literature world, J.K. Rowling's 'Harry Potter' series, we can see how the question of intertextuality mediates core preoccupations about literary value, originality, and authority. Harry Potter is often claimed in journalism and criticism alike to have been a completely spontaneous phenomenon, the offspring of J.K. Rowling's sudden inspiration during a train journey in times of hardship. In the spate of recent criticism on the series, however, many scholars have linked the texts either to specific works of children's literature, from *Tom Brown's Schooldays* to *The Worst Witch*, or to genres (especially the boarding school story) or to myths and fairy tales. Harry Potter, then, is claimed to be both utterly original and part of a literary lineage. Julia Eccleshare, for instance, provides a list of literary parallels:

> Physically, with its dramatic setting and castle-like appearance, Hogwarts owes much to the cliff-top Roslyn in Dean Farrer's classic *Eric, or Little by Little* (1858) as well as to Blyton's altogether jollier 'Malory Towers' stories. [...] The village of Hogsmeade [...] mirrors the pub life in Thomas Hughes's *Tom Brown's Schooldays*. [...] Just as Jennings befriends Darbishire when they both arrive at Linbury Court Preparatory School in Anthony Buckerige's *Jennings Goes to School* (1950), [...] so Harry and Ron become instant friends when they meet on the Hogwarts Express [...].[2]

The inclusion of Hermione as the third element of the group is paralleled to Antonia Forest's *Autumn Term* (1948) and *Kipling's Stalky & Co* (1899), while the figure of the 'ma'm'selle' is read as being subverted by the powerful half giant Madame Maxime, the headmistress of the magical school of Beauxbatons. This reminds Eccleshare of another magical school, that appearing in Ursula Le Guin's *A Wizard of Earthsea* (1968–90), a book defined, however, as being 'far less tethered to the realities of school than *Harry Potter and the Philosopher's Stone'*. Eccleshare, like Marina Warner, links the Harry Potter series to the fantasy genre, whose main representatives are identified as C.S. Lewis, Tolkien, Le Guin, and J.M. Barrie, while T.H. White's *The Once and Future King* (1938) is read as offering a parallel to the Harry–Dumbledore relationship in that between Wart and Merlyn.[3] Wendy Doniger also relates the King Arthur of *The Sword in the Stone* to Harry Potter, pointing out their common abilities to handle a magically heavy sword and to speak with animals.[4] Snow-white's speaking mirror is juxtaposed to the rebuffing mirror in the Weasleys' family house and to 'the Mirror of Erised' in *Harry Potter and the Philosopher's Stone*. The every-flavored beans are linked back to Mary Poppins's 'customised' medicine, the speaking chess figures are read against *Through the Looking Glass and What Alice Found There*, and platform nine and three-quarters as an entrance to the magical world is paralleled to *Alice in Wonderland*'s rabbit-hole. Both journalists and scholars have also linked this to Eva Ibbotson's *The Secret of Platform 13* (1994).[5]

The examples above bring to the fore a characteristic shared by most available criticism on Harry Potter: the parallels drawn between Rowling's series and other texts (mostly, as observed above, children's literature texts) are *generic*, insofar as they are mostly focused on ideas of genre, in the sense of both children's literature and sub-genres such as the schoolboy story or fairy tales.

In this study I would like to explore the function of such generic parallels and examine how they can coexist with claims that Harry Potter is an original, authentic, and spontaneous phenomenon. More specifically, I will look at how Harry Potter's language is often discussed in criticism as being artlessly natural and I will contend that this is made possible by its family resemblances. Many critics and readers assume that the language of Harry Potter is 'natural' in the sense of 'true to life', not adorned or artistically elaborated, or artificially manufactured in some way. Instead, I will be considering here what such claims can mean: how and why do the critics distinguish a language of 'nature' from a language apparently not 'natural'? I will argue further that the idea of this kind of 'naturalness' rests on an idea of family – or generic – relationships, which see this naturalness as that of an offspring snugly nested within the family tree.

Suman Gupta has recently discussed the specific kinds of familiar and yet evasive allusions he sees as traversing the 'Harry Potter' series:

The 'Harry Potter' novels constantly echo the faintly familiar. The names of magical characters, the motifs and rituals of magic, the stories and histories that give body to the magic world appear often to refer back to a shimmering vista of folklore, fairy tale and myth drawn indiscriminately from a range of sources and contexts. [...] The 'Harry Potter' novels remind readers of almost familiar fairy tales, folklores, myths, but do not crystallize the relationship further. I am reasonably sure that after compendiums of allusions are collected, critics would fail to find definite insights from them into these books. Certain general observations might become available: for example, that fairy tales, myths, folklore are alluded to in this way to encode modern values while retaining the traditional effect; or that this is a way of assuming and/or subverting the conventional authority of the story-teller. But such observations, general as they are, are not the province of research into original sources. They do not allude backwards to the past, but sideways from the magic world to our world.[6]

Gupta therefore argues that what he refers to as the 'almost familiar' belongs to a different field from that of 'research into original sources'. The way in which critics discuss allusiveness in Harry Potter is very different indeed from, for instance, the eminent critic Christopher Ricks's recent study on allusion in poetry;[7] nevertheless, both Gupta and Ricks (despite their differences) have to face the problem of 'evasive allusions' – allusions that are somehow 'almost familiar'; while in Gupta they play a major role, in Ricks they are denied the status of allusions altogether, in order to focus on what he describes as intentional allusions. Both solutions highlight how 'the almost familiar' constitutes a central problem within the study of intertextuality, because it raises common questions to do with authority, such as where intertextuality 'originates' (in the intentions of the 'author'?), or which reading can 'authoritatively' identify intertextual allusions and references as such. As we will see in the course of this chapter, the authority and the intentions of the writer are invoked both in the studies focused on what Gupta calls 'the province of research into original sources' and in those concerned with 'evasive allusions'. In the case of Rowling's texts, I will explore how the frequently commented on 'air de famille' in Harry Potter raises issues to do with authority and also enables the two main discourses surrounding it – that of innocent simplicity and spontaneous originality, on the one hand, and traditional literary values, on the other – to coexist.

By looking at Harry Potter in relation to the much-debated issue of relations among texts, I am neither interested in proposing yet another definition of intertextuality nor to discover not-yet-unearthed revealing parallels between Harry Potter and other works of literature. Rather I want to ask why, when the language of the series is read as alluringly transparent in its simplicity and spontaneity, many claims are nevertheless also being made for the intertextual nature of Harry Potter, and how these reflect some more general problems in the theory of intertextuality. This will lead me to reconsider the politics of intertextuality, by focusing on ideas of value and authority.

Children's literature is an ideal arena to explore this link because of its recently attained status of academic discipline; for a long time, in fact, children's literature criticism was regarded at best a pleasant, rather than a serious critical activity, because it focuses on what have been regarded as simple, easy, or not very valuable texts.

John Stephens has defined intertexuality as no longer fashionable, precisely because he sees it as having worked for a long time as a 'fashionable word', which did not imply a new concept, but was just a trendier way to refer to influence. Intertextuality has often been accused of being a new coinage to dress up old-fashioned ideas of influence and source-hunting, again ultimately useless because of its purely cosmetic function.[8] At the same time, however, Julia Kristeva's (and Roland Barthes's) claim that any text is intertextual insofar as it is a 'mosaic of quotation', has often been blamed for being too broad a notion to be critically useful. Indeed, one may argue that the *Tel Quel* notion of intertextuality is more helpful to questioning the validity of source-hunting than in proposing alternative solutions. If we posit any text as a 'mosaic of quotations' (and any text might be said to fit this description), then the productive critical question to ask becomes *why* it is critically relevant to establish differences and similarities between texts.

Rather than declaring intertextuality obsolete or celebrating its critical potential, I will look at intertextual readings of Harry Potter in order to analyse how critics invest in this notion and attribute critical and cultural value to it. Arguments in favor of simplicity and accessibility coexist with arguments in favor of literary value and sophistication in every discussion of Harry Potter as a cultural phenomenon.[9] Since the dizzying figures quantifying the number of books sold and the volume of the market generated by the book (from movies to merchandising) do not elucidate the reasons why this phenomenon has occurred, critics have attempted to provide a number of explanations.[10] And the very idea of explaining the Harry Potter phenomenon is linked to the discovery of sources, as Andrew Blake has noticed: 'Most of the people who have written about the Harry Potter phenomenon (and they are legion) try to discuss these questions by discussing the book's sources.'[11] I would like to begin by looking at the debates on the nature of this literary phenomenon to explore later some of the related problems to do with intertextuality. If some critics writing in Lana A. Whited's volume, such as Roni Natov and M. Katherine Grimes, attribute an intrinsic value to the Harry Potter texts, the vast majority of the contributors to her book (Amanda Cockrell, Jann Lacoss, Pat Pinsent, and Lana A. Whited herself) take the phenomenal measure of the market generated by Harry Potter as proof of the text's value. Cockrell, for instance, asserts that there is a simple reason for Harry Potter's becoming the subject of intense media hype: 'children love it'.[12] She declares Harry Potter's originality by stating that the child, whose innocence is good by definition, can recognize its own innocent goodness in the text. This is followed by the inevitable conclusion that if children love Harry Potter and spontaneously recognize it as good, then the book must be good *for* children. Such approaches posit the child as an intrinsically good entity, which spontaneously chooses the book, proving the book's own goodness, which reflects its own. Indeed, the child is posited here as essential goodness and spontaneity (children's choice to buy the book indicates their spontaneous recognition of their own goodness in the book's goodness). Moreover, the critics place themselves in the position of having to judge a priori what is good for the child. However, if we question, with such critics as Jacqueline Rose, Karín Lesnik-Oberstein, Valerie Walkerdine, and Erica Burman, the assumed intrinsic, a-social and a-historical goodness of the child and the ways in which such claims coexist with all kinds of contradictory claims (a questioning discussed at greater length elsewhere in this volume), the whole proposition disintegrates.[13]

We would be wrong, then, to read those critics who protest against ideas of Harry Potter's literary merit as somehow following a cultural studies approach (as some of these critics describe their critical alliances), because their argument needs to posit literature as 'good' *per se*, rather than to question this assumption. If some concede that this particular book may not be very good, the act of reading certainly remains to them a worthy occupation, unquestioningly linked to literature's power to improve people. If children read more thanks to Harry Potter, then the book is seen as necessarily being a moral one insofar as it helps children to become better citizens. A mass market phenomenon is thus transformed into a self-fulfilling prophecy deriving from the faith in the child's (and literature's) intrinsic goodness. According to this account, then, the phenomenal success of Harry Potter is an utterly spontaneous event; it is an instantaneous moment of recognition between the child (meant as the very site of innocence, goodness and spontaneity) and the book.

Within the children's literature world such claims have, however, been challenged, for instance by Jack Zipes, who highlights how a phenomenon needs to be a popular event, insofar as it can only exist when shared and recognized; as such, it is spontaneous only insofar as spontaneity is constructed as a social and cultural shared meaning.[14] Refreshingly, for Zipes there is no such thing as a spontaneous phenomenon. However, one can detect in Zipes more than a few traces of nostalgia; by harshly criticizing a post-industrial consumerist culture which manipulates needs and desires by producing them, Zipes longs for a more innocent world, as can be observed in the opening of his chapter on Harry Potter, which claims that 'Although there are now four published books in the Harry Potter series, it is difficult to assess them as literature *per se* [...]'.[15] For Zipes the media hype generated around Harry Potter occludes our critical channels and obscures the intrinsic qualities of the books, should it possess any (something Zipes does not believe). For Zipes, clearly, the possibility of judging literature *per se* is there as a possibility, taken away by a capitalist economy focused on profit and exploitation. And this is where these two apparently conflicting claims in favor of and against Harry Potter share a basic theoretical premise; what at first sight might appear as a reading indebted to cultural studies, interested in criticizing the logic which markets the book as product, is undermined, as in the case of Whited, by its ultimate goal, that of being able to find a book which is good *in and of itself*, which in the end amounts to finding a book which is good for the child (cf. Lesnik-Oberstein's critique). Zipes and Whited may appear to represent diverging critical views, with Zipes claiming that the text is not good because it reflects capitalism's reassuringly exploitative logic, and Whited stating that a discussion on the 'literary merits of J.K. Rowling's Harry Potter novels is threatened by the cloud of commercialism encircling the books',[16] but, in my reading, they are in fact driven by the same agenda, focused on finding the book which reflects the child's own unadulterated natural goodness.

One might argue that the recent work of Maria Nikolajeva has challenged both Whited and Zipes's positions.[17] Nikolajeva maintains that one of the reasons for Harry Potter's popularity is to be found not in mere media manipulation, as Zipes claims, but in the fact that Harry is a romantic hero, able to engage readers at different levels:

> After decades of parody, metafiction, frame-breaking, and other postmodern games, it may feel liberating for the readers, young and old alike, to know where to place their sympathies or antipathies. [...] Harry Potter provides the sense of security for the reader that characters such as Lyra or Christopher Chant have subverted.[18]

Nikolajeva's explanation of Harry Potter's popularity is based on the idea of security generated by the ability of readers, or more specifically, child-readers, to recognize good and evil. What at first sight may have appeared as a third way after Whited and Zipes, is in fact a repetition of the theoretical problems encountered in the other two critics. Similarly to Whited, Nikolajeva implicitly reads the book's success as positive because it generates something good for the child and the adult alike. The ultimate goal is shared by all these critics, as they are all looking for the book truly good for children; the only difference is that some identify this with Harry Potter, and some claim that Harry Potter is the opposite of what we should regard as good for the child. Even though these divergent conclusions may have different implications if used as the basis for educational choices, from a theoretical point of view the premises, and the logic, are identical.

These three critics also introduce claims of simplicity, spontaneity, and complexity in relation to the phenomenal aspect of Harry Potter. I would now like to look at how these notions work in similar ways in relation to intertextuality. Assertions such as those made by Cockrell, who maintains that both the child and the book are good, simple, and spontaneous, are contrasted by the many critics who have tried to argue that Harry Potter does not exist in a vacuum, and that its literary relations do not prove its banality or derivative character, but its richness and complexity instead. Pat Pinsent's argument, for instance, maintains that Harry Potter is good because it is genuinely simple but also deeply complex. After a long discussion of thematic parallels between the Harry Potter series and a number of other children's texts such as '*The Worst Witch, Groosham Grange*, or books on a similar theme by Monica Furlong, Ursula Le Guin, and Diana Wynne-Jones', Pinsent asserts that:

> Rowling's books work at more than one level, so that adults readers are able to detect allegorical elements, or may sometimes feel that the complex structures or development of suspense resemble examples of the detective or thriller genre. I am not disparaging Murphy or Horowitz; their intentions and implied audiences are different and their books have been very popular, being awarded prizes, being adapted for film and television, and attracting relatively large sales. Nevertheless, they have not been so popular with adult readers as Rowling's, and must rank largely as entertainment for the young.[19]

The fact that the text can be linked to other texts, proves here that there are layers than can be seen only by certain readers; in Pinsent's argument this works as a classic anti-children's literature claim. While asserting that she is not disparaging certain children's literature authors, she indicates that their limitations lie precisely in their being for children, 'entertainment for the young'. In Pinsent's argument, then, to have additional layers works exactly as in conventional adult criticism: intertextuality, read as the text's multi-layered nature, proves its value by appealing to an adult, that is to say more sophisticated, readership. Paradoxically, this has been one of the classic arguments used to marginalize various kinds of literature, from texts written by women to, indeed, children's literature itself.[20]

In order to avoid circular arguments, we cannot simply equate the child's simplicity and goodness with the text's shared characteristics as Cockrell does. However, we cannot adopt Pinsent's position either, unless we want to discard children's literature as a genre and rescue only those texts that traditionally have – according to the criticism – appealed to an adult readership, thus reiterating a move which for centuries has been at the basis of an exclusionary canon formation.

Does intertextuality, then, represent a blind alley for children's literature? What I am arguing instead, is that, at the very least, this consideration of the critical formulations and problems around intertextuality is helpful to understanding how some of the tenets around which children's literature and its criticism are based are self-contradictory. While doing so, I am also attempting to demonstrate further how the idea of intertextuality as depth is problematic in adult and children's literature criticism alike because it endorses certain ideas of literary value rather than challenging them. Children's literature criticism, therefore, unlike adult criticism, finds itself in a peculiarly difficult position when discussing intertextual references in the text: in criticism, to detect a reference is usually taken to add value to the text by at once proving its complexity and explaining that complexity away; the source has both an enriching and an explicative function. In children's literature criticism this approach (which guarantees the eagle-eyed quickness of the critic while proving the learnedness of the author) encounters a peculiar obstacle in the figure of the child. How can a text such as Harry Potter epitomize childhood's simplicity and spontaneity while being declared as complex at the same time, as we have seen Pinsent, Whited and Nikolajeva would like to claim?

These contradictory positions are maintained, I would contend, through the idea of readers' competence. Let's first of all think about how Cockrell, Nikolajeva, and Pinsent argue that Harry Potter is a text that appeals to its child and adult readership and shows layers of complexity in the text, which are linked to development. Cockrell claims the utter simplicity and spontaneity of the text (and of the text as phenomenon, similarly to Whited). Nikolajeva argues that the text's ability to make readers (children and adults alike) recognize good and evil is to be attributed to its adoption of the figure of the 'Romantic Hero'; and Pinsent, like Philip Nel, claims that intertextual relations do not disprove the text's originality, while also showing its multilayered nature, which appeals to adults and thus proves to be better than other children's texts (at least in terms of complexity). The latter critical position ultimately reinforces the idea of an adult audience as superior or more sophisticated that a child audience, thus reinstating a developmental model which, as I have argued above, is linked to classic literary paradigms that use intertextuality as proof of authority.

In the first case, we have the very problem of how the child can recognize its own innocence. This is the classic Blakean paradox: how can innocence know it is innocence without becoming its opposite, that is experience? How can the child find itself within the book without automatically betraying his self-awareness, and thus its lack of innocence, during this process of recognition? Childhood's innocence, once again, works as the place of the projected and impossible absolute innocence, as both Rose and Lesnik-Oberstein have demonstrated at length.

The second problem, not unconnected to the first, is the idea that a certain simplicity (that of the Romantic Hero as dividing good and evil) is appealing to both child and adult. But how can this happen when child and adult are opposite notions, which seem to exclude each other precisely because the child needs to operate as absolute innocence ('children love it')? The notion invoked in this context is again a developmental one, which claims that children's literature is effective when it makes the adult reader rediscover the child in him/herself (a quality attributed with disconcerting frequency to children's authors too).[21] The book becomes a unity (made of layers) reflected in the developmental unity of the self (a whole made of layers or stages). Erica Burman has persuasively criticized this developmental approach both in the field of child psychology and in that of cultural studies.[22] In the case of Harry Potter, this phenomenon becomes even more relevant because Rowling's series is said to be 'growing up with its initial audience'.[23] The developmental model enables critics to bypass their initial opposition between child's innocence and adult's experience: if the adult can be seen merely as somebody who once was a child, his/her innocence (and the values attributed to it) can be preserved even within a dichotomous framework.

There is another way in which childhood simplicity and adult sophistication are said to coincide in relation to intertextuality, and that is through myth and fairy tales. If Harry Potter is said to reflect both childhood's innocence and adult's experience, critics have been forced both to posit innocence as an absolute value and to argue that to lose one's innocence is part of a normal process of development. This is one of the reasons why Harry Potter is often read as a moral and didactic text that can transform absolute innocence, spontaneity, and simplicity into knowledge of a good kind. In order to do this Harry Potter the book needs to be both spontaneous (original) and part of a tradition (legitimate).[24] This tradition, however, is not envisioned as a legacy of texts to be interpreted, but is constituted as either experience, which is passed on orally (in the case of fairy tales), or as innate values that are rediscovered (in the case of myths and archetypes). Through this move, the original and the legitimate coincide in the notion of the natural. The link between orality and the child is what explains the prominence in children's literature criticism of studies on myths and fairy tales: this can be observed in David Colbert's portentous claims about the links between Harry Potter and Western civilization.[25] However, one may argue that his is a popular volume devoted to a general public with no special claim to pedagogical or academic expertise. More interesting, perhaps, is to note a correspondence between Colbert's assumptions and those of both Elizabeth Schafer in her educationally-oriented volume on Harry Potter[26] and Lana A. Whited in her self-defined academic volume.[27]

One of Shafer's chapters, 'Mythology, Legends, and Fairy Tales', opens with the epigraph by Joseph Campbell, which claims: 'A mythology doesn't come from the head; a mythology comes from the heart.' By claiming that 'myths are stories that reflect cultural beliefs and traditions through symbolism [...]' and that 'connecting diverse groups who share universal concerns, myths offer explanations for such fundamental questions as how the universe was created or why death occurs', Shafer concludes that 'the fundamental Harry Potter plot is universal, appealing to humanity's mythic core and collective imagination. Characters, places, and events have their origins in fairy tales and fables that reiterate cosmic messages and cautionary tales.'[28] From an intertextual point of view, all these claims remain unsubstantiated: the volume first lists a series of classical and English mythological characters, with no reference to how they link to Harry Potter. Only later, in the section 'Analysis of the mythological allusions: Potter as Myth', does Shafer bizarrely suggest that 'Hogwarts could represent Olympus', that Harry can stand for Hercules, and that 'Voldemort is Mars, the god of War', while 'James and Lily Potter could represent Vulcan and Venus'.[29] The only reference that I might be inclined to see in the text is that based on the classically mythical fore-name of Prof. Minerva McGonagall. The links claimed with fairy tale tradi-tion seem hardly less frail to me: 'The novels also present fairy tale imagery. Like Cinderella, Harry escapes from abusive guardians [...] Harry also resem-bles Hansel as told by the Grimm Brothers, trying to outsmart the wicked witch as well as the carnivorous creatures in the forest in his quest for survival or metaphorical maturity.'[30] The omnipresent (in children's literature criti-cism) names of Bruno Bettelheim and Carl Jung are used to prop up the fol-lowing general remarks: 'Bettelheim would have praised the Potter series for demonstrating how children can deal with oppressive situations and coexist harmoniously with frightening and loathsome people'.[31] Jung is also prob-lematically read as having originated a pseudo-scientific hereditary model:

> Carl Jung [...] asserted that all modern beings retain patterns of their ancient ancestors, and that regardless of geography, race, or religion, all people everywhere share common fears and desires. Biologists have long recognized instinctual patterns in lower animals [...] and recent DNA dis-coveries confirm that except for tiny differences in DNA structure, all creatures are biologically similar.[32]

The invocation of DNA to reassert an essentialist view of humanity is at best bizarre from a scientific point of view; it does, however, clearly link the idea of intertextuality to that of descent, showing how intertextuality, at least in the form of general relations with tradition and myth, negotiates the rela-tionship between archaeology and genealogy. This is why, I would argue, in the criticism looking at sources in Harry Potter, we always find references to myths, fairy tales and archetypes, rather than specific discussions on language and structure. These concepts work as the promise of a direct and unmediated connection to the origins – the heart – of civilization (as in Nicolajeva's read-ing of Northrop Frye). They also harmonize the idea of simplicity and com-plexity through an archaeological model which sees spontaneity and tradition coincide. The text, thought of as depth (in itself regarded as a positive quality and synonym of complexity), presents then a surface layer, which in its absolute simplicity corresponds to that of the child; its further strata, however, are myths and fairy tales, corresponding to more 'primitive' stages of civiliza-tion, attributing a third spatial dimension (depth) to this pseudo-Vichian model of historical ages corresponding to human stages of development.

Even those critics who, like Eccleshare, do at times discuss some of these parallels in detail, still resort to ideas of layers and use the intertextual reading as a measure of the text's value: 'Rowling's imaginary inventions are more sophisticated than Blyton's and more extensively developed, but her ability to create a world and a fantasy which children can enter so completely is not dissimilar' and:

> Rowling's opening of *Harry Potter and the Philosopher's Stone* draws closely on Dahl. [...] Like Dahl's, Rowling's children remain children. The school-story setting confirms their status absolutely. [...] But if Rowling is like Dahl in her ability to speak directly to children through her child characters, she has a different view of children's relationship to adults. Where Dahl is largely subversive in promoting the notion that adults should be neither emulated nor respected, Rowling is fiercely traditional.[33]

This discussion reproduces a constant problem in intertextual studies, in which the parallels are necessarily cast within a hierarchical model, thus feeding back into an idea of linear historical progression and additional textual layers: this is a view of literary history in which texts get better and better, or more and more complex over time. Most importantly, however, the ultimate goal remains that of using intertextuality as an explanation for the book's success:

> The Harry Potter stories are a clever fusion of nostalgia for the school-story tradition, laced with high fantasy themes of good and evil that are brought up to date through discussion of rights and race. The interspersing of contrasting contemporary black comedy and social commentary on the late twentieth century provide both context and access.[34]

Similarly, if from a very well identified 'French' point of view, Isabelle Smadja asserts that

> Voldemort neither solely incarnates the Nazi dictator or the Greek Medusa: in fact he represents absolute evil, thus he is the figure of the devil. [...] The multiplication of sources to which Rowling's text refers can, then, explain the universal success of 'Harry Potter': by constantly pointing to at least three kinds of reference, her work is the expression of an imaginary that inevitably goes beyond mere British insularity.[35]

The ways in which readers' competence negotiates ideas of origin, originality and tradition in the cases analysed above indicate how intertextuality can help us to understand logical contradiction at work in the criticism on children's literature while also stressing how many of these issues operate unchallenged within criticism *tout court*. Moreover, these critical examples also point out how the opposite poles of simplicity (equated with innocence) and sophistication need to be maintained as essential to the survival of children's literature criticism while in fact being constantly collapsed into each other.

Just as the text's layers prove both the text's simplicity and its complexity (which reflect that of both the child and the child within the adult), Harry Potter the literary phenomenon is claimed to be at once simple and spontaneous and part of a tradition. Among the claims that argue that Harry Potter is part of a mythical, generic or literary tradition we can detect a further tension between those critics who use this as evidence of the author's knowledge and the text's relevance and those who accuse them of lacking originality or being derivative.

Paul Bürvenich lists in his book a number of possible relations between the Harry Potter series and other children's texts, again mostly of a generic nature, such as sharing the entrance into a magical world with C.S. Lewis's *The Lion, the Witch and the Wardrobe* or the wizards' school with Jill Murphy's *The Worst Witch*,[36] while he plays down José Garcia's argument in favour of the similarities with Tolkien.[37] Bürvenich also describes how Knobloch's intertextual reading of Harry Potter suggests the derivative nature of the parallels between the text and Eva Ibbotson's *The Secret of Platform 13*. The pattern identified at the beginning of this study is here confirmed: many intertextual readings of Harry Potter are of a generic nature, connecting the text with other genres or other texts' themes (rather than with specific linguistic aspects) in order either to prove the book's universality (and universal appeal for children, hence its value) or its derivative nature, reproducing the apparently dissimilar but ultimately comparable positions of Whited and Zipes analysed above.

I also detect constant further anxieties to do with authority in the criticism devoted to Harry Potter and intertextuality. On the one hand this revolves around the idea of how much the author 'actually' knows, and on the other on how every claim to intertextual complexity can easily spill over and turn into a suggestion of derivativeness. In short, two aspects are worth noticing here, one is the opposition between originality and derivativeness, the other is the author's intentions. Let me begin to tackle the issue of originality starting from its opposite: plagiarism.[38] As many critics have pointed out (Whited, Bürvenich), in 1999 Nancy K. Stouffer brought charges against J.K. Rowling, claiming that Rowling had plagiarized her 1987 book *The Legend of Rah and the Muggles*. Paul Bürvenich demonstrates how many of the parallels used by Stouffer as evidence of plagiarism (and appearing on her website) are the result of interpretation. Among the parallels that Stouffer lists on her website, discussed by Bürvenich, is the presence in Rowling of an entry which reads 'knock three times on the oak door', which is argued by Stouffer to correspond, and thus derive, from the fact that in her book too we encounter characters who 'knock three times on the wooden door'. This, Bürvenich argues, just like the location of the castle or the presence of a 'Great Hall' in both texts, cannot be read as constituting plagiarism; they are such common features in literature that their origin cannot be located in one particular text. Moreover, Bürvenich continues, some of the listed parallels appear on closer scrutiny not to constitute parallels at all; what is quoted as 'the book of monster' (as parallel to Rowling's 'the ancient book of tales') never appears as such in Stouffer's text, which has instead 'Monster Book of Monsters' or 'Monster Book'. In this case, then, repetition of some parts of a phrase are argued to amount to a combinatory logic rather than an intentional replication.[39]

Among the strongest claims for legal action was the correspondence in the two texts of 'Muggles' and the similarity of the name 'Larry Potter'. Bürvenich, however, argues that in Stouffer the 'Muggles' are a people living in a continent named Aura;[40] the name has a different meaning and cannot be taken to be derivative, exemplifying his answer to one of the theoretical questions asked above. The statement issued by Scholastic Press in response to Stouffer argues that the frequent occurrence of the words 'muggle' and 'muggles', both as a noun and as a proper name, legally dismantles the case:

> The words 'muggle' or 'muggles' have been used in a variety of ways for many years. In the 18th century the word 'muggles' meant a state of restlessness. These words have also been used in other creative contexts. These include a musical composition by Louis Armstrong entitled 'Muggles' in the 1930s. In 1959 Carol Kendall wrote an award winning book entitled 'The Gammage Cup' which featured a character named 'Muggles'. In the 1990s a book entitled 'Mrs Muggle's Sparkle' was written by Ruth Bragg. J.K. Rowling used the word 'muggles' to describe non-magical people as a derivative of the English slang term 'mug', which means a 'fool' in current usage.[41]

Scholastic Press maintains that the word appears so frequently in discourse that repetition cannot constitute proof of a direct relationship between Rowling and Stouffer's texts. If we want to link this journalistic episode to the theoretical concerns expressed above, we could read Scholastic's statement as a Kristevan argument: the word 'muggles' appears in so many contexts that it indicates how every text is a mosaic of quotations; it then becomes impossible to attribute a specific source to those tesserae.

Another of Bürvenich's points is worth noticing: the similarity between the names 'Larry Potter' and 'Harry Potter' is recognized, but J.K. Rowling's own explanation (that 'Harry' has always been her favorite boy's name, while 'Potter' was the surname of her neighbors) is judged as more persuasive that Stouffer's parallel.[42] Bürvenich's argument moves away from the text (to which he has clung so far in order to prove his points) and resorts to the intentions of the author, thus performing what would be a rather spectacular sleight of hand were it not so common in intertextual criticism.

Repetition, supposedly able to work as evidence, needs to be interpreted in specific ways in order to constitute the basis for legal action, and in the case of Stouffer it certainly did not work.[43] Without entering the moral domain of Stouffer's good faith, Scholastic's legal action, and the marketing effects of all this extra publicity (which have been discussed by Whited and Bürvenich), we can say that Stouffer's list of parallels is very explicitly a reading of what she sees as similarities, against which Scholastic mounts an opposing case (and according to Judge G. Allen Schwartz an ultimately more convincing one). Authority is always a central concern, as can be observed in this case, when Rowling's authority as an author, her 'credibility', is used by Bürvenich to oppose what perhaps may have apparently (if not legally) constituted the most solid among Stouffer's arguments in support of a relation between the texts. In other words, in this case the author's intentions are used to discriminate between plagiarism and invention.[44]

The Stouffer example demonstrates how, in order to construct a case, it is necessary to argue for both difference and similarity. This is not to argue in favor of a slipshod celebration of the breaking of the boundaries between originality and plagiarism; indeed, I agree with Christopher Ricks's magisterial claim 'that moral agreements, though not natural, may be valuable, indispensable, worthy of the respect that they have earned'.[45] However, Ricks also claims that to examine how the drawing of such distinctions is the result of power structures amounts to a defeatist or relativist position, a contention that I have challenged through my analysis of the Rowling case. A critic who does elide the difference between derivativeness and allusiveness (which Ricks wants to defend) is Peter Hunt, who writes:

> To say that the Harry Potter books are built from the furniture of a mind that has absorbed a good cross-section of children's reading (for the purpose of being a child, rather than the writing of children's books) is not to say that the books are derivative (or, fashionably, intertextually rich). Rather (and it would be insulting to the obvious intelligence of Rowling to suggest that this is accidental), she has produced an eccentric blend of the comfortably predictable and the unsettlingly unexpected. Individually, the incidents and characters – the quidditch games, the mysterious messages, the suspicious behaviour of the masters, the gang of bullies – have, in other guises, served many a well-selling author; combined with twenty-first century preoccupations, such as surveillance and the ambiguity of evil, they become new again.[46]

In Hunt we can find a number of issues relevant to our previous discussion: Rowling's mind 'absorbs', just as for Nel it 'synthetises'; either a natural source or a mechanical motor, the author works as the origin of meaning. Moreover, Hunt also claims that the intertextual references cannot be 'accidental' precisely because to introduce even the possibility of lack of control amounts to challenging the author's authority ('it would be insulting to the obvious intelligence of Rowling to suggest' otherwise). Hunt also shares with Stephens a suspicious attitude towards the fashionable term intertextuality; he does not discuss what intertextuality means in relation to these particular texts, thus flattening derivativeness and intertextual richness through a rather flippant move. This is what has pushed somebody like Ricks to claim the following in his recent book on allusion (he would certainly regard the word 'intertextuality' as both stylistically and ideologically unattractive):

> The question of intentions bears upon allusion as it bears upon everything not only in literature but in every form of communication; suffice it (not) to say here that the present writer believes that it is not only proper but often obligatory to invoke authorial intentions, while maintaining that there is (as Wittgenstein proposed) nothing self-contradictory or sly about positing the existence of unconscious or sub-conscious intentions – as in the case of the Freudian slip, where some parts of you may wish to intimate something that another part of you would disavow. Coleridge sometimes despaired of writing 'on any subject without finding his poem, against his will and without his previous consciousness, a cento of lines which had pre-existed in other works.'[47]

Quite clearly, Ricks here wants it both ways. He wants the author to be able to guarantee the accuracy of an interpretation and its distinctive character (its difference from mere sources), and yet he cannot ignore those twentieth-century philosophical and psychoanalytical thinkers (however hard to recognize one may find Ricks's Wittgenstein or Freud) who have revolutionized the concept of the individual as a coherent subjectivity. Ricks is always at his best when close reading, and Coleridge's quotation clearly leads him to question the idea that the author knows what he or she is doing and inscribes these intentions in the texts for the readers to find. Ricks is more than willing to maintain throughout his volume that any text is able to produce a plethora of contradictory readings, and that the lack of consensus is what constitutes literary criticism. Nevertheless, he is not prepared to relinquish intentionality, a notion that allows him to distinguish between a still visible scaffolding (the source) and what is now part of the building (allusion). Interestingly, none of Ricks's readings in his *Allusion to the Poets* necessitates the concept of authorial intentions in order to offer persuasive interpretations of how texts produce their own claims to authority and create their own place within tradition. Authorial intentionality is a way of protesting the validity of the reading too much, and weakens rather than strengthen Ricks's convincing and perceptive readings (which remain to me precisely this, readings, and not absolute truths, however often the author is invoked). Finally, intentionality cannot guard Ricks's 'moral agreements'; as we observed in the case of Hunt it can, on the contrary, contribute to their very demolition.

Intentionality also plays an important role in David K. Steege's recent contribution, which begins with an interesting discussion on how a boarding school story such as Harry Potter does not need to be based in the author's experience, but can be related to a whole preceding tradition. This, however, does not lead him to question the fiction *versus* reality opposition; neither does he question the idea of the author's intentions. Even when critics claim that Rowling may or may not have been aware of certain texts or myths, she is always cast as the ultimate source of meaning and moral of the series insofar as she 'has both used and transformed the elements of [a] basic plot':[48]

> whether or not Rowling was familiar with these prototypes before she began the Harry Potter saga, she supplements her use of the vocabulary of magic and the common themes of the boarding school genre with additional levels of meaning that render the book more attractive to adult readers than those of Murphy and Horowitz.[49]

Even though possibly unaware, Rowling can add layers of meaning: 'Rowling gives the reader terms that are meaningful on a higher level'.[50]

The difference between what Hunt calls 'derivativeness' and 'intertextual richness' does not, therefore, lie in the intentions of the author or in her authority. It can only be argued, case by case, to lie in the ways in which a text constructs portions of itself as belonging to other texts; succinctly put, it is a matter of how texts construct internal differences. This conclusion may not sound as alluringly powerful as Ricks or even Hunt's claims do, but has two distinct advantages: it privileges argument (how a critic can argue for or against the existence of difference in a text) over essence and authority and it reflects on the political implications of claiming to be able to *see* such difference.

Intertextuality can, I am thus arguing, help us to reconsider the politics of literary value. To be able to 'spot the style' (as Samuel Beckett puts it in *Dream of Fair to Middling Women*) or 'to spot the source' (as Wendy Doniger has it) proves the reader's cleverness; no wonder that many critics use intertextuality as a way to justify their role as cognoscenti belonging to a long tradition. Indeed, this is such an effective and well-rehearsed method that few critics pause to think about what allusions and quotations *do* in the text, and what the implications are of claiming that this constitutes an addition of value. In my interpretation of intertextuality, instead, the issue is not one of revealing a source which is necessarily posited as being part of the essence of the text, but to argue how and why a reader can interpret a text as claiming that some portions of itself are to some extent foreign.

For Harry Potter, a text in which, according to many critical claims, the language operates as a familiarly transparent means of communication, intertextuality is seen as a family resemblance, as a generic similarity. We have seen how links to genres or themes are defined in criticism as mythical or archetypal and thus reconnected to orality and innate human character-istics, which enable children's literature critics to bypass the opposition that they have set up between adult and child and innocence and experience. On the rare occasions when single words or specific structures are discussed, it is always while the specter of originality haunts criticism; the issue of pla-giarism is relevant in this context because it highlights how the tracking of references is intimately connected with the need to prove the author's orig-inality (and thus her authority).

In both cases, moreover, intertextuality works to assert the text's value while leaving undisturbed the text's originality and spontaneity. In the intertextual criticism on Harry Potter the archaeological and the genealogi-cal discourses coincide: what is said to be buried and retrieved is in fact the family. Finding what is hidden means finding oneself, as a number of titles and chapter titles of recent critical studies demonstrate: in Edi Vesco's *Il Magicolibro*[51] Rowling is Harry's 'mum',[52] in Marc Shapiro's *J.K. Rowling, The Wizard Behind Harry Potter*[53] the chapter 'Harry is Born' shares its title with a section from Philip Nel's book, while Rowling famously claims that Harry would have been the name she would have chosen for her child, had he been a boy. In Lana Whited's 'Introduction' to her hefty volume, 'Harry Potter' the book stealthily becomes Harry the boy, complete with personal pronoun: 'schools provid[e] that pupils whose parents object to Harry can avoid him [...]'.[54] Intertextuality *is* genealogy in Harry Potter, as the title of one of the sections in *The Ivory Tower* – 'Harry's Other Literary Relatives' – confirms. The book, then, is the boy: innocent, new, a constant source of wonder and yet also the product of a lineage. Rather than reiterating along with the existing criticism that Harry Potter grows with its readers, thus con-firming an organic development of Harry and its readership, I would con-tend that the criticism reproduces the logic of the text, which is based on current ideas of the child. Just as Harry is an orphan with a noble legacy, Harry Potter is in criticism both the spontaneous child and the child of civ-ilization. Harry Potter is original in its innocence, it comes from its 'mum', or, more worryingly, it 'is likely to come from appropriately strong roots, good DNA';[55] however, it also comes from myth, from other stories (but it is better than them); it comes from humble origins but has risen to fame. This way of looking at the role of intertextuality in both texts and criticism enables us to critique the silent assumption that originality and innocence are naturally linked, and to observe how the naturalness of Harry Potter perfectly fits with its legitimacy.

Further reading

Barthes, Roland, *The Rustle of Language*, translated by Richard Howard (Oxford: Blackwell, 1986).

Bloom, Harold, *The Anxiety of Influence* (New York: Oxford University Press, 1973).

Borges, Jorge Luis, 'Kafka and His Precursors', in *Labyrinths. Selected Stories and Other Writings*, Donald A. Yates and James E. Irby (eds), preface by André Maurois (New York: New Directions Publishing Corporation, 1964), pp. 199–202.

Derrida, Jacques, 'Qual quelle. Les sources de Valéry', in *Marges de la philosophie* (Paris: Les Éditions de Minuit, 1972), 325–63; 'Qual Quelle: Valéry's Sources', in *Margins of Philosophy*, translated, with additional notes, by Alan Bass (Brighton: Harvester Press, 1982), pp. 273–306.

Eliot, T.S., 'Tradition and the Individual Talent' (1917), in *Selected Prose of T.S. Eliot*, edited with an introduction by Frank Kermode (London: Faber and Faber, 1975), pp. 37–44.

Foucault, Michel, 'Qu'est-ce qu'un auteur?' (1969), in *Dits et Écrits* (Paris: Gallimard, 1994) 4 vols, vol. 1, 789–820; 'What Is an Author?' (1969), in *The Foucault Reader*, Paul Rabinov (ed.) (Harmondsworth: Penguin, 1984), pp. 101–20.

Kristeva, Julia, *Séméiotiké: Recherches pour une sémanalyse* (Paris: Éditions du Seuil, 1969); *Desire in Language: a Semiotic Approach to Literature and Art*, translated by Thomas Gora, Alice Jardine and Léon S. Roudiez (New York: Columbia University Press, 1980).

Riffaterre, Michael, 'Syllepsis', *Critical Inquiry*, 6 (1980), 625–38.

Segre, Cesare, 'Intertestuale, interdiscorsivo. Appunti per una fenomenologia delle fonti', in *La parola ritrovata. Fonti e analisi letteraria*, C. Di Girolamo and I. Paccagnella (eds) (Palermo: Sellerio, 1982), pp. 15–28.

Notes

1. Cecil Y. Lang and Edgar F. Shannon, Jr. (eds), *The Letters of Alfred Lord Tennyson*, iii (Cambridge, Mass.: Belknap Press, 1990), p. 183; quoted in Christopher Ricks, *Allusion to the Poets* (Oxford: Oxford University Press, 2002), p. 179.
2. Julia Eccleshare, *A Guide to the Harry Potter Novels* (London and NY: Continuum, 2002), p. 38.
3. See Marina Warner, 'Did Harry Have to Grow Up?', *Observer Review* (29 June, 2003), 15.
4. Wendy Doniger, 'Harry Potter Explained: Can you Spot the Source?' *London Review of Books*, 22(4) (17 February, 2000), 26–7. Bürvenich, however, explains that while Arthur inherits the latter from Merlyn, Harry does so from his worst enemy. Paul Bürvenich, *Der Zauber des Harry Potter: Analyse eines literarischen Welterfolgs* (Frankfurt am Main: Peter Lang, 2001), p. 118.
5. Paul Bürvenich, following Jörg Knobloch, also goes as far as suggesting that the idea of the platform may be derivative. For a full discussion of issues of plagiarism and derivativeness, see below. Bürvenich, *Der Zauber des Harry Potter*, p. 150. See also Jörg Knobloch, *Die Zauberwelt der J.K. Rowling: Hintergründe & Facts zu Harry Potter* (Mülheim: Verlag an der Ruhr, 2000). Common parallels are also those which link Harry Potter's struggle between good and evil to Susan Cooper's *The Dark is Rising* sequence (1965–77), Alan Gardner's *Elidor* (1965) and Philip Pullman's *His Dark Materials* trilogy. Often, the phoenix in 'Harry Potter' is related to E. Nesbit's *The Phoenix and the Carpet* (1904) and Elizabeth Goudge's *The Little White Horse* (1946).
6. Suman Gupta, *Re-reading Harry Potter* (Basingstoke: Palgrave Macmillan, 2003), pp. 96–7.
7. Christopher Ricks, *Allusion to the Poets* (Oxford: Oxford University Press, 2002).
8. John Stephens, 'Children's Literature, Text and Theory: What are we interested in now?, *Papers*, 10(2) (August 2000), 12–21.

9. See, for instance Lana A. Whited (ed.), *The Ivory Tower and Harry Potter. Perspectives on a Literary Phenomenon* (Columbia and London: University of Missouri Press, 2002); Andrew Blake, *The Irresistible Rise of Harry Potter* (London: Verso, 2002); John Granger, *The Hidden Key to Harry Potter: Understanding the Meaning, Genius and Popularity of Joanne Rowling's Harry Potter Novels* (Washington: Zossima Press, 2002); Jack Zipes, *Sticks and Stones: The Troublesome Success of Children's Literature from Slovenly Peter to Harry Potter* (New York: Routledge, 2000); Julia Eccleshare, *Beatrix Potter to Harry Potter: Portraits of Children's Writers* (London: National Portrait Gallery, 2002); Paul Bürvenich, *Der Zauber des Harry Potter*; Isabelle Smadja, *Harry Potter: les raisons d'un succés* (Paris: Presses universitaires de France, 2001); Alasdair Campbell, *From Goggle-eyes to Harry Potter* (Swansea: LISE, 1999); Bill Adler (ed.), *Kids' Letters to Harry Potter from Around the World. An Unauthorized Collection* (New York: Carroll & Graf, 2001); Friedhelm Schneidewind, *Das ABC rund um Harry Potter* (Berlin: Schwarzkopf & Schwarzkopf, 2000); Olaf Kutzmutz, *Harry Potter oder Warum wir Zauberer brauchen* (Wolfenbüttel: Bundesakademie, 2001).

10. For figures up to 2001 see Andrew Blake's discussion. Andrew Blake, *The Irresistible Rise of Harry Potter*, pp. 1–3; pp. 58–61.

11. Andrew Blake, *The Irresistible Rise*, p. 3.

12. Lana A. Whited (ed.), *The Ivory Tower and Harry Potter*, p. 17.

13. Jacqueline Rose, *The Case of Peter Pan, or the Impossibility of Children's Fiction* (Basingstoke: Macmillan, 1984); Karín Lesnik-Oberstein, *Children's Literature: Criticism and the Fictional Child* (Oxford: Clarendon Press, 1994) and (ed.), *Children in Culture: Approaches to Childhood* (Basingstoke: Macmillan – now Palgrave Macmillan, 1998); Erica Burman, *Deconstructing Developmental Psychology* (London and New York: Routledge, 1994); Valerie Walkerdine, *Daddy's Girl: Young Girls and Popular Culture* (Basingstoke: Macmillan – now Palgrave Macmillan, 1997).

14. Zipes, *Sticks and Stones*, p. 170 and ff. For an interesting reading of the self-advertising aspects of Harry Potter's language, see Suman Gupta, *Re-reading Harry Potter*, p. 140. Andrew Blake also provides a political reading of 'Harry Potter' as reflecting New Labour's politically dubious creation of the new industries of leisure, entertainment, and education, where 'creativity and the imagination are to be made more completely at the service of capitalism', just like the Weasley twins do. Blake, *The Irresistible Rise*, p. 65. A persuasive analysis of the role of class in relation to Englishness in 'Harry Potter' can be found in Farah Mendelsohn, 'Crowning the King: "Harry Potter" and the Construction of Authority', in Whited (ed.), pp. 159–81.

15. Zipes, *Sticks and Stones*, p. 170.

16. Whited, *The Ivory Tower*, p. 12.

17. Maria Nikolajeva, 'Harry Potter, A Return to the Romantic Hero', in Elizabeth E. Heilman (ed.), *Harry Potter's World. Multidisciplinary Critical Perspectives* (London and New York: Routledge Falmer, 2003), pp. 125–40.

18. Nikolajeva, 'Harry Potter', 139.

19. Pinsent, *The Ivory Tower*, pp. 48–9.

20. An almost identical argument can be found in Philip Nel, who writes: ' "Why are the books so popular?" [...] One reason why this question may seem so difficult to answer is that the "Harry Potter" novels represent the creative synthesis of a lifetime of reading, and Rowling is very widely read. Another reason is that the books operate on many levels, with many layers of meaning.' Philip Nel, *J.K. Rowling's Harry Potter Novels*, p. 28.

21. 'Like many famous children's authors J.K. (Joanne) Rowling, author of the brilliant and phenomenally successful Harry Potter books, remains in close touch with her own childhood.' Alison Lurie, *Boys and Girls Forever. Reflections on Children's Classics* (London: Chatto and Windus, 2003), p. 113.

22. See Erica Burman, *Deconstructing Developmental Psychology* and 'Childhood, Sexual Abuse and Contemporary Political Subjectivities', in Sam Warner and Paula Reavey (eds), *New Feminist Stories of Child Abuse. Sexual Scripts and Dangerous Dialogues* (London and New York: Routledge, 2003), pp. 34–52; see especially Burman's analysis of the recent Barnardo's advertisement campaign, pp. 45–6.

23. Cockrell, *The Ivory Tower*, 25. The idea of the book developing with the child is at the basis of pedagogical projects aimed at improving the child's learning abilities through 'Harry Potter'. For instance, 'Harry Potter' is used to teach English to German children in Barbara Maria Zollner, *Langenscheidts grosses Zauberwörterbuch für Harry Potter-Fans. Englisch–Deutsch* (Berlin: Langenscheidt, 2001).

24. For an interesting discussion of the relationship between the natural and the legitimate in English poetry, see Ricks, *Allusion to the Poets*, p. 76. The idea of genealogy is central to Ricks's study, in which the first section is titled 'The Poet as Heir'.

25. David Colbert, *The Magical Worlds of Harry Potter. A Treasury of Myths, Legends, and Fascinating Facts* (London: Puffin, 2001).

26. Elizabeth D. Shafer, *Exploring Harry Potter* (London: Ebury, 2000).

27. See also *Im Bann des Zauberlehrlings? Zur Faszination von Harry Potter*, (ed.) Kaspar H. Spinner (Regensburg: Friedrich Pustet Verlag, Themen der Katholischen Akademie in Bayern, 2001). 'Harry Potter' is said in this book to 'belong' to the Katholische Akademie, because of its moral message. 'Harry Potter' is also read as an archetype and compared to Jesus.

28. Shafer, *Exploring*, pp. 128–9.

29. 'Characters in the novels have similar names or traits to certain gods. Harry, Hercules.' Shafer, *Exploring*, p. 146.

30. Shafer, *Exploring*, pp. 150–1.

31. Shafer, *Exploring*, p. 156.

32. Shafer, *Exploring*, p. 160.

33. Eccleshare, *A Guide to Harry Potter's Novels*, pp. 35–6.

34. Eccleshare, *A Guide to Harry Potter's Novels*, p. 36.

35. 'Voldemort n'incarna pas uniquement le dictateur nazi ni même la Méduse des Grecs: il représente en réealité le mal absolu, dont il est la figure diabolique. [...] La multiplications des sources auxquelles renvoie le texte de Rowling peut alors expliquer l'universalité du succès de "Harry Potter": s'appuyant constamment sur un minimum de trois types les références, ses ouvrages sont à la rencontre d'un imaginaire qui, inévitablement, ne pouvait que déborder la seule insularité britannique.' Smadja, *Harry Potter: les raisons d'un succés*, p. 44 ; the translation from the French is mine.

36. Bürvenich, *Der Zauber des Harry Potter* , p.151.

37. Bürvenich, *Der Zauber des Harry Potter*. The reference is to Garcia's article 'Die total Potter-Manie', *Tagespost*, 123 (31) (14 October, 2000), 9.

38. Ricks interprets plagiarism as the opposite of allusion: 'But allusion has to be the contrary [...] of plagiarism, since allusion is posited upon our calling the earlier work into play, whereas the one thing that plagiarism hopes is that the earlier work will not enter our heads. [...] allusion is a defence that must stanch the accusation of plagiarism.' Ricks, *Allusion to the Poets*, pp. 231–2.

39. Bürvenich, *Der Zauber des Harry Potter*, pp. 139–40.

40. Bürvenich, *Der Zauber des Harry Potter*, p. 142.
41. Bürvenich, *Der Zauber des Harry Potter*, p. 143.
42. 'Even the American copyright form states that one cannot protect "titles, names and short phrases"', Françoise Meltzer, *Hot Property: The Stakes and Claims of Originality* (Chicago: University of Chicago Press, 1994), p. 74; quoted in Ricks, *Allusion to the Poets*, p. 225.
43. Whited also discusses how Stouffer, 'to demonstrate her books' circulation, introduced shipping invoices later determined to be invalid', p. 5. For a detailed discussion of the case, see Whited, *The Ivory Tower*, pp. 4–5.
44. Bürvenich also reports how Richard Jenkyns claims more than one textual source in *Happy Potter* from Geoffrey Willan's *The Complete Molesworth* (1999); 'in one of the adventures in the series – "How to be Topp" – the name "the Hogwarts" appears as a cod play by Marcus Plautus Molesworthus and reappears as Hoggwart as the name of the headmaster of Porridge Court, a rival academy to St Custard's', Richard Jenkyns, 'Potter in the Past', *Prospect*, 56 (October 2000), 38–43, 40.
45. Ricks, *Allusion to the Poets*, p. 223.
46. Peter Hunt, *Children's Literature* (Oxford: Oxford University Press, 2001), p. 123.
47. Ricks, *Allusion to the Poets*, p. 4; the quotation is from Samuel Taylor Coleridge, *Collected Letters*, ed. E.L. Griggs (Oxford: Clarendon Press, 1956–71), iii, pp. 469–70.
48. Steege, *The Ivory Tower*, p. 156.
49. Pinsent, *The Ivory Tower*, p. 27.
50. Lacoss, *The Ivory Tower*, p. 71.
51. Edi Vesco, *Il Magicolibro. Zuccologia, gufologia e autentica stregoneria: la guida più completa al mondo di Harry Potter* (Milan: Sperling&Kupfer, 2002).
52. Vesco, *Il Magicolibro*, p. 3.
53. Marc Shapiro, *J.K. Rowling, The Wizard Behind Harry Potter* (Harmondsworth: Penguin, 2000).
54. Whited, *The Ivory Tower*, p. 4.
55. Pharr, *The Ivory Tower*, p. 54.

9
National Identity. Where the Wild, Strange and Exotic Things Are: In Search of the Caribbean in Contemporary Children's Literature

Jacqueline Lazú

Islands offer a unique space within which to construct the most fantastic worlds imaginable – ones that offer limitless adventures for young travelers in children's books. This phenomenon, however, is certainly not unique to children's literature. In fact, within Caribbean studies, island images continue to be important literary and theoretical, discursive spaces in which to identify wider issues of (post)colonialism particularly in relation to representation. With the few but significant contributions in children's literature scholarship dedicated to the critical analysis of island symbols, the historical/literary continuity with 'adult literature' and its symbolic system is evident. These images have been both sustained and challenged by *native* Caribbean authors in both adult and children's literature.

An interesting context emerges in the contemporary transculturation of island tropes, particularly how US Caribbean authors have attempted to subvert the aggressive agenda of popular culture and both contemporary and classical representations of islands. The works of several contemporary US Caribbean authors stand out as exemplary contributions to this discussion. Judith Ortiz Cofer's collection *An Island Like You* (1995), Anilú Bernardo's *Jumping Off to Freedom* (1996), George Crespo's *How the Sea Began* (1993) and Julia Alvarez's *The Secret Footprints* (2000), offer a panorama of diverse approaches to subverting and rearticulating images of islands. Their stories address popular images and narratives and make room for the complex experiences of a young Diaspora. In a time of rapidly changing demographics and increasing youth consumer power, mass culture on the whole is forced to meet the demands of this constituency and strategically consider politics of representation.

Traditional islands and postcolonial appropriations

For many critics, multicultural children's books perform a dual function. From their viewpoint, authors attempt to provide a source for imagining and reflecting heritage and for validating a unique culture. These books are a window into another's world, a means of gaining knowledge and understanding of peoples different from themselves.[1] Consequently, it is important to consider what it is that the island trope has represented in children's literature, how and why it has become a set of images that is contested, particularly for writers of the Diaspora.

First, it is important to understand the contexts from which the trope of islands as sites of encounters with strangeness and adventure emerges in children's literature as well as 'adult' literature. Islands may be constructed in terms of a geography of isolation and self-sufficiency, depending on ideas of an autonomous self and isolation as a human condition. Island heroes may be seen to discover their identities apart from a society or community. Island stories come in many genres, but are also related through this production of islands.[2]

The most influential and imitated island story is Daniel Defoe's 1719 classic, *Robinson Crusoe*. Versions of this story proliferated to the point where the term 'Robinsonnade' came to define a new literary genre. Perhaps the second most influential island story is by Robert Louis Stevenson, a Robinsonnade writer who followed the tradition of Defoe in *Treasure Island* (1883).[3] In Stevenson's adventure, however, the island is not uninhabited. The hero chooses to go to the island and the focus of the story is on finding a treasure versus the Robinsonnade objective of survival. Rooted in the imagery of the civilized and primitive exposed by postcolonial theorists, the island imagery in these texts can be explained through the exploration of the trope's historical context.

Images of the New World in general and the Caribbean in particular around the time of The Conquest emerge as an exoticist discourse developed in Europe. This allowed an *avant-garde* of writers and intellectuals to escape to strange places and romanticize the liberating otherness of new colonial possessions. Perhaps the single most important text in relation to this theme in postcolonial criticism is Shakespeare's *The Tempest*. *The Tempest* became one of the most important sources used to establish a paradigm for postcolonial readings of canonical works. Specifically, the character Caliban, the half-human, half-beast offspring of a witch (original inhabitant of an island) who was forced into servitude by Prospero and his shipwrecked crew has become representative of conquest and transformation to establish some kind of order.[4] Although there is no direct reference to the newly encountered world in Shakespeare's last play, it was within this imaginative space that the Americas were essentialized and a pattern of cultural and moral dichotomies was established.

Around the 1960–70s, Caribbean intellectuals began positioning Caliban as a complex symbol. To these writers, Caliban epitomized the intermingling not only of indigenous, African and European races but also of African oral and European written traditions, local dialects and standard European languages, a history of colonial oppression and a regional culture of resistance.[5] In effect, the archetypal duo of Prospero, the shipwrecked king and colonizer of the story's island and Caliban has evolved as a socio-political metaphor for colonialism and cultural imperialism. The figure of Caliban (the symbolic cannibal) in particular has been reshaped according to culturally specific situations.[6]

How, then, can these island texts and offspring be read? And how or why are contemporary writers responding to them? For some, island stories are a vehicle for a complete value statement on growing up: the gaining of strengths and confronting of weaknesses by the self. The island's paradoxes are seen as integral to readers' attraction to the theme. Desert and paradise, shipwreck and home, nightmare and daydream, limitation and refuge are seen as a reflection of the paradoxes of life itself. A microcosm of society and macrocosm of self, it is the end of innocence and the death of childhood; the beginning of experience and the birth of maturity.[7] However, I assert that the messages of this and any looping signifier are dependent upon their historical moment. In today's postcolonial, neocolonial and transcultural societies, island images both remain the same and reveal new interpretations.

In the United States discourses about people of color and those deemed *foreigners* have produced them as representations of *otherness* in relation to a *mainstream* (white, middle-class, Protestant, heterosexual) gaze. A long and profound history of Euro-centric/Western conceptualizations of exoticism shapes depictions of those who are marginalized. The increasing discursive and material emergence of the non-European 'Third World' diasporic communities in North America has led to the construction of complex, hybrid identities. In this acculturation process, it is reasonable to conclude that an immigrant's selfhood could be intertwined with the stories, legacies and the immigration heritage of his or her respective ethnic group. These narratives are intimately bound up with the formation of an individual immigrant's identity.[8]

Image, representation and their objectives or who are these island people, anyway?

In the context of the United States the images of islands have provided important material, not only for children's books but also for popular culture production in general. As a society that is economically and to some degree socially dependent on the production and dissemination of entertainment and popular culture, islands have been important spaces from which to create contexts for Hollywood movie stars, Disney animated creatures, amusement park rides, or sideshow exhibits, to name just a few of the most popular examples. What is propagated within these spaces is a complex trope for the American imaginary. This trope is often the only reference point for talking about island cultures within the US cultural context. Taken alongside the fact that the US has the largest Spanish-Caribbean (Cuban-American, Puerto Rican and Dominican) communities outside of the Caribbean, as well as many of the largest communities of West Indian and Pacific Islanders outside of those regions, and that Latinos in general are the largest growing demographic in the US, questions of identification and representation are more relevant than ever.

One of the most immediate observations that can be made about the works of many US Caribbean writers is the inability to categorize their 'island' stories within the confines of the Robinsonnade. In fact, more often than not, the hero reflects the phenomenon of 'insider/outsider' that is better aligned with the complexities of US Latino cultures. In these stories, one can witness the construction of novel hybrid, borderland cultural practices of 'Third World' Diasporas in 'First World' communities suggested by postcolonial critics as representative of minority literatures.[9] One of the objectives of postcolonial projects is to study specifically how colonial and neocolonial practices and policies are deeply intermingled with the present-day diasporic experience. In the works of Judith Ortiz Cofer, Julia Álvarez, Anilú Bernardo and George Crespo, this translates to strategies that reveal and attempt to counter what critics have called 'omissions and misrepresentations' recognized as early as the mid-1960s in children's literature.[10]

In Western/Euro-centric representations of islands they are often detached completely from identifiable sociological or geopolitical contexts, making it difficult to categorize them as referring to any specific ethnic or cultural group. For example, perhaps the most popular contemporary representation of islands and what has been proclaimed as one of the most popular children's books written is Maurice Sendak's *Where the Wild Things Are*.[11] Also containing many of the characteristic elements of the classical island representations, the plot involves a young traveler, Max, whom upon disobeying his mother and threatening to 'eat her up', is sent to bed without supper. Max's room is transformed into a forest and then an ocean where he sets sail for the island home of the 'wild things'. Max becomes king of the wild things, taming them by similarly keeping supper from them. Eventually, despite pleas from the wild things for him to stay, Max decides to return home where he finds his supper waiting for him. This story is in many ways a prototype. The ocean voyage and encounter with the wild things are metaphorically linked to Columbus's voyage and accounts of the magnificent creatures of the Indies. Similarly, the story is Robinsonesque, with the hero preparing to take a new role in his 'society' (home) informed by his encounters in the utopic space. Max's control of the island society is unquestioned and automatic upon his arrival. Yet, the island home of the wild things is never named beyond the description of its inhabitants, making it generic and transferable. This point is key in Cofer and other diasporic writers' approach to countering the Eurocentric island imagery.

New narratives and complex practices: How Caribbean writers write themselves

For US Puerto Rican (Nuyorican) author Judith Ortiz Cofer, the geopolitical location of her island story becomes central to the entire collection of young adult stories from the very title onwards. *An Island Like You: Stories of the Barrio* reveals a series of important issues concerning her diasporic community. In 12 stories that take place in a neighborhood in Patterson, New Jersey, Cofer captures a moment in the life of a Puerto Rican teenager. Like many characters in children's and young adult's literature, these are on a course toward discovering themselves in relation to their family and society on a whole. As Latinos, however, they are also trying to discover who they are in relation to the Puerto Rican community and to mainstream US society. Aligned with a more traditional reading of an island metaphor, Cofer's island (the island of her characters), as suggested by the title and her heroes' insightful and omniscient voices, seems to represent the individual's search for the self, and strength and potential for achievement. Like an island, the characters additionally search for their position in relation to their world. Like the Caribbean island in question in Cofer's stories, characters search for who they are in relation to two societies, the island colony and the mainland nation state.

In the first story of Judith Ortiz Cofer's collection, 'Bad Influence', Rita travels to Puerto Rico one summer to visit her grandparents. After getting caught in a lie to her parents, they give her a choice between going to a Catholic girls' retreat and going to the countryside home of her relatives on the Island. For Rita, the punishment is that there will be no other younger relatives with whom to make this a vacation. She will have to follow her grandparents around in their normal routines, which, to her having grown up far from many island traditions, are strange and foreign. Rita says 'My whole life, I had seen my grandparents only once a year when we went down for a two-week vacation, and frankly, I spent all of my time at the beach with my cousins and let the adults sit around drinking their hot *café con leche* and sweating, gossiping about people I didn't know.'[12] Without her cousins, Rita feels isolated, yet longs for the privacy that she associates with mainland culture.

The true adventure and ultimate lesson for Rita begins when she is 'forced' to go with her grandfather to a client's house where he is to perform a *trabajo*, a spiritual cleansing, for a girl about Rita's age who is suffering from a mysterious ailment. Papá is a spiritist, practitioner of one of the Island's popular religious practices; a syncretism of European spiritism and santería. Rita initially asks her grandmother if that means that her grandfather sacrifices chickens and goats. Her connection to the rituals at that point in her life is limited to 'voodoo priests who went into trances and poured blood and feathers all over everybody in secret ceremonies'· and 'a black man from Haiti in [our] neighborhood who people said could even call back the dead and make them his zombie slaves.'[13] Shocked, her grandmother responds that her grandfather works with God and His saints, not Satan. Rita then thinks to herself: '...I really should have been given an instruction manual before being sent here on my own.'

The estrangement that Rita feels and that is reflected in this last thought is slowly transformed. As her grandfather works to find the *mala influencia* that possesses the girl, he uses Rita to help create a bond with his clients. Eventually discovering that the bad influence was the girl's stepfather, Papá successfully cures the girl, impressing Rita and allowing her to accept and realize the power of individual beliefs. Rita becomes good friends with the girl, Angela, and eventually discovers the *mala influencias* in her own life – the things that estranged her from her family in her life back in Paterson.

Interestingly, 'Bad Influence' follows in many ways the trajectory of a classic island story. The hero searches for answers to questions of the self in relation to society, which she will then use to return home and change her position in society. There are some key differences, however, in how Cofer writes the personal discovery of her characters that distinguish and challenge traditional readings. While Rita initially finds the customs of her family on the island to be strange to her, the personal growth that occurs for her involves a realization of how familiar it actually is to her. Having grown up in the mainland, albeit surrounded by her ethnic community, her exposure to 'life on the Island' is limited to short yearly vacations. By breaking away from the superficiality of the holiday, she is exposed to the 'real thing'. Unlike the Robinsonesque characters, it is essential to Rita's growth to realize how much of Puerto Rico's culture she owns. Simultaneously, however, Cofer's message is one that contests cultural nationalist rhetoric in which there is no room for the experience of migration. In fact, transculturation is an important part of Rita's discoveries. Her experiences as a Puerto Rican girl growing up in the inner city in the United States' mainland are what lead her to her adventure in the first place. The resulting experiences on the Island presumably lead her to begin new adventures, with a new understanding of her life back in Paterson. Neither Island culture nor mainland culture is privileged, but the hybridity resulting from the shared experiences.

The term *hybridity* is recognizably an important one in talking about the experiences of diasporic, minority communities. I assert that the term is of particular significance when talking about recent generations and minority youth culture in the United States. While recognizing its dialogic and ambivalent aspects critics have now long explored its applicability to the situation in the Americas, which has been described as *postcolonial* in various ways. Homi K. Bhabha's theories of cultural hybridity, postcolonialism, Third Space and subversion have been commonly applied to the fields of diasporic culture border culture and Latino cultures by using examples from pop culture and literature. In these spaces, people negotiate their cultural identities as citizens of the First World while retaining a strong identification with the culture of their home country. Diasporic identity is shaped by and linked to the cultural and political issues of race, gender, colonization and power that are present in the hostland and the homeland. For Puerto Rican migrant parents and their mainland-born, for whom travel to and from the Island is not limited by issues of citizenship, identity formation is a constant negotiation of their multiple, and often conflicting, dialogical voices, histories and *I* positions.[14]

The complexities and constant negotiations we see in Rita and the other characters in *An Island Like You*, ultimately prove that the experience of the *native* traveler to and from the island of Puerto Rico is not one that is isolating, homogenous and/or for a privileged outsider. For these characters, it is part of a specific cultural phenomenon informed by very specific historical accounts, the depiction of traditional ceremonies and/or rites of passage, and journeys that focus not only on the adventure but on the geographic and socio-political context within which the journey takes place. As the title suggests, the experiences may be unique and individual, like the insularity of an island, but it is 'like you' and thus reflective of a specific cultural experience. Similarly, the work of Cuban immigrant writer Anilú Bernardo insists that identities are not fixed to universal properties, rather they are constantly changing and embedded in many cultural and historical processes, conceptually challenging the tropes of island experiences. For Bernardo, whose family fled from the revolution in 1961, the experience of exile informs the events of her young adult novel *Jumping Off to Freedom*.[15] In this story, young David Leal and his father embark on a dangerous journey to escape the dictatorship in Cuba. Joined by thousands of other *balseros* on rafts, they hope to reach the Florida coast and the promise of a new life. The danger involved in the journey forces them to leave half of the family behind with the promise of sending for them after they are established in Florida. There are elements in this psychological thriller that are reflective of the traditional island narrative. The protagonists are pitted against the forces of nature, storms, sharks, hunger and chaos and ultimately, the lessons of youth on a journey toward adulthood. Yet it is impossible to ignore or generalize the historical background, characterization, and the text's orientation in this story that are linked to and shaped by the specific experiences of Cuba from the perspective of the exile community in the United States.

Like perhaps no other island in the world, Cuba has represented to the United States imaginary sets of ironic and conflicting symbols. Before the revolution, Cuba was the Paris of the Caribbean. It was the quintessential locus for the exotic, the tropical and the uninhibited as well as the symbolic cultural center of the Caribbean and, arguably, Latin America. This image drastically changed, of course, after the communist takeover of the Island.

After decades of disconnection with Cuba, Americans rely on narratives fueled by language barriers, Anglo-centrism and Cold War mentality. Alfredo Prieto González, director of the Popular Communications Department of Havana's Martin Luther King Jr Memorial Center, has studied the ways that Cuba is represented in the US media. He explains that although the Cold War is over, the image of Cuba continues to be permeated by a web of narratives that derive from that time. In the post-Cold War world, Cuba has lost her 'charm', becoming just another – albeit *peculiar* – Caribbean country.[16]

From the perspective of the exile community, however, images are informed by experiences at the moment of departure from the island. As Cuban exile has had various different identified stages since the revolution, each one has had very different and complex motivations and sets of images attached to its narrative. For David and his father Miguel in *Jumping Off to Freedom*, the Cuba they are escaping is a fairly contemporary one. It is not the Cuba immediately after the revolution. The narrator explains that the Leal family was once very comfortable. Now, Miguel feels that his family will not survive the political repression and hunger they are experiencing as they survive on meager rations and face the possible arrest of their son on false charges of theft of government property. Cuba for the Leal family promises a continued life of fear, suspicion, violence and repression. While Bernardo draws from her own experience of having immigrated to the United States in 1961, it is clear that her experience as an exile of that particular generation informs her narrative above all. Ultimately, the historical specificity and thriller in this adventure story constructs contrasting points of view that challenge traditional representations and speak more directly for a diversity of Cuban experiences.

The story opens with David being arrested and held for questioning in the case of a theft involving a cow slaughtered for meat. David's bicycle is found at the crime scene. One of the family's most valued possessions and only form of transportation, David allowed his friend to borrow it. Unbeknownst to him, Pepe along with co-conspirator, Tomás, uses it to carry the meat to feed their families. After temporarily resolving the problem, Miguel begins his plans to leave with his son on a raft to the US. The two are unwillingly convinced to bring along two more companions, Luis and 'Toro'. After days of confronting hunger, sickness, sharks and storms and facing the deterioration of his father on board the makeshift raft, David, who is often described as 'hot headed' and immature, grows to be more tolerant and responsible, largely due to his interactions with the two other men. It turns out that Toro is actually Tomás whom David had threatened to meet and take revenge on for getting him in trouble with the police. By then, Toro has proved his friendship and commitment to his fellow travelers and in the process helped David realize his own weaknesses. This is in many ways both a story of survival, coming of age and one in which the travelers ultimately seek the treasure of freedom.

What differentiates *Jumping Off to Freedom* from traditional island and sea adventure stories is precisely its commitment to the history of Cuba and the communist regime from the perspective of the exile community, and providing a context within which the ultimate message of growth and maturity for the hero will take place. The generic quality of traditional island adventures is erased by the images of a people faced with the hunger of embargo, the fear and threat of repression and helplessness. At the same time, it is interesting to compare and contrast this narrative with that of other Cuban-American children's literature authors. Nancy Osa, for example, author of the young adult novel *Cuba 15* (2003)[17] approaches the idea of rites of passage in a very different manner, from a different political perspective, ultimately adding yet another dimension to the very complex text of Cuban images of Cuba.

In Osa's story, Violet Paz is celebrating her *quinceañero*. The celebration of her fifteenth birthday is an important cultural tradition marking her entrance into womanhood. Half Cuban and half Polish, Violet identifies, above all, as American. Her reference points to Cuba are her family's passion for playing dominoes, smoking cigars and dancing to salsa music, yet she is forced to accept her grandmother's plans for the *quinceañero*. This begins her quest to find out more about the tradition and other aspects of her Cuban heritage. For her grandparents, Cuba and Fidel Castro elicit sadness and anger. Violet's Aunt Luz, however, is more open-minded, leaving her confused about how she should feel toward Cuban politics. With this new rite of passage, however, come the responsibilities of adulthood, including that of forming one's own opinion on things, even when it means confronting your own family. The novel, told from the vantage point of a Cuban-American living in Chicago, offers another dimension to the contemporary images of Cuba from a *native* perspective. Like Bernardo, Osa is offering the perspective of insider/outsider. They are able to represent both the marginalized and the privileged and how in many ways the perspectives have formed and shaped each other. Behind the tropes lie complex ideologies from which these images have stemmed as well as the social and political uses to which they have been put.

These stories can be read to provide cultural relevance and points of commonalities without conforming to generic models. With a few regional exceptions, mass media's construction of Latino cultures is in fact similarly generic and homogenized into a single category 'Latin' (or Hispanic) that presumably includes Spanish Caribbean peoples. Yet the Caribbean, void of contemporary people, also has its set of images informed by Hollywood and the myriad adventure stories mentioned.

Myths and representation: Challenging the simple, the strange and the exotic

For the last two texts in this study, the source for their challenge to the problematic of island representation lies in the use of myths and indigenous folktales. Creation myths and stories of the perseverance of native cultures are especially popular among Caribbean children's literature authors. During the two centuries following Columbus's first voyage in 1492 whole societies disappeared as large portions of the Caribbean were depleted of indigenous people. The destruction of native societies was especially grim in the Greater Antilles where in only a few decades whole societies and hundreds of thousands of people were killed by disease and violence. While there were native people who survived and joined together to form new viable ethnic groups, native people like the Taínos of this region are considered to be extinct. For these authors, rescuing the history and legends of indigenous cultures is the key to informing young readers about the complex history of Caribbean pre-Columbian societies that in fact form an important part of the identity and identification of contemporary societies.

Myths are an important cultural phenomenon in the Caribbean and its Diaspora. Yet myths are also elusive and subject to time, translation, and interpretation, among many other factors. For Alvarez and Crespo, writing for younger audiences than Bernardo and Osa, the retelling of myths associated with indigenous people or tales is part of a history involving first oral tradition and later writing stories to pass from generation to generation. Folk literature explores many varied phenomena, which include natural occurrences such as weather conditions to religious beliefs. This literature is seen to provide people with a doctrine by which they run their daily lives, and also an explanation of any given event that affects the world.

In *How the Sea Began*,[18] Crespo tells the story of a place called Zuania where there are four great mountains. One of the mountains is called Boriquén, the indigenous name of Puerto Rico. The story revolves around a family including the son Yayael, a skilled hunter, and his parents Yaya and Itiba. Yayael helps sustain his tribe with his skillful hunting with a tabonuco wood bow and arrow that his father has carved for him. After an encounter with Guabancex, the goddess of hurricanes, Yayael perishes in the storm leaving his people to survive on their own without his hunting skills. It is not until Yaya discovers that his son's bow and arrow, which he preserves in a gourd, still hold the power of the tabonuco tree and yield large fish with which to feed the whole village, that the tribe sees good fortune again. One day while several boys of the village play near the gourd that holds Yayael's bow and arrow, they drop and break them sending massive amounts of water flowing into the village. The water tastes of salt, like the salt of tears and is full of fish and all kinds of sea life that fills the land and turns Boriquén, and the other mountains, into separate islands.

Meanwhile, in Julia Alvarez's *The Secret Footprints*, it is not the origin of a people that is emphasized but the survival. In this island there is a tribe of people called the ciguapas who make their homes underwater and come out on land only to hunt for food at night, fearful of humans. While the ciguapas look exactly like humans, they are obviously different in that they can live underwater and that their feet are on backward, allowing them to leave footprints in the opposite direction and ensuring their secret existence. This security is challenged when a young ciguapa named Guapa is led by curiosity to interact with a family from one of the villages. Trying to escape after stealing some food from their picnic, Guapa falls and the family assumes that her feet are broken. As they search for help, she is able to talk the son into giving her time to escape back to the safety of her home. No one can trace her again since the prints led back to the same spot where they first found her. Bringing samples of food from the kind family to her people, she is given more freedom by her elders to explore the land carefully and make an occasional, secret visit to the boy and his family.

I would like to consider how myths and folktales like these serve as a means for reading Caribbean cultures. First of all, they construct ideas of family and community, and secondly, they provide narratives of traditions from the islands which are reread in the United States. About his story, for example, Crespo explains that it is a Taíno creation myth by the Arawak people of the Orinoco Basin in South America who migrated to the Greater Antilles around the year 1000. Zuania was the Taíno name for the South American mainland. Boriquén was, again, what is now known as the island of Puerto Rico. The other three mountains in the story became Cuba, Jamaica and the Dominican Republic/Haiti. Crespo explains to his readers in the appendix that the Taíno believed that the natural world was inhabited by a variety of spirits and that it was a custom to keep the bones of dead relatives in a gourd hung from the ceiling of a hut in the same way that Yaya and Itiba keep Yayael's possessions. Fray Ramón Pané collected *How the Sea Began* in Hispaniola in its original form nearly 500 years ago when Columbus commissioned him to record the beliefs and customs of the Taíno people. Pané's work *Relación acerca de las antiguedades de los indios*, is the only existing document on Taíno mythology and the first ethnological study done in the New World.[19]

In the retelling and illustration of the story from the perspective of the creation of Puerto Rico, Crespo emphasizes what is native and original to an island about which little is known from the vantage point of the US beyond its status as a colonial possession. The heroic character of Yayael provides a role model and the power of the gourd's contents a belief system which constructs a Puerto Rican narrative of identity and heritage, particularly in a context where few of these narratives are available. Similarly, Alvarez, in an appendix to her story, explains that she first heard about the ciguapas when she was a little girl in the Dominican Republic. Throughout the years she would hear many different versions of the ciguapa story. The common denominator is that the creatures originated a long time ago in the Dominican Republic. Some say that they had golden skin and others say black skin. In some versions, they are small and in others they are as tall as humans. Some say they lived in caves under water and other versions say they lived in the woods and that they were an all-female tribe. All agree that they only came out at night to hunt. Alvarez explains that some writers think that the ciguapas also came from the legends of the Taínos. Interestingly, the author explains that her mother and aunt would try to scare her at night by saying that if she did not go to sleep quickly, the ciguapas would come and take her away. Today, she says that she still pays homage to them by leaving a piece of candy or apple in the pocket of her pants or jacket when she leaves her clothes on the line to dry like the family in the story did for Guapa. She finishes the appendix by saying 'I know it's a long way from the Dominican Republic to Vermont, especially if your feet are on backward. But I have to tell you, sometimes that piece of candy or apple is gone from that pocket in the morning.'[20]

Many contemporary Latino writers, like Julia Alvarez and Judith Ortiz Cofer, are also successful authors of 'adult' literature. Much of their 'adult' work has been characterized as autobiographical and shares with their children's stories a commitment toward capturing a neglected history; stories of their communities and the strategies migrant and US-born Puerto Ricans and Dominicans use to create a space between two cultures.

In postcolonial studies, research has emphasized the mixing and moving, continuous and ongoing process through which many non-Western/ non-European immigrants reconstitute and negotiate their identity. From a dialogical point of view such negotiations involve multiple mediations with a larger set of political and historical practices than both one's 'homeland' and ones 'hostland'.[21] Mohanty points out that the history of the immigration and naturalization in the US parallels the process of racialization that spans the annihilation of Native Americans, the history of slavery and the civil rights movement.[22] Subsequently, tales of discrimination, hardships and sheer exploitation are kept alive in most non-European immigrant communities through personal remembering and shared histories. Like the contextualizations of Cofer and Bernardo, the use of myths by Crespo and Alvarez function as tools for communicating these memories. For them, it is important to communicate a message beyond the portrayal of customs and culture as being exotic or strange.

The political economics of identity formation and the 'right' stories to tell the kids

Postcolonial scholarship provides us with insight about how any study of the diasporic self needs to be investigated within the ideological contexts of race, colonial and postcolonial history, and contemporary asymmetrical power relationships between cultures. I assert that similar models can be applied to children's literature and all cultural production aimed at young consumers. Marilyn Halter explains in *Shopping for Identity: The Marketing of Ethnicity*,[23] that the 1960s marked a pivotal point in the formation of the contours of American ethnic identities today. Social movements by people of color spearheaded by Black Nationalism and followed by the American

Indian Movement and then the Chicano Movement unearthed occluded histories and forced the celebration of distinctive heritages.[24] In 1974, Congress passed the Ethnic Heritage Act to help fund initiatives promoting cultures and histories of American ethnic populations. Halter explains that this so-called 'roots' phenomenon accounts for the increase in ethnic celebrations, interests in genealogies, travel to ancestral homelands and interests in ethnic artifacts, cuisine, music, literature, and of course, language. Cobb asserts that during the period of the late 1960s to late 1970s, considerable research was conducted concerning the representation of minority populations in children's textbooks as well.[25]

There are two important things that we have to keep in mind, however, before considering how consumer capitalism evolved to meet this demand. The first is how, within the symbolic fields of America's racial/ethnic hierarchies, ethnicities are invested with different social values. Symbolic capital is different for each group and dependent on their position in this hierarchy. Groups at the top have higher social prestige, that is, more economic opportunities and access to economic capital. Groups at the bottom have negative social prestige and are usually tied to a negative public image.[26] Images of the 1960s and what was 'in' in terms of ethnic representations did not involve the Dominican or Puerto Rican. And Spanish only recently has been viewed as a valuable language to study – because of the changing demographics (only for second-language acquisition – not bilingualism and, of course, only particular varieties of Spanish that are more like 'real' Spanish (Castilian)).

The second important factor is that the bases of paternalist discourse are also irreconcilable with the social phenomena associated with the decades of popular rhetoric in the Caribbean in the 1940s, 1950s and 1960s. Culture was constructed as objects that could be displayed as art or tradition and not a way of life and everyday culture. It was defined in opposition to the 'other', the commercial culture of the United States. Since difference then had to be combined into a common idea of peoplehood this meant that those things (and people) that were both inside and outside of the ideal must be defined. This process of detecting knowledge and authenticity are part and parcel of the struggle to perpetuate a status quo. Pierre Bourdieu argues that those in the dominant positions 'operate essentially defensive strategies designed to perpetuate the status quo by maintaining themselves and the principles on which their dominance is based'.[27] This process of homogenization, which is linked with nationalism's Western heritage, in particular the Enlightenment concepts of nations as authentic and unique entities, has contributed to the questions of nationality in the development of the 'canonical male literary proto-nationalist production'.[28] This left no room for the representation of diasporic communities, the urban experience, or discussions of any gender politics in what were considered national literatures (adult or child).

In the 1970s, the parameters of the American marketplace, however, were shifting. Mass marketing was decaying as a strategy in many sectors of the economy. The parity in the production and technology of consumer goods had, for the most part, been achieved, so that customers were felt not to be able to differentiate any more between the values of services between competitors. Companies had to find new ways to hook consumers on to their particular brands. They turned to segmented marketing approaches and the relationship between ethnic identity formation and consumer culture was cemented. Through the consumption of ethnic goods and services, people modify and signal ethnic identities in social settings not limited any longer to the boundaries of their ethnic or migration experience.

Today, it is clear how important it is for big companies to focus especially on young consumers. Halter explains that in keeping with prototypical generational modes of adaptation, adolescents in California's Mexican-American immigrant community during the 1920s were seen to be most likely to be the first in the family to break away from traditional customs, clothing styles, foods, or entertainment and to Americanize by participating in mass-consumer society. This pattern has only been judged to have increased since then. The figures on Latino youth's purchasing power are so outstanding that ethnic marketers now hold training sessions specifically focused on reaching Latino teenagers, such as 'Latino Youth Power', a corporate conference that uses case studies from companies like Coca Cola, Target Stores and MTV to teach business executives how to go about winning this market. Currently estimated at $380 billion, the purchasing power of Latinos in the United States is said to exceed the GNP of any one Spanish-speaking nation in all of Latin America. Consulting firms that specialize in Latino marketing always stress the importance of teenage buyers within this consumer base; almost 40 percent of the current population is between the ages of 16 and 34. More than any other age cohort within the Latino community, the young people are seen to live in two worlds – Spanish and English speaking. Today, however, they are viewed as most likely to identify themselves first as Mexican or Puerto Rican or Cuban, second as Hispanic or Latino, and only third as American, reflecting an idea that young people privilege the *ethnic* experience above any other.[29]

Currently there are countless numbers of children's books aimed at the Latino reader. To some degree, this displays a turn toward the generic, all encompassing experience that can seem homogenizing, problematic and against the grain of consumer demand as witnessed by the statistics privileging ethnic identification. Moreover it seems to reproduce the objective of collapsing the differences between and among colonial/racial subjects, gendered subjects and the racist, sexist representation of these subjects in the Euro American imaginary. Simultaneously, however, there is also a movement toward the specificity of the ethnic experience as witnessed by the works of the authors in this study. I suggest that both are important in how they are indigenously performed throughout the stages of self-identification and the circulation of representation. *Latinidad* is a significant word in the emerging field of Latino and postcolonial studies. This analytical concept is a category of early identification, familiarity, and affinity that the singularity of ethnic identification may not necessarily match. It is a noun that modifies a subject position, being Latina/o in a given space.[30] Agustín Laó-Montes explains that *Latinidad* is historically rooted in discourses of 'Latin Americanism establishing a historical sense of identity in the modern world as well as in the mass migrations, political exiles, conquests of peoples and territories, and processes of uneven development and unequal exchange that characterize the relations between Anglos and Latino/ Americans both within and beyond the territorial boundaries of the United States'.[31]

Conclusion

More than filling in historical blanks, the central, constitutive role of specifically Caribbean cultural production in the US is in, as critic Juan Flores puts it, the making and breaking of the nation in the twentieth century.[32] Contemporary theorists of diasporic, transnational identity agree that geographic separation and distance don't eliminate altogether the sense of community and origin, but that instead the opposite effect can be seen in the form of a heightened collective awareness of belonging and affirmation. Flores insists that it is not enough to glue pieces together by naming forgotten names and events. The seams and borders of national experience need to be understood not as absences or vacuums but as sites of new meanings and relations.

While for many writers, including the writers of contemporary Caribbean children's literature in the United States, many of the issues that emerge are an extension of island-based discourses, most focus on the complexities that emerge from their characters' diasporic experiences. The emphasis in these stories is placed on the hybridity of nationalities. Even when focusing around ideas of recapturing ancient myths and legends, as with authors like Julia Alvarez and George Crespo, their historical consciousness is better understood from the perspective of the migratory experience. For young travelers like Rita and David, their translocal nature does not erase the efficacy of space. Boundaries still exist – there is still a 'here' and 'there'. In these island stories, not only is the written text read but the appendages of national history and the history of images is made available to readers. In a time when youth culture and young people have reached an unprecedented position in consumer culture and the projections claim that at least one-third of all children's books published should be directed at minority audiences,[33] the challenge of literacy for a diverse culture is pressing, to say the least. The issues and problems of the concept of culturally relevant materials must be addressed.

Further reading

Affergan, F., *Exotisme et altérité: Sa essai sur les fondements d'une critique de la antropologie* (Paris: Press Universitaire de France, 1987).

Aparicio, F. and S. Chávez-Silverman, *Tropicalizations: Transcultural Representations of Latinidad* (Hanover: Dartmouth College, University Press of New England, 1997).

Barradas, E., *Partes de un todo: ensayos y notas sobre literatura puertorriqueña en los Estados Unidos* (San Juan, P.R.: Editorial de la Universidad de Puerto Rico, 1998).

Brathwaite, K., *Islands* (London: Oxford University Press, 1969).

Canclini, N.G., *Hybrid Cultures: Strategies for Entering and Leaving Modernity* (Minneapolis: University of Minnesota Press, 1995).

Cesaire, A., *Une Tempete; D'aprés 'La Tempete' de Shakespeare. Adaptation pour une theatre négre* (Paris: Editions du Seuil, 1969).

Davies, C.B. and E.S. Fido, *Out of the Kumbla: Caribbean Women and Literature* (Trenton, N.J.: Africa World Press, 1990).

Lie, N. and T. D'haen, *Constellation Caliban: Figurations of a Character* (Amsterdam, Netherlands: Rodopi, 1997).

Oboler, S., *Ethnic Labels, Latino Lives: Identity and the Re(Presentation) in the United States* (Minnesota: University of Minnesota Press, 1995).

Retamar, R.F., *Caliban and Other Essays* (trans. Edward Baker) (Minneapolis: University of Minnesota Press, 1989).

Notes

1. S. Cox and L. Galda, 'Multicultural Literature: Mirrors and Windows on a Global Community' in *The Reading Teacher*, 43 (8), 1990, 582–9.
2. C.R. Goforth, *Desert and Paradise: Paradox in Island Stories for Children*. MA Thesis, Clemson University, 1984, p. 1.
3. See also J. Hillis Miller's chapter on *The Swiss Family Robinson* in this volume for a further discussion of the 'Robinsonnade'.
4. M.J. Dash, *The Other America: Caribbean Literature in a New World Context* (Charlottesville: University Press of Virginia, 1998), p. 30.
5. C. Lopez-Springfield, 'Revisiting Caliban: Implications for Caribbean Feminism' in *Daughters of Caliban: Caribbean Women in the Twentieth Century* (Bloomington and Indianapolis: Indiana University Press, 1997), p. ix.
6. See J. Lazú, *Nuyorican Theatre: Prophecies and Monstrosities*, Ph.D. Thesis, Stanford University, 2002.
7. Goforth, *Desert and Paradise*, p. 81.
8. S. Bhatia, 'Acculturation, Dialogical Voices, and the Construction of the Diasporic Self' in *Theory and Psychology*, 12 (1), 2002, 55–77, 56.
9. See G. Anzaldúa, *Borderlands/ la frontera* (San Francisco, CA: Spinsters/Aunt Lute, 1987), and H. Bhaba, *The Location of Culture* (New York: Routledge, 1994).
10. J.B. Cobb, *Images and Characteristics of African Americans and Hispanic Americans in Contemporary Children's Fiction*, Ph.D. Thesis, The University of Tennessee (Ann Arbor, MI: UMI Dissertation Services, 1992), p. 4.
11. M. Sendak, *Where The Wild Things Are* (New York: Harper and Row, 1963).
12. J.O. Cofer, *An Island Like You: Stories of the Barrio* (New York: Orchard Books, 1995), p. 1.
13. Cofer, *An Island Like You*, p. 10.
14. See Bhatia, 'Acculturation, Dialogical Voices, and the Construction of the Diasporic Self'.
15. A. Bernardo, *Jumping Off to Freedom* (Houston, TX: Piñata Books, 1996).
16. See A. Prieto González, 'The Image of Cuba in the US Mass Media' in *Conexiones: Voices of Cuba* (April/May 2000, at: http://isla.igc.org/Conexiones/conexiones.html).

17. N. Osa, *Cuba 15* (New York: Delacorte Press, 2003).
18. G. Crespo, *How The Sea Began* (New York: Clarion Books, 1993).
19. R. Pané, *Relación acerca de las antiguedades de los indios: el primer tratado escrito en América* (Santo Domingo: Ediciones de la Fundación Corripio, 1988).
20. J. Alvarez, *The Secret Footprints* (New York: Dell Dragonfly Books, 2000), last page of section 'About the Story' (no page numbering).
21. See Bhatia, 'Acculturation, Dialogical Voices, and the Construction of the Diasporic Self'.
22. See T.M. Mohanty, 'Cartographies of Struggle: Third World Women and the Politics of Feminism', in C.T. Mohanty, A. Russo and L. Torres (eds) *Third World Women and the Politics of Feminism* (Bloomington: Indiana University Press, 1991).
23. M. Halter, *Shopping For Identity: The Marketing of Ethnicity* (New York: Schocken Books, 2000).
24. Halter, *Shopping For Identity*, p. 4.
25. Cobb, *Images and Characteristics of African Americans and Hispanic Americans in Contemporary Children's Fiction*, p. 6.
26. R. Grosfoguel and C.S. Georas, 'Latino Caribbean Diasporas in New York' in *Mambo Montage: The Latinization of New York* (eds) Agustín Laó-Montes and Arlene Dávila (New York: Columbia University Press, 2001).
27. P. Bourdieu, *The Field of Cultural Production: Essays on Art and Literature* (Cambridge: Polity, 1993) p. 83.
28. A. Dávila, *Sponsored Identities: Cultural Politics in Puerto Rico* (Philadelphia: Temple University Press, 1997), p. 3.
29. See Halter, *Shopping For Identity*.
30. A. Laó-Montes and A. Dávila (eds), *Mambo Montage: The Latinization of New York* (New York: Columbia University Press, 2001), p. 3.
31. Laó-Montes and Dávila (eds), *Mambo Montage*, p. 7.
32. J. Flores, *From Bomba to Hip Hop: Puerto Rican Culture and Latino Identity* (New York: Columbia University Press, 2000), p. 49.
33. Cobb, *Images and Characteristics of African Americans and Hispanic Americans in Contemporary Children's Fiction*, p. 7.

10
Landscapes: 'Going foreign' in Arthur Ransome's *Peter Duck*

Sarah Spooner

> Literature … reminds us that we understand, create and experience not only the world around us but also the world of our dreams, desires and fears, in terms of the very language we learn to articulate.[1]

> [O]ne can gain a powerful insight into a culture's sense of identity precisely through its fantasies of 'Otherness', rather than simply those of 'Home'. Identities of place are formed through a constant process of negotiation between fantasies of Self and Other, of Home and Away, of Here and There. Who we think we are is inextricably connected to who we think we are not. How we imagine where we are is directly related to how we imagine other places.[2]

In much children's literature criticism, there is an idea that place or location is important to children's literature. These places and locations are then often discussed as either part of a familiar and recognizable landscape, or as part of existing but strange and new places. In this chapter I argue instead that in texts notions of 'the real' and 'the fantastic', of the 'exotic', and of 'home' and the 'foreign', and by extension of 'the child' are very precisely ideas, not self-evident fact. Furthermore, I argue that these ideas are produced in a constant and never-ending process of negotiation, using each other to define themselves and vice versa. I use Arthur Ransome's novel *Peter Duck* as an example and, critiquing some of the ways this text has been positioned in the past, hope to demonstrate how *Peter Duck* is engaged in this process of negotiation, producing one place in relation to another, offering multiple ways of reading landscape and 'home'. Along the way, I also try to demonstrate the problems with claims of any kind that children's literature and its language offer a simplicity or transparency that somehow provides a direct view of a world just as it is.

Of the 12 texts going under the name of the 'Swallows and Amazons' series, three have been termed as 'fantasies': *Peter Duck*, *Missee Lee* and, perhaps more contentiously, *Great Northern?*[3] Peter Hunt groups the three texts together in the 'Fantastic Voyages' chapter of *Approaching Arthur Ransome*, Victor Watson says that two of the texts took the protagonists 'to distant exotic seas and involved them in adventures of a more or less fantastic nature', while Hugh Shelley (and, following him, Christina Hardyment) describes *Peter Duck* and *Missee Lee* as 'realistic fantasy' rather than Ransome's usual 'fantastic reality'.[4] As the term 'fantasy' may not appear to be one most obviously applicable to the work of Arthur Ransome, associated as it usually is with a specific genre of other worlds and supernatural events, it is notable that Peter Hunt has to explain and qualify his use of the term. It is the assumptions that seem to be at work in this explanation that provide a useful introduction to the issues I wish to discuss in this chapter as they raise a number of questions concerning not only the definitions of 'realism' and 'fantasy' as literary genres, but also the nature and status of a literary 'series'.

Peter Hunt's explication of his own fantasy definition begins to acknowledge some of the problems. He notes that a general definition of 'fantasy' as 'something out of the ordinary' could include all fiction, while a more narrow genre definition of 'fantasy literature' as to do with magic and 'wondrous events' would exclude the Ransome texts. He therefore suggests that 'romance' may be a more appropriate term. Nevertheless, he persists with a 'fantasy' definition, insisting that the three texts 'deal with the shadowy area between the improbable and the impossible'.[5] This can direct us to the problems inherent in genre criticism, where the emphasis is placed on taxonomical classification and which has little to offer those texts that do not fit neatly into one of its delineated categories.[6] Lucie Armitt in *Theorising the Fantastic* writes that fantasy is 'like all other literary modes, fluid, constantly overspilling the very forms it adopts, always looking, not so much for escapism but certainly to escape the constraints that critics…inevitably impose upon it'.[7] In the light of this, Shelley's depiction of Ransome's work as realistic fantasy/fantastical reality is both more interesting and useful as it acknowledges further layers and shadings between the genre extremes of 'fantasy' and 'realism'. This acknowledgment in itself serves to blur the genre boundaries, and its application to Ransome suggests that the *Swallows and Amazons* texts negotiate genre and cross borders in a much more fluid and flexible way than Hunt's terminology can provide for.

But what factors have led these particular three texts to be defined as fantasy in the first place? From my reading of the criticism it would appear that the two key factors in the definitional process are setting – the place in which the action of the text is sited – and the relationship to the rest of the series. These two elements can actually work in combination. Of the 12 books which make up the series, five are set in the Lake District, two in the Norfolk Broads and two centre around the Pin Mill and Harwich area of Suffolk. The three 'fantasies' each have a setting shared by none of the others in the series; respectively, an island in the Caribbean, islands off the coast of China, and a non-specified location in the Inner or Outer Hebrides of Scotland. Christina Hardyment writes that these three books are 'different from the rest' and on this rationale largely omits them from her book of investigation into the 'real places' 'behind' the Ransome texts. As these books are not seen to be based around 'real places', then she need not trace the sources to China, the Caribbean or the Hebrides, but need only go to the Ransome archives in Leeds to find the 'truth' behind the texts.[8] The fact that each of these three texts has a location not returned to in any of the other texts in the series seems to work in combination with the exotic foreign-ness of those locations to create the fantasy definition. Indeed, for some critics the exotic location is enough on its own. Victor Watson writes that *Missee Lee*'s opening in a 'noisy Japanese harbour' shows that 'this adventurous seagoing novelist has again broken free of the realistic conventions of children's books'.[9] Here it is the Japanese harbor setting that leads directly to the claim of Ransome having 'broken free of realistic conventions'. The implication is that there is something intrinsically non-real about Japan or China that makes any novel set there into a non-real, a fantasy text.[10]

However, the lack of such apparent exoticism in the Scottish setting of *Great Northern?* – the presence of the 'savage Gaels' notwithstanding – and its apparent realism leads Peter Hunt into telling difficulties regarding his definition of it as one of the fantasy texts. He describes it as a fantasy, 'although clothed in realistic clothes', largely because the characters are not seen to grow (John and Nancy are ostensibly around 16, yet do not comply with his ideas of teenage behaviour) and therefore are not seen to be 'subject to the laws of the real world'. He argues that the shape of *Great Northern?* is adult because of its lack of apparent closure, and that this then jars with what he sees as 'the childishness of the characters'. He states, '*Great Northern?* has, consequently, a feel of not being related to the rest of the sequence at all', and this perceived lack of continuity with the rest of the series ultimately seems to be the primary source of his definition of this text as fantasy. This element can, in fact, be extended to cover both *Peter Duck* and *Missee Lee* also. In *Approaching Arthur Ransome*, Hunt refers to the other nine texts in the series – the non-fantasy nine – as 'the main sequence of the books'. As with *Great Northern?* the two other 'not-main' texts do not adhere to the narrative of character development and skill-acquirement that Hunt perceives in the movement of the other books. This appears to lead him to regard these three books as lesser achievements. The division of the series into 'main' and 'not-main' carries with it assumptions about value, implying that the three 'fantasy' texts are somehow diversionary, less serious, less important. In the hierarchy of the 'main' and the not-main, fantasy comes firmly into the latter category. Ultimately 'fantasy' here seems to function as a label with which to contain – and sideline – events or behaviours that do not contribute to a tidy or coherent reading of the series as a whole.

However, returning to the issue of setting as it arises in the fantasy definitions, I intend to look at how these exotic landscapes are set up as such within these 'fantasy' Ransome texts, focusing particularly on *Peter Duck*, and how these exotic landscapes are made to appear as such through references to and comparisons with the 'home' landscape. As divisions between 'fantasy' and 'reality' – or even the purely generic divisions between 'fantasy' and 'realism' – are far from clear, so I wish to demonstrate that boundaries between home and away, familiar and unfamiliar, reliable and unreliable, land and sea, become equally shifting and unstable. These texts show how difficult it is to obtain clear knowledge about the true place of anything, even the land upon which you are standing.

One thing instantly noteworthy about the settings of these three texts is how nebulous and unspecific they are. It is striking in the context of a series so concerned with exploration, discovery and mapping that that these locations are so pointedly 'un-mappable'. All of them in fact either begin or end as secrets. This remains the case even in the most ostensibly familiar of these locations, the Scotland of *Great Northern?*. As part of his definition of this text as a fantasy, Peter Hunt comments: '[t]he meticulous Hebridean setting should not mislead us into assuming that the plot line bears any relationship to reality.'[11] But, importantly, this 'meticulousness' does not include specifics such as real names or a map location and, while this can also be said of much of the Lake District settings used in other texts, in *Great Northern?* attention is drawn to this fact. Ahead of chapter one and following two maps, one a very large-scale one of the west coast of Scotland and the Inner and Outer Hebrides, and one a small-scale one of the two valleys in which the events take place, is this note:

Every effort has been made (short of falsifying the course of events) to prevent the inquisitive reader from learning the exact place where the *Sea Bear* was scrubbed and the Ship's Naturalist made his discovery. Persons who pester the author for more information (whether or not they enclose stamped envelopes with their letters) will not be answered. Further, should anyone with particular knowledge of the Hebrides identify the loch where the Divers are nesting and be the means of disturbing them, they will make enemies of John, Susan, Titty, Roger, Nancy, Peggy, Dorothea and Dick, as well as of the author, who will in that case be sorry he has written this account of what happened.

This continues within the text with a claim of made-up names for the Gaelic characters because '[i]f the real name were to be printed here, it would tell everybody who read it exactly where the Great Northern Divers had their nest. It was necessary, therefore, to change it for use in this book'.[12] These two notes serve to add an aura of authenticity to the text by implying that the events really occurred (and are still occurring; note the use of the present tense in reference to the Divers nesting), that the characters really exist, and that the location is 'out there' able to be discovered by any reader with 'particular knowledge' of the region. However, the notes also work to justify the lack of specificity about the location by rendering it a deliberate secret, the breaking of which will entail a kind of breaking of faith with the characters and events described, and even with the author himself. The location has to be kept secret in order to protect vulnerable wildlife and so participates in the discourse of wildlife preservation at work in the rest of the text. So the lack of specificity in this 'fantasy' landscape becomes highly visible and is made an important part of the text.

This same emphasis on secrecy can be seen in the other two 'fantasy' texts under consideration. Indeed, we can see the same idea of protection at work in *Missee Lee*. The frontispiece map to *Missee Lee* contains a note ostensibly from 'Nancy Blackett (Capt.)' stating that much of the map is guesswork as there was no time to do a 'proper survey', and concluding:

> We are not putting in the lat. and the long. because if the government knew it might send gunboats and people to shoot Miss Lee or even put her in prison because of what she is doing. This would be very unfair as she is only doing it because of her duty to her ancestors... We have put in junks instead.

The three islands off the coast of China where the novel is set are being run as a form of protection racket known about by the Chinese, but that has to be kept secret from the English for fear they will send 'gunboats' to break it up. Again this secret of location is an important element around which the plot turns, and the characters' escape from the islands is conditional upon a promise not to break the secret. So, as in *Great Northern?*, the lack of specificity, the 'un-mappable' and indeterminate nature of the setting is stressed and made into an important plot device. In *Peter Duck* the case is slightly different. It is Crab Island's status as a treasure island rather than any desire to protect it which leads to secrecy about it, and once the treasure is gone, there is no longer any necessity to keep it a secret. But in both *Peter Duck* and *Missee Lee* the knowledge of latitude and longitude, figures that allow the plotting of exact location onto a map, becomes physically dangerous. I have already noted that the latitude and longitude figures are omitted from the map in *Missee Lee* on the grounds that they would give away the specific location of the islands and thus jeopardize Miss Lee, but the possibility that the Swallows and Amazons may be able to calculate these figures places them in danger within the text. The instrument – a sextant – used to calculate the figures is seen and recognized by one of the islands' rulers who, as a result, realizes that these English visitors constitute a very real threat to the future of the three islands. In the case of *Peter Duck*, the latitude and longitude of the treasure island are written down by the men who buried the treasure, memorized and then written down again by the young Peter Duck, and ultimately stolen by the novel's villain Black Jake, whose resultant knowledge of the island's location becomes dangerous for all concerned. As Peter Duck had memorized the figures – 'couldn't forget them if I tried' – it is the writing down of them that is seen as the mistake and which he comes to regret. The writing of the bearings onto the 'scrap of paper' gives the island a traceable entity, which can then easily fall into the wrong hands. So it can be seen that in all three of these texts, knowledge of the specifics of location is depicted as a danger, either to the characters or to the place itself.

Peter Duck, although in chronological order of publication the third of the texts, is set up as following on from *Swallows and Amazons*, and there are a number of references to the events of that text, and particularly to the area in which they took place:

> 'Swallows and Amazons for ever!' John, Susan, Titty and Roger shouted back, remembering how they had shouted that over the water to each other as their little boats, the *Swallow* and the *Amazon*, were sailing home on the last day of those holidays on the lake in the north.[13]

Indeed, that far-away 'lake in the north' comes to signify 'home' and normality, and serve as a measure of the current 'strange' surroundings and of how far the characters have come from that site of familiarity: ' "We never thought when we were sailing home from Horseshoe Cove that this year we'd be landing in her on a desert island." '[14] At the crisis point of the text the lake is introduced as something to hold on to when everything else appears to be spinning out of control:

> They would have said just that if they had got out of time while rowing together on the lake at home. They said it now, though they were rowing at dusk to an island of landslide and earthquake and half-mad pirates roaming about with stolen guns. Still, some things were the same as usual. Wherever you were you said 'Sorry' if you bumped 'stroke' in the back with the bow oar, and you said it was your fault if you had happened to change the time unexpectedly because you were thinking of something else.[15]

Here, the lake and its associated behaviours evoke a kind of safety in the midst of danger because of its familiarity and ritualized activities. The landscape of that previous text serves as the benchmark through which to see and judge any other landscape. 'He thought of Lowestoft harbour and of the lake among the hills at home, and then he looked at the green feathery tops of palm trees, the green forest climbing the slopes of Mount Gibber, and the open sea.'[16] As that landscape is normal, familiar, and pointedly specified as 'home', so any place that differs from it is exotic, foreign, strange. Sometimes there are points of similarity: 'Some of the trees were very like pine trees and reminded Titty and Roger of the woods above the lake in the far-away country at home.'[17] But it is still notable that they are 'very like' pine trees rather than fully qualified pine trees in themselves. These points of similarity and recurring references to 'home' and its activities – which include the act of sailing itself and comparisons to the harbor on Wild Cat island – actually work to underline and constantly reiterate that this is not 'home', and indeed that 'home' is 'far-away'. References to the distant familiar draw attention to, and emphasize through comparison, the strangeness of the current surroundings.

Many of the references to 'home' occur in relation to the ship *Swallow*, which functions as a point of contact between the two texts and the two settings. It is *Swallow* that is sailed on the lake at home and at the tropical island. However, another ship in *Peter Duck* also provides a connection to 'home'. The *Wild Cat* is a green schooner that only features in the 'fantasy' texts *Peter Duck* and *Missee Lee*. Not only does she function as a kind of home for the characters in these texts, 'a regular house of a ship', a place that provides them with a base and a sanctuary and a vehicle of escape from the exotic, strange places when they become too threatening, but her connection with the 'home' landscape of *Swallows and Amazons* is made explicit in *Peter Duck*. On joining the ship, hitherto only identified as 'the green schooner', the Swallows are asked what she is called: ' "*Wild Cat*" said Titty. "She's called after our island", said Roger.'[18] By this naming then, the key site of the 'home' landscape, Wild Cat island, the place that functions as 'home' within *Swallows and Amazons*, is present by proxy. Christina Hardyment refers to this ship as 'the island come to life'.[19] The name of the ship functions as a constant reminder of that other home. It is significant, then, that this ship only appears in the two texts with the most obviously 'othered' or exotic landscapes, namely the China of *Missee Lee* and the Caribbean of *Peter Duck*.

In relation to this, another notable feature that only occurs in these two texts is the joint presence of both the parrot and the monkey. Although the parrot is present in both the preceding 'non-fantasy' texts, *Swallows and Amazons* and *Swallowdale*, Roger's monkey, Gibber, bought for him after the treasure-finding episode in the first book, is only referenced as having gone to the zoo for the holidays to explain its absence from *Swallowdale*. Peter Hunt notes this recurrent absence: 'but the fact that monkey and parrot only appear together in the fantasy novel *Missee Lee* suggests that Ransome knew their place in the literary scheme of things.'[20] For him, then, it would seem that the monkey and parrot together, evoking as they do for him 'the kind of exotic gifts so often found in wish-fulfilling (and impractical) children's stories', belong naturally in the fantasy texts. This specific placement of the 'exotic' as more appropriate in the fantasy realm ('knowing its place') is telling, and reiterates the connection made between the exotic and the non-realistic by Victor Watson which I quoted earlier. However, this alignment of the parrot and monkey alongside the fantasy element is also performed in *We Didn't Mean To Go To Sea*. In this passage, the Walker family, left alone on a ship in Felixstowe harbor, pretend they have just returned from a much longer voyage.

'John,' said Titty. 'Where've we come from?'

John started. It was as if she had heard him speak his thought out loud.

'River Plate,' he said. Dover seemed too near, if Titty also was thinking they had come in from the sea.

'Months on the voyage,' said Titty. 'Isn't it lovely to be in home waters at last?' ... 'To think that last time we anchored there were palm trees on the banks, and crocodiles. I say, it's an awful pity we haven't got the ship's parrot with us, to sing out "Pieces of Eight!" and make things seem more real.'

'Gibber, too,' said Roger. 'He'd be simply fine sitting on the cross-trees and much happier than in the Zoo.'

Titty, looking up at the cross-trees, found it easy to see the monkey and the parrot perched up there side by side.[21]

Here, the parrot and monkey function as imaginary visual aids to make the equally imaginary return from foreign seas 'seem more real'. Titty is not wishing to have actually returned from the river Plate, she is wishing for the presence of the monkey and parrot to lend veracity to an illusion of having done so. It is as if some intrinsic 'exotic-ness' about these non-native-English animals serves to bring other exotic elements closer. By this token, the *Wild Cat* in *Peter Duck* and *Missee Lee* could be said to have a touch of the exotic or foreign aboard already, in the shape of the parrot and the monkey, before the ship even leaves Lowestoft harbor. Indeed, in *Peter Duck*, these animals are connected to the new, foreign landscape the ship sails in search of. Gibber sits looking out at other ships in the harbor before they leave because 'so many masts all together reminded him perhaps of forests at home'.[22] While the 'perhaps' here sounds a note of speculation and implies a limit to the narrator's knowledge, this statement nevertheless makes the point that Gibber's 'home' is not the same as the 'home' of the other characters. This serves to introduce the idea that 'home' is a relative and positional concept, rather than one that is set in stone. The same connection is made regarding Polly the parrot when the *Wild Cat* arrives at Crab Island. 'There was a sudden screaming flight of parrots, that brought an answering scream from Polly.'[23] Polly 'answers' the scream from the island with one of her own, thus making the similarity between the two explicit. If these two animals do function as links to the exotic tropical island, or work to signify the exotic in the seemingly more prosaic 'home' (be that 'the island in the north' or Lowestoft harbor), then their very presence in the 'home' environment of the *Wild Cat* could serve to destabilize any clear cut division between 'home' and 'away' or the 'familiar' and the 'exotic'. Although the *Wild Cat* sails away from the tropical island, the presence of the parrot and the monkey on board means then that it does not leave every trace of exoticism behind it.

The initial response to arrival at the island is told through the new child character, Bill:

> Bill watched the island but did not say a word ... to come to this green island, with its beaches of bright sand, its black, cliff-like peaks, rising out of feathery palms swaying and blowing in the trade wind, this was indeed going foreign, and Bill would not trust himself to speak lest, for once, he should let the others see he was surprised. It was better to see all he could and to say nothing. These children would say everything that wanted saying.[24]

This sets the tone for much of the subsequent response to the island. It is as if, in confronting this island, the characters are being shown something truly and undeniably strange, something utterly divorced from any previous experience. The text states that 'this was something different', and the surprise is such that Bill does not 'trust himself to speak'. Bill's characterization up to this point in the text has been as someone who has seen everything, an apparently experienced and even cynical counterpoint to the naïve romanticism of the other children. So the fact that even this character is stunned into silence in the presence of the strangeness of this landscape – 'this was indeed going foreign' – serves to further emphasize its status as alien. The presence of this island acts to highlight the limitations of any prior definition of Bill – or anyone else – as 'experienced'. Bill opts for silence in the face of this new experience as he is afraid any utterance may betray his surprise. 'It was better to see all he could and say nothing.'[25] It could even be held that Bill's response is somehow 'truer' or more genuine precisely because of his inability or unwillingness to put it into words. However, the text acknowledges that Bill's silence is not duplicated by the other characters who 'would say anything that wanted saying', and who 'chatter about this and that they saw on the island shores'[26] while Bill maintains his silence. That said, it is nevertheless Bill's silence in the face of the island that is foregrounded. Indeed, the text partially re-enacts his silence by not incorporating the 'chatter' of the other characters.

Other early depictions of the island in the text appear to repeat the idea of the limitations of words or words alone to properly convey a sense of this foreign land. The characters 'watch ... the island shores slip by, one strange, wild picture after another framing itself in the galley doorway'.[27] Here the island appears as a series of pictures and thus as a visual spectacle, an art work. A view of the island becomes a series of pictures by appearing framed by parts of the ship. A frame serves to set boundaries or limits and thus in many ways works to define whatever is held within it.[28] A frame provides a context through which to view the picture. So in this case, it is notable that the pictures of the island are framed by the doorway of the ship's kitchen. The island scenes appear as doubly 'strange' and 'wild' because of the prosaic nature of the place from which they are viewed. It is also notable that the pictures are described as framing *themselves* in the doorway: 'one strange, wild picture after another framing itself against the galley doorway.' The sentence ascribes the agency to the pictures themselves – or the landscape out of which they are made – rather than any more external organizational power. This makes the framing doorway seem only a passive recipient for whatever picture decides to appear there.[29] The pictures are not only 'strange' – as in odd, different, unfamiliar, alien – but also 'wild'. This latter term introduces further ideas of nature untamed, of lack of civilization. The two terms together indicate that the pictures are wild because they are strange, and strange because they are wild. The conjunction of the two ideas suggests that 'strangeness' and 'wildness' depend upon each other for definition in this text. Again, ideas of 'strangeness' rely upon notions of 'normality' – or the not-strange – in order to work. Here, the 'wild' is allied with the 'strange' to become unfamiliar and alien, something not normal. As in the viewing of the island pictures through the kitchen doorway, it all depends from where you look.

On the first morning on the island Titty gets up early to re-enact the iconic first glimpse of the new world: 'it was really there, with colours even brighter than she had seen them in her mind.'[30] One of the hallmarks of the descriptions of the island is this emphasis on its extreme nature. We have already seen that the island is represented as something beyond Bill's capacity with words, and here the colors of the island, although only specified as green and black, become brighter than even Titty's imagination has been able to make them. Although the description itself only runs to 'green trees' and 'black rocks', the idea of the scene as dazzling is emphasized by the reiterated word 'bright' and the associated 'burning', 'blazing', 'sparkling'. However, the *Wild Cat* makes her final anchorage in the dark, where the strangeness of the place is conveyed by an emphasis upon sound. 'Everybody was speaking in a whisper, so as to hear the noises of the land.' The parrots scream, the palm trees 'creak' and 'rustle', tree-frogs 'whistle', and they also hear 'the sharp crac-crac of the grasshoppers'. However, this arrival in the dark concludes with a return to the visual:

And then, suddenly, millions of lights showed along the edge of the forest, moving all the time. It was as if millions of small bright sparks were dancing there in the dusk.

'Fireflies,' said Captain Flint.

'It can't be,' said Titty.

'This is the real thing at last,' said Nancy.[31]

This final sighting, or partial sighting, of the fireflies elicits both the statement of disbelief: 'it can't be', and the statement of total belief or recognition: 'this is the real thing at last.' Here it is the new world, the exotic tropical island of the 'strange' and 'wild' pictures that becomes the yearned for 'real thing', 'at last'. In a series of texts so dedicated to the destabilizing of any settled categorization of the 'real' and the 'not-real', it is highly fitting that the sight of the 'small bright sparks ... dancing there in the dusk' generates such apparently contradictory responses.

However, elements of this early idyllic depiction of this tropical island are carefully problematized. Titty's desire to be alone in her experiencing of the desert island 'she had been looking forward to ... ever since she could remember' is upset by the presence of Peter Duck, already up and on the deck before her. She momentarily ignores him and 'pretended to herself that she had sailed alone across the ocean'. Her interaction with this longed-for experience has now become partially simulation. The presence of another person means that it is not as much of a desert island and is something of an undercutting of expectation. Peter Duck is up early and in place to disappoint Titty because he is doing some fishing. It is not the 'rainbow-coloured' fish that he wants but rather the more ugly-sounding grey 'big-mouths' which feed on the brighter fish. Whenever he catches one with a ' "Joseph's coat" ', Peter Duck throws it back as ' "[t]here's not chewing for a mouse on him" '; ' "All bones he is, and a gay coat on the back of them." ' It is the larger, more drab-looking ones that can provide the better meal, while the ones with the prettier surface have little substance. The initially bright attractiveness proves to be deceptive. This pattern can be said to be re-enacted on a large scale with the apparently idyllic island itself. This same fishing episode provides an early hint of this. Captain Flint is the next to emerge on this first morning on the island and immediately dives into the water for a swim only to get instantly attacked by a shark. 'A big, triangular fin, above a huge dim shadow in the water, was moving fast towards the swimmer ... a long grey shadow flashed white in the water, and the shark turned over and a horrible mouth snapped only an inch or two below his foot.'[32] The shark is here repeatedly described as a shadow. The water that had been 'clearer than good glass' only moments before, enabling a clear view 'five fathoms' down to the rainbow fish in their 'underwater forests', seems much less transparent when it comes to the shark which can only be seen as a fin and a 'dim shadow'. Even the very transparency of the water becomes deceptive. While seeming clear, it works to blur the dangers contained (or even concealed) within its 'brilliant world'. A comparison is again made with the events of the earlier text and, by extension, with the 'home' landscape of that text: ' "[d]o you remember looking for sharks over the side of the houseboat, that day you made me walk the plank? You were afraid the sharks wouldn't be big enough to eat me." '[33] As Roger acknowledges, ' "[t]his is different" '. The dangers that had to be imagined in *Swallows and Amazons* have become real in this exotic and apparently idyllic landscape. ' "Giminy!" said Nancy. "It really was a shark. Look!" They all saw that three-cornered fin cutting through the water seventy or eighty yards away.' Although it is stated that 'after that, oddly enough, they never saw another', one is enough to sound the warning. Right from this first morning on the island, the impression has been given that it is not as idyllic as it appears to be.

The first expedition on land still stresses the 'gorgeous' and colorful dimension of this strange landscape, with butterflies 'as big as saucers', 'birds so small that at first Titty thought they were biggish bees' and 'many strange flowering trees the names of which they did not know'.[34] Here again the things appear strange through the comparison with things familiar and known: butterflies as saucers and birds as bees. The comparison with more mundane but familiar objects might appear to render the subject of the comparison more recognizable, but actually serves to make it more alien by dint of the very mundanity of the thing to which it is compared (and in the case of the butterflies as saucers reference, make it seem like one of Lewis Carroll's Looking-Glass insects). The trees appear to be classified as 'strange' largely because they do not know the names for them, naming here, as elsewhere in the series, functioning in a discourse of knowing and controlling. However, even here among the flowering trees and the blue, purple and red bee-sized birds, there are intimations of danger. The children are told to wear shoes and make a noise while walking in order to avoid snakes; and ' "[i]t's not only snakes you'd best be looking for. There's them hairy spiders. Don't you let one of them things grapple and board." ' But the most problematic of the animals encountered in *Peter Duck* are the crabs after which this treasure island is named. These crabs feature large in the young shipwrecked Peter Duck's memories of the place as large, numerous and threatening, particularly the ones that appeared during the night. In comparison with this, the crabs that appear in this text initially appear few and of a 'disappointing size'. They become a lesson in the deceptive-ness of memory and storytelling: ' "they seems so small to what they was. Maybe they growed with me thinking about them and spinning the yarn so often" ',[35] and the problems of perception: ' "[t]hey'd seem big enough if you were on the island by yourself ... I bet they'll have grown a bit when you come to tell your grandchildren about them ... they probably seemed bigger in the dark." '[36] The repeated 'seems' and 'maybes' in this speech further emphasize notions of provisionality and doubt. The crabs come to be an ever-present pest rather than an active danger, requiring constant vigilance over fire, food and belongings. Yet they represent a further hint that this island is not as beautiful as it seems, as the crabs may be smaller and less physically dangerous than anticipated, but they are nevertheless cannibalistic. As soon as one of the humans kills one, the other crabs 'pull it to pieces'. The characters learn that the best way to distract the crabs from their possessions is to throw some of the dead crabs away and 'instantly some of the other crabs lost interest in the fire and turned on the dead bodies of their relations'.[37] The projection of a human familial relationship onto the crabs here makes obvious an idea of almost incestuous cannibalism, and the human analogy makes clear the lack of human morality at work among these crabs. 'The crabs themselves had no hearts at all. They grabbed at each other and tore each other to pieces, and the noise of crunching which they made was horrible in itself.' It is this element to the crabs which remains true to Peter Duck's fearsome memories of them, and prompts him to say 'Quite like old times'. Aside from the lack of physical threat posed by the crabs, their cannibalistic presence is inherently disturbing to the characters and serves as a constant reminder of a non-benign idea of nature. Again, we can see in the instance of the crabs that this is a place, a landscape, that is deceptive.

With the entrance of the storm, the island moves from being merely deceptive to being actively dangerous. As the storm approaches and continues there is a reiterated idea of something being 'wrong'. Sometimes the wrong-ness is specifically attributed to the weather or to the sea, and at other times it is just left to stand as 'there was something wrong'. From the regular warm temperatures and steady winds of the early days on the island, the weather becomes erratic, shifting, unpredictable. Preliminary indications of a change in the weather are given by the wildlife: the crabs vanish, the birds 'all at once rose screaming above the trees' and the monkey shivers and whimpers.[38] The humans are slower to register the 'wrong-ness', but soon notice an abrupt change in temperature, and the difference between them and the other animals shrinks: 'all the explorers…shivered like the monkey.'[39] The 'wrong-ness' of the storm is characterized by suddenness, irregularity and by elements out of their proper place. The winds do not come from one direction, but 'swing all round the compass' so that the land no longer works to protect the *Wild Cat* from the prevailing winds, but becomes a danger, so that the ship has to take to the open sea in order to be safe. The progress of the storm is abrupt and unpredictable, swinging from one extreme to another; from noise to silence, from raging wind to quaking earth, from suffocating dry dust to drenching wet rain. 'The squall had stopped as suddenly as it had begun… there was silence again…and it was as if Susan, for no reason at all, was shouting in an empty room.'[40] Nothing is where it should be. The air becomes dust and unbreathable: 'the feathery green palms were fading in a ruddy brown haze as if they were behind a veil of coppery silk', while the wind takes on a physical entity and is able to be leant against 'as if it was a wall'. Most strikingly of all, the 'wrong-ness' of the storm is emphasized by the metallic, 'unnatural' imagery used to describe it. The initial cloud indicating the presence of the storm is 'the colour of a bright copper kettle' and is a 'great, hard-edged copper-coloured fan' that spreads to cover the blue sky 'as if it were cut out of sheet metal'. A 'curious chemical smell' follows the earthquake, and the waterspout is also described in terms of man-made metals and machinery:

[A] narrow band of light showed under the black cloud that stretched above it, hard-edged as a bar of iron. And across that narrow band of light a thin black thread seemed to join the cloud to the sea … That thread of dark colour between cloud and sea was thicker now. The cloud itself seemed now to roof the sky. The waterspout was changing shape with every moment. It was like a tremendous indiarubber tube joining sky and sea. It widened at the top where it met the cloud, and the bottom of it spread out like the base of a candlestick.

'It's twirling like a corkscrew,' said Titty.[41]

These references to 'hard-edged', 'copper' and 'iron', to kettles, fans, corkscrews, candlesticks and indiarubber tubes, produce the storm almost as a man-made thing upsetting the proper balance of nature. It 'cuts' in, against the prevailing winds and the natural pattern of things. Where the previous weather was 'healthy', the storm weather is sick. 'The sea was somehow slack and sulky. It was grey like the sky. It was a sea stirring in its sleep, troubled by some uneasy dream.'[42] 'The colour of the island had faded, and it seemed that its noises, too, were hushed.'[43] This storm is undoubtedly 'wrong', an aberration, an unnatural thing. In this context, the placing of the storm in the tropics is again significant. These 'busters' or 'snorters' are explicitly positioned in the tropics in a comment from Captain Flint: ' "What if we get a circular storm? We're in the tropics, mind you." '[44] The implication is that the tropics is a place prone to such unnatural events. This specific placing of a dangerous, unpredictable and unfamiliar meteorological phenomenon is discussed by Peter Hulme in *Colonial Encounters*. He discusses the term 'hurricane' as one specific to the colonial Caribbean region and as a word derived from the local Arawak *hurakan*, implying that neither the Spanish or English languages had a word appropriate for an event so fundamentally alien to them. Hulme states: 'Arguably no phenomenon – not even the natives themselves – characterized so well the novelty of the New World to Europeans.'[45] As the storm in *Peter Duck* approaches, again there is a reference to comparative events in *Swallows and Amazons*: ' "just remember the hurricane we had our last night on Wild Cat Island." ' As with the shark episode, the reference to the previous text serves to emphasize how far away from it *Peter Duck* has come and how different this tropical storm is from the one in the Lake District.

One essential difference here is that this storm manages to completely change the shape of the landscape. The wind has blown down all the trees, and the earthquake has caused the island's chief landmark, Mount Gibber, to fall down.

The very shape of the hills had changed. The green island had turned a dusky greyish brown, with the ruin of the forest and the falling dust of the earthquake and the landslides. There were still three hills, but no one could have recognised Mount Gibber from out here, at sea, if he had not known what had happened. It was now hardly higher than the others.

The tremendous landslides caused by the earthquake had carried the whole of that precipitous black peak headlong down over its wooded lower slopes. Where the green forest had climbed...there was now nothing but a dreadful chaos of raw earth and rock.[46]

The early idyllic exoticism of the tropical island has now become a 'chaos' of shifted earth and torn greenery. A 'ruin'. 'It was a dismal sight, the forest that only the day before had been rich and green...[t]he trees had been tossed this way and that, and in their fall had crushed the ferns, and brought down with them all those gay curtains of flowers.'[47] The vanishing of the mountain that had been the identification mark for the island to those approaching by sea, as well as the fall of the tall palm tree that acted as a harbor mark, entails a complete loss of bearings. The signs in the landscape that enable the finding of the harbor and the identifying of the island have been shown to be worryingly impermanent. '"Nobody would think it was the same place," said John. "Nobody would think it was the same island," said Titty.'[48] The features that made this island distinguishable from any other, that made it specific, have gone. Gone are the blazed trees that act as markers, gone is the path through the forest, and, indeed, gone is the freshwater spring upon which they rely. 'It was as if Nancy's spring had never been.' If you cannot rely on mountains to stay in place over time, then what can you rely on? Again there is an instructive contrast with the landscape presented in *Swallows and Amazons*. In that text, John turns to the hills around the lake as comforters in a time of difficulty:

But the big hills up the lake helped to make him feel that the houseboat man did not matter. The hills had been there before Captain Flint. They would be there for ever. That, somehow, was comforting.[49]

Here it is the very permanency of the hills that acts as the comfort and brings about a shift in perspective. The thing – person – that was worrying him is made to seem less important through the longevity and stability of these hills. The hill in *Peter Duck* cannot provide this reassurance. Far from 'being there for ever', the key hill here falls down within days of their first seeing it. This foreign landscape is not one that can provide stability or safety.

However, it is not simply the earthquake which shows this foreign island to be shifting and unstable. Rather, it has been shown to be so much earlier in the text. This is made most obvious in the changes that have occurred in the 60 years between Peter Duck's first experience of the island and his second, which is taking place in the text. '"It don't look the same"' Peter Duck says. The changes he sees could be a statement about the problematic and provisional nature of memory (as could also be the case regarding the crabs), but it nevertheless provides an idea that this land is not reliable, is changing. On their first trip across the island they find evidence of previous landslides, '[t]hey could see that all this side of the hill must have slipped down across the old course of the stream',[50] and hints are provided that there are further landslides to come: ' "I shouldn't like to be up here when there's another bit of a shrug and the next lot comes down." '[51] When Peter Duck complains of the lack of 'motion' on islands, Captain Flint points to this earlier landslide as evidence to the contrary: ' "[t]his island's had plenty of motion at one time or other." '[52] But even without landslides, this island is still on the move. Near where the *Wild Cat* is anchored a 'spit of land' is discovered to divide into two 'what had seemed to be a single bay'. They work out that 'at some time the stream had shifted, leaving its old bed dry and making a new one for itself. The spit of land had built itself between the old outlet of the stream and the new.'[53] As in the case of the landscape 'framing itself' through the ship's galley doorway, this phrasing produces the land and the stream as performing these actions of their own volition. This land has a mind of its own. Aspects of this landscape seem at first glance to be one thing and then turn into another. This vision of the landscape is repeated in a subsequent view of the island from the sea.

> The shape of the island seemed to be changing all the time. The little hill … stood out for a time … then … it had gradually seemed to be part of Mount Gibber, and now … had disappeared altogether … The peak of Mount Gibber changed, too. At one time it looked like a smooth black cone rising out of the forest. At another they could see chasms in it and black precipices above the trees …[54]

The character of the island changes according to the point from which it is looked at. Although this is a cliché of all landscape views, the emphasis on movement, time and on 'seeming' in this passage draws attention to the provisionality of any perspective of this landscape. What the landscape 'seems' to be is subject to change at any given moment. The ultimate source of stability and reassurance in *Swallows and Amazons* – the hills – has here become provisional and unreliable, alien.

The trees on Crab Island can likewise provide no stability. Undistinguishable from each other, the palm trees are 'as like as belaying pins'. ' "They're as like as links in chain cable. There's no man alive could tell t'other from which." '[55] Peter Duck had seen the treasure buried under the tree in which he was sleeping, and assumed he could use the tree as a marker with which to find it again. But again, the features of this landscape prove to be unreliable, nothing stays still. ' "I was thinking I'd have to be picking out my old bedroom tree, and with all them trees as like as clincher nails I was feeling like a man making the Finnish coast without a chart." ' In the 60 years since Peter Duck last saw his tree, it may have ' "grown up, fallen down, been eaten by ants, rotted into fibre and blown away in dust … I don't know how long palm trees live" '. In this landscape, the evidence of a person's eyes or of the trees is no guarantee to finding the treasure. The chosen ground for digging for the treasure is then selected according to its proximity to an apparently more stable natural feature: the rocks that make the harbor of Duckhaven. But, as we have seen with Mount Gibber and the landslides, even the rocks in this place cannot necessarily be relied upon: the rocks of Duckhaven also shift during the earthquake into more unnatural positions: '[t]hey no longer seemed to be growing out of the sand.' But even before the earthquake, the finding of the treasure is problematized by the movement of the island itself.

> It may well be that in these sixty years the sea's gone back a little, or piled up the sand, and the earth and the forest may be gaining on the shore. Perhaps all those trees at the very edge of the forest weren't there sixty years ago, and we'll find the stuff a little further back, where the edge of the forest used to be.[56]

The borders of this land itself, the boundaries between the land and the sea, are here produced as in flux, constantly changing.

There are further moves made in *Peter Duck* towards instability, towards a blurring of boundaries. While the Caribbean island is produced as something moving rather than stationary, something rocking and crumbling, – '"This shore simply won't keep still" said Roger'[57] – the sea is frequently described as a kind of land. We have already seen that the masts of the ships in Lowestoft harbor are likened to a forest, while the *Wild Cat* is 'a regular house of a ship'. In an extension of this, the English Channel becomes a kind of street – a 'highway' – with the lighthouse flashes functioning as 'the signposts of the sea'.[58] Black Jake's trailing of the *Wild Cat* down the Channel is likened to 'being followed about by some stranger in the street',[59] while the lights of a liner are 'like a runaway town in the dark' – another thing out of place. While still in the Channel, the swell is like 'smooth hills and valleys of greenish-grey water', but out in the Atlantic, it grows into 'the mountain ranges of the sea'. '[T]he *Wild Cat* raced for the south among rolling seas that seemed like mountains.'[60] By the time they get to the island, these mountains have names: '[g]one, now, were those mountain ranges of water, Andes, Pamirs, Sierras, rolling in from seaward in the evening sunshine.'[61] When they first set sail, it is not the ship that is described as moving, but the land. 'The land seemed to sway up and down as they rushed along … the land would drop to the bulwarks … and the land seemed to leap up the sky.'[62] When they arrive at Crab Island and leave the ship for the shore, again it is the land not the sea that feels to be moving: 'something had gone wrong with their legs, or else with the shore … [b]ut the shore settled down presently.'[63] It is significant that this wobbliness occurs in the transition period between ship and shore, as these references to the sea as land serve to further destabilize an idea of clear and fixed boundaries between the two. In *Peter Duck* the land is shifting, unstable and ultimately dangerous, while the sea takes on these missing qualities of the land to become a site of safety from both earthquake and human violence.

Distinct boundaries between land and sea are further problematized in the wreck episode during the storm. The wreck is a boat out of place on land. In colliding with the land it has ruined itself, made itself useless, and presumably also brought about the ruin of the people on board. Only the barest remnants of it are left:

> [j]ust the bows of it were visible, sticking up out of the sand. The caulking had rotted away and you could see between the planks. A great gaping hole had been smashed in one side of it.[64]

It has been made increasingly unwelcoming by the fact that it is now the home of the cannibalistic crabs. Yet it is this wreck that becomes a place of refuge during the storm. The crabs vanish and, when their tent is blown away, the children seek safety from the wind, rain, darkness and moving earth in the remains of the old boat. Both the boat's old role and current distance from it are emphasized: 'nothing but the grey ribs and the dry, splitting planking of what had once upon a time lifted across the seas.'[65] The phrasing of the wreck's past as a 'proud' ship as 'once upon a time' makes this past non-specific, the proper subject of fairy tales. Yet this boat on land provides a protection from the storm that the land itself cannot, in the same way that the *Wild Cat* sails as far away from the island as possible in order to be safe. The haven it provides lasts only as long as the storm itself. With the resumption of 'normality' the crabs return and the wreck is as inhospitable as it ever was. But with the land rolling like the sea, the old boat is produced as an ideal place to ride it out. This structure is thus both wreck and haven, and, occupying an uncertain position between land and sea, works to corrode and wreck any attempt to pose clear distinctions between the two.

Captain Flint positions the movement of the land as strange: ' "Queer thing it is, the way these islands keep changing all the time." '[66] This whole comment positions a changing landscape as a 'queer thing', something not normal. The idea of landscape as a permanent, timeless, unmoving entity – as in the Lake District hills of *Swallows and Amazons* – is here the usual one, and deviations from this are not normal, are 'queer'. The comment also sites this 'queer-ness' explicitly; it is '*these* islands' that are changing, and therefore '*these* islands' that are 'queer'. The specificity of the reference to 'these' gives the 'queer-ness' a location, placing it firmly in the realm of the foreign, exotic Caribbean islands and retaining definitions of normality for the stable, reassuring home landscape which doesn't move about in this 'queer' way. Here again, 'queer' equals the foreign, the not-home.

Ironically, in *Peter Duck*, it is the earthquake and the destruction of the land that enables the finding of the treasure. The treasure is found under the torn-up roots of the tree that had been 'the landmark of Duckhaven'. So it is the loss of recognizable fixed markers or bearings that actually brings about the desired result and the end of the search. However, the revelations of the violence that this place is capable of not only change the physical shape of the island, but also alter the characters' response to the place. The dangerous storm and the advent of other humans in the shape of the violent and equally dangerous pirates turn the exotic island into a different place. 'Everything seemed just as they had left it and yet altogether different, because they could no longer think of the island in the same way.'[67] Here it is to do with possession: '[i]t was no longer their island and theirs alone.' The advent of other humans has changed their relationship to the land itself. 'Earthquake and landslide had not been enough to make this kind of difference. It was the coming of the *Viper* that had changed the island for them.' Other humans complicate ideas of ownership and possession, which are bound up with ideas of safety and protection. Yet that notwithstanding, it is the island itself that is again constructed as being visually deceptive: 'everything *seemed* just as they had left it.' Again the island seems to be one thing and is another. Another point worth noting here is the primacy placed on the mental or emotional construction of the land. Everything becomes different 'because they could no longer think of the island in the same way'. This is an important gesture within the text towards the idea that the land and the human relationship with it is a creation of the mind. The way they think of the island governs their attitudes and responses to it and their actions within it.

From 'the happy place it had been', the island has now become 'a horrible place to be alone in'.[68] It is not just the presence of the pirates, but the island itself that has become 'horrible'. The noises that they liked or ignored when in the earlier large group now seem oppressive and almost menacing. This is a further indication of how the perception of landscape alters according to circumstance. A landscape is not simply one static thing but shifts according to point of view.

> And there lay the island, silent, secret in the fading light of the evening. What was happening there?...They could get no answer by looking at the island. It might never have known the footsteps of man, so indifferent, so desolate it looked.[69]

By the end of the text, the island has moved from an exciting idyll to an unknown mystery. However, in both cases, the response to the island hinges on its 'unknown' status. At the end it is secret, silent, desolate, and seems to have shrugged off their presence and returned to a virgin state. The island has an ambiguous relationship with humans. While the island's 'desert' state was part of its initial attraction, here its apparent freedom from the 'footsteps of man' is positioned as fearful, part of its silence and refusal of answers. The emphasis is now on its savagery. Yet elsewhere, as we have seen, it is the presence of humans other than themselves that has altered the island for them and in fact prompts the questions that the island seems to refuse to answer. It is positioned as 'indifferent' to them, almost actively refusing to participate with them in its denial of answers. Despite all their best efforts in marking, mapping and pathfinding it has remained silent, secret and unknowable. The unknowability that was enticing on their first arrival has become something much more threatening as the island resists European attempts to grasp and control it. Yet it is finally still the European that sees and sets the terms of that unknowability. Although the island and attitudes towards it may go through many changes in *Peter Duck*, its status as Other remains unchanged and thereby remains the feature through which it is defined.

Further recommended reading

Clifford, James, *The Predicament of Culture: Twentieth-Century Ethnography, Literature, and Art* (Boston: Harvard University Press, 1988).
Matless, David, *Landscape and Englishness* (London: Reaktion Books, 1998).
Miller, Hillis, J., *Topographies* (Stanford: Stanford University Press, 1995).
Rose, Jacqueline, *States of Fantasy* (Oxford: Oxford University Press, 1998).
Schama, Simon, *Landscape and Memory* (New York: Alfred A. Knopf, 1995).

Notes

1. Lucie Armitt, *Theorising the Fantastic* (London: Arnold, 1996), p. 18.
2. Peter Bishop, 'Shangri-la Revisited: Imperialism, Landscape and Identity', in *Landscape and Identity: Perspectives from Australia – Proceedings of the 1994 Conference of the Centre for Children's Literature, University of South Australia* (Adelaide: AusLib Press, 1994), 21–32, 21.
3. The 12 texts, in chronological order of publication, are *Swallows and Amazons* (1929), *Swallowdale* (1931), *Peter Duck* (1932), *Winter Holiday* (1933), *Coot Club* (1934), *Pigeon Post* (1935), *We Didn't Mean To Go To Sea* (1937), *Secret Water* (1939), *The Big Six* (1940), *Missee Lee* (1941), *The Picts and the Martyrs* (1942) and *Great Northern?* (1947).
4. Peter Hunt, *Approaching Arthur Ransome* (London: Jonathan Cape, 1992). Victor Watson 'Poetry and Pirates – Swallows and Amazons at Sea', *Signal*, 66 (1991), 154–68, 154. Hugh Shelley, *Arthur Ransome* (London: The Bodley Head, 1960), p. 38.
5. Hunt, *Approaching Arthur Ransome*, pp.147–9.
6. 'Obsessed with classifying and categorizing, differentiating and counter-differentiating between fantasy, science fiction, space opera; or between faery, fantasy and fable, they continue to make redundant distinctions. Few genuinely enable readers to relate better to the narratives with which they engage' (Armitt, *Theorising the Fantastic*, p. 18). Lucie Armitt's criticism of the taxonomical impulse of the bulk of fantasy theory and criticism seems to me highly pertinent. There may be a need for a criticism which can engage with the 'fantasy'/non-realist elements of a text like *Peter Duck*.
7. Armitt, *Theorising the Fantastic*, p. 3.
8. Christina Hardyment, *Arthur Ransome and Captain Flint's Trunk* (London: Jonathan Cape, 1984), p. 26.

9. Victor Watson, 'Poetry and Pirates – Swallows and Amazons at Sea', 159.
10. M. Daphne Kutzer in *Empire's Children: Empire and Imperialism in British Children's Books* (New York & London: Garland, 2000) seems to perform a similar move: 'the swift movement of [*Coral Island*] from coastal England to exotic Pacific island is similar to the swift movement from the real world to the fantastic in children's fantasy.' Here the connection between foreign and fantasy is again being made, with the 'exotic Pacific island' and 'the fantastic' occupying the same position in the analogy being made.
11. Hunt, *Approaching Arthur Ransome*, p. 82.
12. Arthur Ransome, *Great Northern?* (Harmondsworth: Puffin, 1980), pp. 304–5.
13. Arthur Ransome, *Peter Duck* (Harmondsworth: Puffin, 1982), pp. 16–17.
14. Ransome, *Peter Duck*, p. 218.
15. Ransome, *Peter Duck*, pp. 350–1.
16. Ransome, *Peter Duck*, p. 254.
17. Ransome, *Peter Duck*, p. 224.
18. Ransome, *Peter Duck*, p. 16.
19. Hardyment, *Arthur Ransome and Captain Flint's Trunk*, p. 24.
20. Hunt, *Approaching Arthur Ransome*, pp. 98–9. The statement is not absolutely correct in that he omits *Peter Duck*, which also contains both parrot and monkey.
21. Arthur Ransome, *We Didn't Mean To Go To Sea* (Harmondsworth: Puffin, 1985), pp. 86–7.
22. Ransome, *Peter Duck*, p. 29.
23. Ransome, *Peter Duck*, p. 208.
24. Ransome, *Peter Duck*, p. 205.
25. This idea of the inadequacy of words to depict the strange or sublime or wonderful nature of a new scene is one frequently seen at work in tourist literature. You don't 'merely' see but 'experience' a place and words are then seen as unable to convey sufficiently the sense of 'being there'.
26. Ransome, *Peter Duck*, p. 206.
27. Ransome, *Peter Duck*, p. 206.
28. See *The Rhetoric of the Frame: Essays on the Boundaries of the Artwork*, ed. by Paul Duro (Cambridge: Cambridge University Press, 1996).
29. This not only produces an idea of the picture content making its own arrangements – having the power – but also emphasizes an idea of that content being continually on the move, shifting even as it is being looked at: 'one … picture after another framing itself ….' This idea of the scene being in a state of flux and instability is a recurrent one throughout the text.
30. Ransome, *Peter Duck*, p. 211.
31. Ransome, *Peter Duck*, p. 209.
32. Ransome, *Peter Duck*, p. 214.
33. Ransome, *Peter Duck*, p. 214.
34. Ransome, *Peter Duck*, pp. 224–5.
35. Ransome, *Peter Duck*, p. 242.
36. Ransome, *Peter Duck*, p. 267.
37. Ransome, *Peter Duck*, p. 269.
38. It is notable that at this point, Gibber, who has hitherto been referred to as 'he', suddenly becomes an 'it'. 'The monkey whimpered. Its lips drew back from its chattering teeth … It shivered so violently.' It is as if this prior warning of the storm makes Gibber less humanized, non-gender-specific, more animal. 'He' becomes 'it', the familiar becomes strange.

39. Ransome, *Peter Duck*, p. 286.
40. Ransome, *Peter Duck*, p. 298.
41. Ransome, *Peter Duck*, pp. 372–3.
42. Ransome, *Peter Duck*, p. 323.
43. Ransome, *Peter Duck*, p. 327.
44. Ransome, *Peter Duck*, p. 287.
45. Peter Hulme, *Colonial Encounters: Europe and the Native Caribbean 1492–1797* (London: Methuen,1986), p. 94. He traces the changing use of the existing English term 'tempest' and new native term 'hurricane' in the English colonial literature about the region, displaying instances where the English discursive framework appears to be inadequate in the face of this new phenomenon. He places the term 'hurricane' alongside 'cannibal' as words from the Caribbean which 'ultimately displaced words from an established Mediterranean discourse that were clearly thought inadequate to designate phenomena that were alien and hostile to European interests' (p. 100).
46. Ransome, *Peter Duck*, p. 323.
47. Ransome, *Peter Duck*, p. 309.
48. Ransome, *Peter Duck*, p. 312.
49. Arthur Ransome, *Swallows and Amazons* (Harmondsworth: Puffin, 1980), p. 171.
50. Ransome, *Peter Duck*, p. 226.
51. Ransome, *Peter Duck*, p. 228.
52. Ransome, *Peter Duck*, p. 247.
53. Ransome, *Peter Duck*, p. 219. In the modern maritime 'true-life' narrative that is Sebastian Junger's *The Perfect Storm*, Sable Island, subject to the Atlantic Ocean, is similarly described as 'prowl[ing] restlessly around the Scotian Shelf, losing sand from one end, building it up on the other, endlessly throughout the centuries… it has melted away beneath the foundations of six lighthouses.…' (*The Perfect Storm* (London: Fourth Estate, 1997), p. 133.) This produces the island as relentlessly mobile and somehow insubstantial ('melted away…'), moving around almost by its own agency. It is this movement that makes the island such an active threat to shipping.
54. Ransome, *Peter Duck*, pp. 259–60.
55. Ransome, *Peter Duck*, p. 238.
56. Ransome, *Peter Duck*, p. 283.
57. Ransome, *Peter Duck*, p. 220.
58. Ransome, *Peter Duck*, p. 101.
59. Ransome, *Peter Duck*, p. 130.
60. Ransome, *Peter Duck*, p. 179.
61. Ransome, *Peter Duck*, p. 323.
62. Ransome, *Peter Duck*, p. 90.
63. Ransome, *Peter Duck*, p. 220.
64. Ransome, *Peter Duck*, p. 239.
65. Ransome, *Peter Duck*, p. 300.
66. Ransome, *Peter Duck*, p. 258.
67. Ransome, *Peter Duck*, p. 351.
68. Ransome, *Peter Duck*, p. 352. Again, this is worth comparing to *Swallows and Amazons*, where Titty is extremely eager to be alone on Wild Cat island in order to feel more fully like Robinson Crusoe.
69. Ransome, *Peter Duck*, p. 346.

Index